T0318266

Regulation and Development

In *Regulation and Development* Jean-Jacques Laffont provides the first theoretical analysis of regulation of public services for developing countries. He shows how the debate between price-cap regulation and cost-of-service regulation is affected by the characteristics of less developed countries (LDCs) and offers a positive theory of privatization that stresses the role of corruption. He develops a new theory of regulation with limited enforcement capabilities and discusses the delicate issue of access pricing in view of LDCs' specificities. In the final chapter he proposes a theory of separation of powers which reveals one of the many vicious circles of underdevelopment made explicit by the economics of information. Based on organization theory and history, and using simple empirical tests wherever possible, Professor Laffont offers a comprehensive evaluation of the different ways to organize the regulatory institutions. An authoritative book from one of Europe's leading economists, it makes a significant contribution to the field.

Jean-Jacques Laffont was Professor of Economics at the University of Toulouse and at the University of Southern California. He published extensively in public economics, incentive theory, development economics, and the economics of regulation. He died in 2004.

Federico Caffè Lectures

This series of annual lectures was initiated to honour the memory of Federico Caffè. They are jointly sponsored by the Department of Public Economics at the University of Rome, where Caffè held a chair from 1959 to 1987, and the Bank of Italy, where he served for many years as an adviser. The publication of the lectures will provide a vehicle for leading scholars in the economics profession, and for the interested general reader, to reflect on the pressing economic and social issues of the times.

Regulation and Development

Jean-Jacques Laffont

CAMBRIDGE
UNIVERSITY PRESS

CAMBRIDGE
UNIVERSITY PRESS

University Printing House, Cambridge CB2 8BS, United Kingdom

One Liberty Plaza, 20th Floor, New York, NY 10006, USA

477 Williamstown Road, Port Melbourne, VIC 3207, Australia

314-321, 3rd Floor, Plot 3, Splendor Forum, Jasola District Centre, New Delhi - 110025, India

103 Penang Road, #05-06/07, Visioncrest Commercial, Singapore 238467

Cambridge University Press is part of the University of Cambridge.

It furthers the University's mission by disseminating knowledge in the pursuit of education, learning and research at the highest international levels of excellence.

www.cambridge.org
Information on this title: www.cambridge.org/9780521549486

First published 2005

A catalogue record for this publication is available from the British Library

Library of Congress Cataloging in Publication data
Laffont, Jean-Jacques, 1947–2004
    Regulation and development/Jean-Jacques Laffont.
      p. cm. – (Federico Caffè lectures)
    Includes bibliographical references and index.
    ISBN 0-521-84018-X – ISBN 0-521-54948-5 (pbk.)
    1. Municipal services–Developing countries.   2. Municipal services–Government policy–Developing countries.   I. Title.
    II. Series.
HD4431.L34 2004 363.6´01–dc22   2003069754

ISBN 978-0-521-54948-6 Paperback

Contents

Publisher's acknowledgment

Regulation and Development was being typeset at the time of Jean-Jacques Laffont's tragically early death in May 2004. The Publisher wishes to acknowledge with gratitude the help of Jean-Jacques' friends and colleagues who, working on both sides of the Atlantic, between them read and corrected the page proofs: Bharat Bhole, Isabelle Brocas, Antonio Estache, Hossein Farzin, David Martimort, and Jean Tirole. In their note attached to the corrected proofs they write;

> Because life did not leave Jean-Jacques time to read the proofs, several persons were involved in reading and sometimes correcting them, keeping in mind the desire to provide a final version of the book as close as possible to what Jean-Jacques would have liked himself.
>
> We all hope that we have done a good job but are fully conscious that Jean-Jacques would have done much better by himself.

Foreword

François Bourguignon

Jean-Jacques Laffont's book on "regulation and development" is to be praised on two grounds. It is the first comprehensive book to revisit the theory of regulation and incentives from the viewpoint of the needs and constraints of developing and transition countries. Following the liberalization, deregulation, and privatization trends that significantly modified industrial structures in developed countries in the 1980s, and in the wake of the "structural adjustment" and the "transition" from socialism, a powerful set of reforms was set in motion in developing and transition countries during the 1990s. Positive results are starting to show up in transition countries as they overcome the adjustment costs of the transition. But, in both developing and transition countries, satisfaction with the reforms is far from uniform. In several cases, liberalization and privatization have been severely criticized by some for having led to practically unregulated private monopolies that charge unduly high prices and do not necessarily improve quality. Today, it is increasingly recognized that, in many instances, the problem was that reformers disregarded the functioning of regulatory institutions, assuming implicitly they would work as in developed countries.

Chief Economist and Senior Vice President, Development Economics, World Bank.

Regulatory institutions do not always function well in rich countries; however, the problems confronting developing countries are both more numerous and more serious. Offering a theory of regulatory institutions specific to developing countries is therefore a major contribution to development economics.

Second, this book is authored by one of the best specialists of the theory of regulation and incentive theory in the world, a major contributor to this branch of economics who did much to bring it at the forefront of the discipline, where it belongs. His 1993 book with Jean Tirole on the *Theory of Incentives for Procurement and Regulation* continues to be the undisputed reference for anyone working on the theory of regulation. It was then followed by many more publications and books. All represented a breakthrough not just for economic theorists but also for policymakers as Jean-Jacques increasingly allocated his energy towards addressing policy issues directly.

Among Jean-Jacques's many contributions to the theory of regulation and incentives, early work had already touched upon specific applications to developing countries. His work on the relationship between monopolists and the state as a contract with specific goals and informational constraints was particularly relevant here. In particular, it forced Jean-Jacques to question much of the received wisdom from the traditional public economics literature on the real control that the government can exercise on the behavior of monopolistic providers of public services. The relevance of cost and demand uncertainty for the choice of a regulatory regime also led him to question the standard recommendations by consultants advising reforming governments in developing countries to adopt an incentive-based regulatory regime under all circumstances. The analysis of access pricing and interconnection charges and other entry issues in competition policy also made him question the superiority of the Efficiency Component Pricing Rule under a wide set of circumstances relevant to developing countries. We should also mention several other contributions which were of relevance for developing countries. For instance, Jean-Jacques' application of econometrics to various aspects of industrial organization theory includes new insights into the design of auctions and a critique of many practices in the allocation of the use of natural resources, and in the award of public contracts or of licenses for the delivery of public services. In particular, he actively participated in the debate on the way in which licences in the telecoms sector should be awarded, both in France and in developing countries. He saw cost modeling work in the telecoms sector as an effective instrument to reduce the cost inefficiencies resulting from the information asymmetries critical to a number of important regulatory decisions (including the pricing of the Universal Service Obligations, USOs, and of access to the basic common infrastructures). His analysis of agency problems in multiprincipal-multiple agency contexts was also crucial to the public sector institutions, including regulatory agencies.

Over time, his trips around the world from Argentina to China, to many sub-Saharan African countries and to Eastern European countries, eventually led Jean-Jacques to develop a research agenda that focused on developing countries. Five of his previous books dealt fully or partially with developing country issues. Three of the books he co-authored in the 1990s were actually published in China, where his theoretical contribution was widely known and where he was a frequent lecturer at the University of Wuhan and at a research center he helped establish at the Chinese Academy of Social Sciences in Beijing.

The present book very much reflects Jean-Jacques' research agenda on development and may be seen as a first attempt at synthesizing what he had learned in a number of key areas. For instance, he held rather strong – and most welcome – views on the costs and benefits of privatization of network industries and he was concerned about the pragmatism and the cost effectiveness of the way in which social issues were addressed in the design of regulatory regimes in developing countries. This included research on the financing of USOs and on the case for cross-subsidies when tax systems are unable to generate the appropriate levels of resources to finance social programs. His work also included reflections on corruption and capture by private operators and their interference with reform processes and the way governments are meeting their obligations to the poorest. The agenda also covered the need to reconsider the role of the state in the context of reform and to assess the limits of standard reforms when civil servants are not benevolent and use their power to meet their own objectives, political or otherwise.

Doubtless, there was more to come. Much more. In the discussions I regularly had with Jean-Jacques over the last couple of years, he was always telling me how, at the stage he had reached in his career, he saw economic development as the single most important global issue and how he intended to devote most of his future work to this area of economics. We both shared the same passion for development, and we were both convinced that rigorous economic analysis was key to accelerate it. We differed only in the field that should be given priority. On this point, I remember that Jean-Jacques constantly argued that the regulation of the price of public services and utilities was central for the reduction of poverty and that people like us in the World Bank, specializing in poverty and inequity, should pay much more attention to these issues. I am happy that his concern is very much taken care of in the research work pursued today in the World Bank. I would be still happier if we could have enjoyed his continued collaboration. Alas, this will not happen. It is a tragedy that such a prolific research career, such a talent, such a commitment for effective development policy, had to come so dramatically to an end. We are missing not only a dear friend but a deep and active thinker on key aspects of development.

We are fortunate that Jean-Jacques had the time to finish this book, a major work that will doubtlessly inspire and influence development thinking in the future and certainly the most obvious testimony of his profound commitment and contribution to the cause of development.

Y. Hossein Farzin

Perhaps the most satisfying thing for an economist is to see his or her research making an impact on economic policy-making and, ultimately, on the well-being of people. This is even more true if the economist happens to be a theorist and the people are very poor and living in developing countries. Jean-Jacques Laffont's vision was to improve life for poor people in developing countries, and this motivation was evident during informal discussions at conferences and on other occasions. The desire to improve the lives of poor people in developing countries was the major motive for writing this book, since Jean-Jacques believed that the well-being of people in poor countries depended largely on basic infrastructure such as a reliable water supply, electricity, transportation, telecommunications, postal service, and health and education services. Governments traditionally provide or regulate these services, and Jean-Jacques argued that one important way to improve the living standards of poor people was to create and enhance the capabilities of governments to improve and expand the delivery of basic services.

Through personal experience, Jean-Jacques became aware of the inadequacies and imperfections of public institutions to manage basic services efficiently and equitably. As he notes throughout this book, public institutions can be plagued with corruption, lawlessness, unaccountability, imperfect information, inadequacy of physical and financial infrastructure,

University of California at Davis; Associate Editor, *Review of Development Economics*.

and shortage of human and financial resources to design and implement the necessary regulations, and high costs to raise funds to provide basic public services.

Jean-Jacques' direct observations of the basic service problems of developing countries, and the urgent need to design policies tailored to their specific institutional features, prompted him to review critically the existing economic models of public incentives and regulations that underpin the regulatory policies of the industrial countries. This critical assessment of existing theories, together with Jean-Jacques' pragmatism and sensitivity to cost effectiveness in addressing social concerns in developing countries, led him to revise and extend traditional public economic theory to make it more relevant to their needs. These new theoretical developments and their empirical tests are evident throughout the book, especially in chapter 2, where he derives optimal regulations taking into account the characteristics of developing countries, in chapter 3, where he identifies and tests conditions for effective privatization in developing countries, in chapter 5, where access pricing rules for developing countries are derived, in chapter 7, where the design of regulatory institutions in developing countries is addressed, and in chapter 8 where the need for separation of regulatory powers in developing countries is descussed.

It is unfortunate that Jean-Jacques' untimely death did not let him see the full fruits of the establishment of one of the world's best economic research institutes, IDEI in Toulouse. However, Jean-Jacques' work on regulation and economic development will have a lasting impact on development economics – and, more importantly, on the daily life of the world's poor.

Preface

This book is an expanded version of the Caffè Lectures I gave in 2001 at the University La Sapienza in Rome. I thank the Department of Economics of La Sapienza for inviting me to give these prestigious lectures and for making my stay in Rome such an enjoyable experience. Along the years I have benefited from discussions with Antonio Estache, Paulina Beato, Luis Guasch, and Ioannis Kessides on the topics of this book. I have also used joint work with my former students Cécile Aubert (chapter 7), Mathieu Meleu (chapters 3 and 8), and Xinzhu Zhang (chapter 6). I thank Hossein Farzin for useful comments on the final draft.

Finally, I thank once more my outstanding secretary Marie-Pierre Boé for typing the manuscript.

Los Angeles, December 2002

Introduction

Using incentive theory elaborated in the 1980s to model regulation as a problem of control under incomplete information, the new economics of regulation (Loeb and Magat, 1979; Baron and Myerson, 1982; Laffont and Tirole, 1986, 1993 (hereafter LT)) has provided a useful normative framework for the reforms of public services in developed countries. However, this literature has paid no attention to the specific characteristics of developing countries.[1]

Simultaneously, the privatization, deregulation, and liberalization movement of the 1980s which started in the United Kingdom and the United States and then extended to Europe and some countries of Latin America (Chile and Argentina in particular) has provided a lot of useful experiences. Under the pressure of international banking institutions (IMF, World Bank), developing countries have been forced to liberalize their public services as the developed world had just done.

Advisers in LDCs could rely only on the experience of the developed countries and on an intellectual framework also designed for those countries. Not surprisingly they have essentially repeated the precepts designed for the developed world and paid little attention to the characteristics of LDCs.

---

[1] We will use the expressions "developing countries" and "less developed countries" (LDCs) interchangeably.

Some economists at the World Bank were quite aware of the risk early on and have accumulated precious knowledge on some of the leading reforms in the world often hidden in internal reports but increasingly available in academic publications.[2] In terms of countries, Argentina and Chile have generated more than their fair share of empirical assessments of regulatory problems resulting from reform.[3] In terms of sectors, the telecommunications sector was generally the first to be subject to major reforms, followed closely by the electricity sector, and both sectors have encountered major regulatory crises reflecting the importance of the issues discussed in this book.[4] To put things in perspective, it may be useful to quote an estimate of the welfare gains from utilities reform in Argentina.[5] Relying on a general equilibrium model, Chisari, Estache, and Romero estimated that the welfare gains from privatization and deregulation added up to at least 0.9 percent of GDP if all efficiency gains from reform were transformed into rents for the new owners of the utilities sector. Effective regulation which would ensure the redistribution of the gains from reform to the users through lower tariffs would eventually add the equivalent of 0.3 percent of GDP in welfare, with most of these gains accruing to the poorest.

It is the purpose of this book to start the work of building a theory of regulation for LDCs. In this effort, I could rely on little or no literature. The results reported in this book should be considered as only a first step towards a more comprehensive theoretical framework. They relate to the impact of various characteristics of LDCs on the theory of regulation,

[2] For general overviews see Basanes and Willig (2002), Estache (2001), Guasch and Spiller (2002), or Ugaz and Waddams-Price (2003).

[3] On Argentina, for instance, see Chisari, Estache, and Romero (1999); Abdala (2001); Artana, Navajas, and Urbiztondo (2002); Estache (2003), and, on Chile, see Bitran and Serra (1998).

[4] For overviews on telecom, see Berg and Gutierrez (2000); Wallsten (2001); Estache, Valletti, and Manacorda (2002); for electricity, see Estache and Rodriguez-Pardina (2000); Bacon and Besant-Jones (2001).

[5] See Chisari, Estache, and Romero (1999).

which struck me as important in my limited experience in Africa, Latin America, and China. I hope they will provide useful starting points for more in-depth studies, or further study.

The analysis is essentially theoretical because I feel that the greatest weakness of the current situation is the lack of a theoretical framework. Sometimes I have ventured to perform some quantitative analyses, which are very exploratory and designed to illustrate the theory rather than proving empirically robust results.

Chapter 1 gives an overview of the major regulatory issues in LDCs. The liberalization of an industry of services distinguishes segments which can be opened to competition from segments which remain natural monopolies and must be regulated. First, we discuss the structural issues raised by the design of the regulatory agencies and those concerning the design of the proper market structures. For the segments that remain natural monopolies the main question is then: what use can be made of the new incentive regulation introduced in developed countries? The success of promoting competition in some segments of the industry (such as electricity generation, or long-distance telephony) relies crucially on the proper pricing of access to the segments which remain natural monopolies (such as the transmission grid in electricity or the local loop in telephony). The various paradigms of access pricing are reviewed. What kind of competition policy is the next important issue of a deregulation program. Finally, we discuss how universal service obligations can be maintained in a competitive environment.

Chapter 2 deals with the essential rent extraction–efficiency trade-off present in the regulation of a segment of the industry which remains a natural monopoly. Indeed, asymmetric information obliges the regulator to give up costly information rents to regulated monopolies and distorts efficiency to mitigate those rents, for example by pricing above marginal cost. After presenting a simple model of regulation and reviewing the relevant characteristics of LDCs affecting this question, we discuss how these characteristics affect the rent extraction–efficiency trade-off. Data about concession contracts in Latin America are then used to illustrate the determinants of this trade-off.

Privatization of services is also often recommended by the economists at the World Bank and many of the other multilateral and bilateral aid agencies. After reviewing the literature which examines the pros and cons of privatization we develop in chapter 3 a positive theory of privatization. We argue that politicians in power privatize only when the benefits they derive from privatization are greater than those they previously obtained from public firms. This leads to the conjecture that the rate of privatization has an inverted U-shape as a function of the level of corruption. This conjecture is tested with African data.

An implicit assumption of the theory of regulation for developed countries is that regulatory contracts are enforced by a Court of Law. However, this assumption of perfect enforcement presumes a quality of institutions which does not exist in LDCs. Accordingly, we propose in chapter 4 a theory of imperfect enforcement. Sometimes the regulator cannot prevent opportunistic renegotiations by firms. Countries invest in enforcement to limit these costly renegotiations. The theory yields a structural equation for the level of enforcement expenditures which is tested with cross-country macrodata and microdata.

As already noted, access pricing is a complex issue crucial to the success of liberalization. Chapter 5 discusses the different types of problems arising in pricing access from the point of view of LDCs. Should vertical disintegration be preferred to vertical integration of the incumbent monopoly? Which kind of pricing rule is best for the one-way-access problem, such as access of long-distance operators to the local loop? When competition of infrastructures is possible (mobile telephony, for example), should reciprocal access prices be regulated, and how?

In chapter 6 a model of optimal development of the network in rural areas for public services such as electricity or telecommunications is proposed to illustrate the universal service issues relevant for developing countries. Particular attention is devoted to the possible capture by interest groups of regulators for this politically highly sensitive issue.

The design of proper regulatory institutions is a key question for developing countries, which start from scratch and have the opportunity to use historical experience. Chapter 7 discusses the various trade-offs that theory has uncovered for choosing between centralized versus decentralized regulatory institutions, multi-industry or mono-industry regulation, multifunctional or monofunctional regulation. In each case we examine how the characteristics of LDCs affect these trade-offs.

Finally, in chapter 8 we study more formally the question of the separation of powers for regulatory institutions. We construct a model to see how a duality of regulators can help deal with the crucial issue of capture. Again, we pay particular attention to how the characteristics of LDCs affect the optimal choice between one or two regulators.

A conclusion (chapter 9) summarizes our basic findings and discusses the need for further research.

1

Overview of regulatory issues

1.1 Introduction

This book focuses on public utilities, telecommunications, electricity, gas, water, transportation (roads, railways, buses, ports, airports, . . .) and the postal service which are sometimes referred to as "economic infrastructures." It does not concern itself with the so-called "social infrastructures" such as education and health, or with financial infrastructures. This chapter will discuss the specific questions surrounding the regulation and liberalization of public utilities in developing countries.[1] We first review the characteristics of developing countries that have a bearing on the analysis of regulation and competition policy.

An essential concept is the marginal cost of public funds – that is, the social cost of raising 1 unit of funds. This cost includes in particular a deadweight loss[2] because governments raise revenues by means of distortionary taxes. It is estimated that this deadweight loss amounts to around 0.3 in developed countries, meaning that it costs citizens 1.3 units of account every time the government raises 1 unit. The inefficiency of tax systems in developing countries, coupled with the corruption that is sometimes also present, makes

---

[1] See chapter 3 for a discussion of privatization in developing countries.
[2] The deadweight loss depends on the type of tax used, because the tax systems are not usually optimized.

it extremely difficult for governments to invest in infrastructures and affects the cost of all types of public interventions, in particular, regulation and competition policy. According to World Bank data, the deadweight loss in developing countries is well beyond 1.0. It has been estimated at 1.2 in Malaysia and 2.5 in the Philippines, while in Thailand it ranges between 1.2 and 1.5 (Jones, Tandon, and Vogelsang, 1990). In developing our analysis we take the high cost of public funds as a given because, although tax reforms are necessary in many developing countries, it is unlikely that they will be in place quickly owing to the many financial, human and political constraints involved.

An essential instrument of regulatory and competition agencies is the ability to audit costs. Yet, developing countries are hampered by the absence of well-developed accounting and auditing systems (Trebilcock, 1996; Campos, Estache, and Trujillo, 2003). This is due to the lack of proper training programs; to the political and social difficulties that hamper the payment of incentive salaries to auditors to reward effort and discourage corruption; to the lack of up-to-date technology such as computerized systems (which makes it harder to discover cost padding and evaluate real costs); and to the inability to impose high penalties in cases of documented wrongdoing (because of the strong limited liability constraints of most economic agents).

Many developing countries also suffer from widespread corruption due, in particular, to the low internal costs of side transfers. When two parties (such as a firm and an auditor or a bidder and the auction organizer) arrange a private deal, they must take into account the costs of being discovered and the need to use indirect compensation (which is less efficient than direct compensation). The cost of these side-transfers is expected to be lower than in developed countries because they are more difficult to identify and, in addition, social norms may place a positive value on some types of side transfers (for example, when they take place within families, villages, or ethnic groups). Accordingly, it is more difficult to fight corruption (Tirole, 1992).

Inefficient credit markets and the sheer lack of wealth make limited liability constraints more binding in developing countries. It is important to stress this point because many of the problems in regulation and competition policy result from difficulties in borrowing and attracting foreign capital. It is also worth highlighting the complementarity of general competition policy and good banking sector regulation. When the banking sector is inefficient and makes borrowing costly or impossible, an effective competition policy may destroy the rents that allow firms to invest, or may create instability.[3]

Other characteristics that hamper public utility regulation concern the government. In particular, two characteristics of developed countries that are often missing in developing countries are constitutional control of the government and some degree of ability to enter into long-term contracts. The lack of the checks and balances typical of well-functioning democracies (supreme courts, government auditing bodies, separation of powers, independent media[4]) makes the government an easier prey to interest groups and patronage. The lack of democracy and well-functioning political institutions increases the uncertainty of future regulations and makes it difficult for the government and the regulatory institutions to make credible commitments to long-run policies. Consequently, the economic policies of developing countries are even more sensitive to ratchet effects and renegotiations.

Another shortcoming of developing economies is the weakness of the rule of law. Poor enforcement of laws and contracts

---

[3] Mishkin (1997) concludes that "developing countries may need to move slowly in financial liberalization in order to keep a lending boom from getting out of hand."

[4] See Besley and Burgess (2001) for an empirical study of government responsiveness to media activity.

biases contracting towards self-enforcing contracts or leads to costly renegotiations.

Finally, it is essential to stress that the liberalization and deregulation of public infrastructures in developing countries often fails to attract the level of foreign capital that is necessary.

These features will be kept in mind throughout the discussion that follows, and when necessary specific advice for dealing with these difficulties in regulating and promoting competition in public utilities will be presented.

Section 1.2 discusses the structuring of regulatory agencies that favor competition, and the trade-offs involved in choosing whether or not to engage in the vertical disintegration of incumbent monopolies between the competitive segments and the natural monopoly ones. Section 1.3 presents the regulatory rules required by the monopoly segments in developing countries. The crucial issue of the management of the interface between the monopoly segments and the competitive segments is addressed in section 1.4 where access-pricing rules adapted to developing countries are discussed in greater detail. Section 1.5 is devoted to competition policy *per se* for the segments opened to competition. Universal service obligations are discussed in section 1.6. Concluding comments are offered in section 1.7.

1.2 Structural issues

The structure of regulatory agencies

A first consideration in structuring the government entity that will have responsibility for regulation and competition policy is whether these functions should be allocated to one integrated agency or separate ones.[5] In this regard, recent experiences in Australia and New Zealand are enlightening.

---

[5] Useful readings on the design and structure of industries include Abdala (2001) on Argentina, Bhatiani (2002) on India, and Mueller (2001) on Brazil.

New Zealand developed a very novel approach to regulation, relying only on general competition laws enforced by the courts and by an industry-wide competition authority. This approach was first used to regulate telecommunications and then electric power. The notion of self-regulation by industry was also introduced. In this case, industry participants form councils to negotiate the main rules and access conditions.

Although the New Zealand experiment was not an immediate failure, the government recognized, after some years, that there was still a need for regulatory control of industries that are not competitive enough. Indeed, this proved necessary even in telecommunications, which is the most competitive industry of the ones we are considering here. The concern is that light control of the industry is not sufficient to contain abuse of dominant position. The number of cases brought before the courts shows that rapid technological change and the technology-intensive nature of the industry make it difficult to find a firm guilty of abuse of dominant position. Moreover, the procedures involved make for very long delays. As a result, relying solely on competition laws has proved inefficient even when these laws are well developed and enforced. On the basis of this experience, therefore, we can conclude that eschewing regulation is not the right option.

Integrating general competition policy and regulation into a single agency is possible only if the regulatory agency is a multi-industry one, as in Australia. Australian regulation is organized around a federal multisectoral agency (the Australian Competition and Consumer Commission, ACCC), specialized agencies, and regional regulation. The ACCC is composed of sectoral and functional bureau and coordination entities. The Commission deals with product safety, consumer protection, access, mergers, and restrictive trade practices in all the sectors under study in this report.

The ACCC was created in 1995 following the recommendations of the Himler Report. It has taken over a significant part of the duties of specialized regulators by acquiring responsibility for promoting competition in a larger sense. For example, the regulatory body responsible for telecommunications was closed after the creation of the ACCC. The Utility Regulators Forum, created in 1997, is responsible for coordinating regulatory activities within the ACCC. The Australian case involves integration at the federal level of regulation and competition, even if regional agencies are also used. This system can be contrasted with the one prevailing in the United States, where multisectoral ruling takes place at the state level, specialized regulation is the rule at the federal level, and competition policy is dealt with separately.

The integration of regulatory agencies is an attractive option for developing countries because they face an extreme shortage of adequately trained personnel. This is especially the case for the telecommunications, electricity, and gas industries. While there are substantial economies of scope between the regulatory institutions of those industries, they seem much less important between regulation and competition policy. To avoid creating too powerful an institution, we would generally favor a separate competition agency and, except for very large countries, integrated regulatory agencies at the federal level. The only exception might be water, which could remain at the local level. In general, technological intensity requires federal regulation to reduce costs, but accountability requires more decentralized institutions.

Good advice on this structural issue must take into account political constraints, initial conditions, and industry specificities. The variety of solutions implemented in developed countries and the experience of the different Latin American countries (Argentina, Chile, Peru, Brazil, Bolivia...) suggest that the trade-offs are complex (see box 1.1). They involve balancing differentiation versus coordination; creative versus destructive competition between regulators; better enforcement by local authorities versus better control by the government; local corruption versus federal corruption; industry-specific expertise versus sharing resources; and diversifying the risks of institutional failures versus coordination (Aubert and Laffont, 2001; Smith, 2000).

Box 1.1   Structure of regulatory agencies

Specialization in Argentina

In Argentina,[1] each sectoral restructuring was accompanied by the creation of a sector-specific regulatory agency. But the specific approach adopted by each sector was quite different. While the creation and staffing of the electricity and gas regulatory agencies followed the international best practice and they had no major problems in fulfilling their obligations, the experience of the other regulatory agencies or authorities has been much poorer. The most problematic were the telecoms and water regulators, where there were not only staffing problems but also concerns with the lack of transparency of the decision making process. As for transport regulators, who have recently been merged into a single regulatory agency, the main issue has been the lack of independence from the political power.

A compromise between coordination and specialization: Bolivia

Bolivia's regulatory system constitutes a balanced compromise between a multisectoral agency and specialized regulators. It is composed of sector-specific branches operating under the supervision of a coordination entity. The structure is very similar to that of a multisectoral agency with specialized bureaus, yet it affords more independence to the branches. This, in turn, makes it more acceptable to the ministries, which might be reluctant to turn their regulatory power over to a multisectoral agency. Such an organization may help reduce the threat of capture of regulators by the industry but may fail to insulate the agency from political interference in view of its strategic importance.

The structure of regulatory agencies in China

Generally speaking, China has a mixed structure of regulatory agencies consisting of both industry-wide and sectoral agencies (ministries or departments) at both central and regional levels.

According to the law, the State Development and Planning Commission (SDPC) is the government body in charge of price regulation of public utilities. Another major SDPC responsibility is to regulate market entry and investments in public utilities. In addition to the SDPC, there are also some sectoral-specific ministries that complement the SDPC, including the Ministry of Information Industry (the regulatory agency for telecommunications) and the Ministry of Railways, etc. The latter are generally the implementation bodies.

Another structural feature of the Chinese regulatory agencies is the hierarchical structure between the central and local regulatory bodies. First, there are regional SDPCs in each layer of administrative governments. Similarly, there are some implementation bodies, either industry-wide or sectoral, at each local government level, that complement regional SDPCs. The separation of powers between the SDPC and local SDPCs is that the former is usually in charge of the control of entry and investments for big projects and the approval of price adjustment proposals submitted by local SDPCs while local SDPCs take care of smaller projects and make price adjustment proposals.

The general trend in the reform of regulatory structure is to delegate more and more of the regulatory power to regional governments. For instance, to provide incentives for the regions to make investments in electric power, the central government has given to local governments the authority to approve entry and investments in generation. It also allows the local governments to make price-purchase arrangements with independent power producers, subject to the approval of the SDPC. As a result of decentralization of regulatory power, installed generation capacity has increased rapidly and substantially so that since 1998 China has solved the shortage of energy, a problem which had plagued the economy. It is also the case in telecommunications (where, except for basic telecoms services including fixed-line and mobile phone services, not only has extensive deregulation taken place nationally, but also, when regulations remain), local regulatory agencies have gained much more discretion in terms of approval of market entry and investments and price regulations. Similar delegation has also happened in the gas and transport sectors.

With respect to the structural choice between industry-wide and sectoral regulators at the central government level, the trend is not clear, since until recently the reform of regulatory agencies has focused on separating management from regulatory and policy making functions and the attempts to set up independent regulatory agencies have only recently begun. Indeed, the government has announced that an electricity regulatory agency will be created, the first of its kind in China, at least judging by its name and status. But this event has arisen within a specific institutional setting, because unlike telecoms, railways, and transport, etc., there is now no specific regulatory body in charge of electricity regulation in China.[2] In other words there is a vacuum of power in electricity regulation. So it is really difficult to judge at present whether it will be another old-style implementation agency just bridging this power gap or is going to be a real institutional innovation, signaling that the government is determined to take a sector-specific agency approach which would eventually take the regulatory power of electricity away from the SDPC.

[1] This discussion of the case of Argentina (as in chapter 7) was valid until the crisis of January 6, 2002, which has essentially frozen the effective functioning of all Argentina's regulatory institutions.

[2] The Ministry of Water Resources and Electricity was restructured and disappeared in 1998 and the regulatory functions were taken over by the State Economic and Trade Commission, another government agency which mainly takes care of the management of state-owned enterprises (SOEs).

The structure of the industry

The industries under consideration were formerly public or regulated private monopolies providing services such as telecommunications, electricity, gas, or transportation. Segments of these industries are now viewed as potentially competitive. Some examples are long-distance telecommunications services and electricity generation. These are, therefore, the segments open to competition. Other segments continue to be considered natural monopolies. These include, for example, the electricity transmission grid, railway tracks, and to some extent so far, the local loop in telecommunications. These industry segments remain regulated and may eventually face new forms of regulation (see section 1.3).

Three types of market structures can be envisaged for these industries: (1) vertical disintegration, (2) vertical integration, and (3) competition in infrastructures. Under vertical disintegration, the firm controlling the "bottleneck" (the natural monopoly segment) is not allowed to compete in the services using the bottleneck as an input. For example, the local telephone company owning the local loop is not allowed to compete in long-distance service using the local loop to access consumers. In the case of vertical integration, the firm controlling the bottleneck becomes one competitor among many service providers using the bottleneck as an input. Finally, in the case of competition in infrastructures, competition then takes place between vertically integrated firms, each of which controls restricted access points and provides services.

The comparison between cases (1) and (2) contrasts the economies of scope that vertical integration makes possible and the problems of favoritism it raises. The bias in developing countries should be towards vertical disintegration because the economies of scope are likely to be independent of the characteristics of these countries (at least for given technologies), while favoritism is more difficult to counter.[6] The choice between cases (2) and (3) rests on a comparison of the fixed costs associated with competition in the provision of the bottleneck (like local telephony) and the gains one may expect from this competition (Auriol and Laffont, 1992). The comparison is difficult for developing countries where the high cost of public funds makes both the duplication of fixed

---

[6] This should be balanced with another consideration, which is the importance of *transaction costs*, which will be higher in case (1) due to the lack of enforceability of contracts and the lack of commitment which produces constant renegotiations. (See also Ordover, Pittman, and Clyde, 1994.) Another consideration in small countries, and some industries such as electricity, is that only a vertical structure may provide a critical level of business attracting the interest of foreign investors.

costs and the information rents resulting from a monopolistic provision of the bottleneck more expensive.

These comparisons are further complicated by the dynamics of the industry which may be moving towards case (3), as in the telecommunications industry. Then, vertical disintegration may in fact slow down the emergence of competition among vertically integrated firms providing both local and long-distance telephony. Recommending vertical disintegration may then be particularly inappropriate. However, for railways,[7] gas, or electricity, vertical disintegration of the track, the pipelines, or the electricity transmission grid from transportation or generation may be recommended if competition in services is introduced.

In all these cases there is a choice between a single regulated entity that owns the tracks, or the pipelines, or the grid, or shared ownership of the bottleneck by users who agree on rules for using it. The comparison is here between the inefficiency of regulation and the free-rider problems of joint ownership. In a country where regulation is easily captured, one may favor the second alternative, despite the lack of consumer representation that it often entails.

A particular problem for the gas industry is the market power of producers, especially when there are foreign producers involved. The bargaining power of consumers with respect to producers may be enhanced by the existence of a vertically integrated network operator who also owns gas fields. This argument is used in Europe with respect to the supply by Algeria, Russia, and Norway, and also in Argentina where YPF (now acquired by Repsol) sells more than 60 percent of the gas produced.

More generally, there is a question about the affordable competitiveness of the market structure, given that developing countries also need to attract foreign capital (see box 1.2).

---

[7] Except perhaps where competition by roads or (for large countries) competition between vertically integrated firms interconnected with reciprocal access rules is possible.

Box 1.2   Market structure

Market structure of telecommunications infrastructure providers

Zambia aimed at a very competitive industry with two fixed-link telephony providers and three mobiles, but was unable to attract any investors. Ghana issued two licenses for fixed-link telephony but the weakness of regulation allowed foreclosure behavior by the incumbent monopolist so that the second operator is not operational. Côte d'Ivoire was criticized for granting a seven-year monopoly for fixed-link telephony, but the network is now expanding as scheduled.

The telecommunications sector in Peru was privatized in 1994 and a seven-year monopoly in fixed-link phone services was granted to force large investments that increase coverage and penetration and allow for a smooth restructuring of tariffs. In 1998 the monopoly (Telefónica) and the Peruvian authorities renegotiated the contract and opened all services to competition.

The structure of the industry in China

The general trend is to separate the monopolistic segment from the competitive ones. In other words, vertical separation is taken to be the mainstream restructuring form of industrial structure. Mobile services were separated from the incumbent, China Telecom, in the restructuring reform of the telecoms sector in 1998. In electric power, the government approved a new restructuring plan to separate generation from transmission and distribution even though transmission and distribution will remain integrated for a while. As can be expected, this move is driven by the desire to facilitate efficient regulation and prevent favoritism.

However, the government did not approach restructuring uniformly. Indeed, other forms of industrial structure such as vertical integration and competition in infrastructures have also been implemented or allowed to exist. In this regard, it is interesting to contrast the different restructuring approaches in electricity and telecommunications.

In the power sector, entry in generation has been permitted for independent power producers since the mid-1980s, while the

State Power Company (SPC) owned not only the monopolistic transmission and distribution networks but also competitive generation assets. Given the general situation of shortage of generation capacity, everything proceeded smoothly until excess capacity of generation and capacity constraints of transmission arose in 1998. Then, serious problems of favoritism were claimed when the SPC no longer wanted to dispatch the power from independent power producers. Indeed, the power markets have become quite segmented among different regions and power exchanges among provinces count for only about 20 percent of total transactions, which is not considered reasonable given the huge geographical differences – Eastern China is the load center and has no generation assets while Western China is endowed with much of the resources for power generation (rivers and coal mines). Worries about the serious favoritism problem, particularly when more stations such as the Three Gorges Project begin to generate power, and the desire to build an integrated national market have contributed to speed up restructuring reform in the power sector. The government has approved a new reform package in which separation of generation assets from transmission and distribution is one of the main elements. Vertical separation will then be adopted in the power sector.

In the case of telecommunications, however, a different approach was adopted from the beginning. Competition in infrastructures was created in the telecoms sector, implemented in two ways. On the one hand, entry was liberalized in the competitive services and competitors need to buy access from the incumbent. Beginning in 1994, when China Unicom was created, competition was introduced in long-distance, mobiles, and data services even though China Telecom still held the dominant position in local services, access to which was needed by its rivals in competitive markets. This did cause some problems in creating competition in local services, because China Unicom (which can, as a matter of principle, provide local services) has until recently deployed a network in only three cities or regions – Tianjin, Chongqing, and Sichuan. Given the natural monopoly feature of local services, this should not come as a surprise. However, such institutional arrangements did achieve an important policy goal of increasing the access to telecommunications services. Indeed, the penetration rate of fixed lines reached 21 per 100 persons, a remarkable achievement by any standard.

On the other hand, competition in infrastructures has also been introduced through restructuring of the existing operators. After the implementation of major restructuring in 1998 in which operation was separated from the government functions and some services such as mobile services were divested, the Chinese government initiated a new restructuring reform in 2001. The main theme this time was to separate China Telecom on a geographical basis, dividing it into the South part which inherited the brand name and the North part which will be integrated with China Netcom, originally a carrier and widely considered to be politically well connected. In addition, each company was allowed to enter each other's territory. Both China Telecom and China Netcom can now provide long-distance and local services. China Unicom had been granted a license in local services before, but had chosen to exercise it to only a limited extent. It seems that the government is not convinced by the natural monopoly argument of local services. Fueled by a desire to create competition in local services but also worried by the network expansion needs, the government has now chosen a horizontal restructuring approach which will not only create competition in the market but also keep it viable.

1.3 Regulation of natural monopolies

The regulation of natural monopolies requires striking a balance between efficiency and the cost of information rents. High-powered incentive schemes (such as price caps) which induce cost minimizing behavior yield large rents to the most efficient firms, while low-powered incentive schemes (such as cost-of-service regulation) control those rents but create weak incentives for minimizing costs.

The high cost of public funds

As stressed above, a major characteristic of developing countries is the high cost of public funds. It is easy to see that this high cost calls for higher prices of the commodities produced by the natural monopoly and for lower-powered incentive schemes (high shares of cost reimbursement). Before presenting the intuitive reasoning for these results, it is important to emphasize that we are assuming here perfect observability of cost and full commitment of the regulator.

Intuitively, we know that the higher cost of public funds means a higher cost of giving up rents and also a higher cost of inefficiency. However, the relative cost of rents increases faster because when an additional rent is given up to a particular firm to support an efficiency improvement, the same incentive must also be provided to all the more efficient firms. The optimal regulation sacrifices some efficiency in order to decrease such rents. This is an argument in the direction of cost-plus schemes relative to fixed-price schemes – or, in the language of regulatory theory, rate-of-return regulation versus price caps (see box 1.3).

A higher cost of funds also means that it is more valuable to price above marginal cost, i.e. to use public utilities prices to finance fixed costs and the government's budget. In particular, it is a mistake to advocate marginal cost pricing for public utilities in developing countries.

The implied difference in pricing between developed and developing countries can be substantial, since a move from a cost of funds of 0.3 to 1.0 translates into a relative deviation from marginal cost which is double in the second case. Since effort levels also decrease as cost reimbursement rules are tilted towards cost-plus schemes, marginal costs are higher and, therefore, prices should be even higher in developing countries.

Box 1.3   Cost-plus or price caps

Pricing of telecommunications in Côte d'Ivoire

In the 1997 concession contract, CItelcom was granted a seven-year monopoly for the services delivered by fixed-link telephony. The guidelines for pricing are as follows:

- In 1998, a price cap maintained the global level of real prices with the possibility of adjusting each price by 10 percent.
- From 1998 to 2001, the price cap required a 7 percent per year decrease of real prices.
- After 2001, the price cap chosen each year guaranteed a rate of return on capital to be negotiated, with the goal of reaching tariff levels and structures similar to those in Europe and in neighboring countries. Indeed in 2002 a rate of return of 15 percent was decided.
- Note also the following provisions: If after 2002 the rate of return exceeded 25 percent, the price cap could be revised downwards. If after 2002 the rate of return was below 8 percent for at least two years, CItelcom could ask for an increase of the price cap.

The high cost of public funds in China

The high cost of public funds may imply that it is better to finance the fixed cost and contributions to government revenues through tariffs rather than through general taxes. That is, industrial-wide budget balancing should be maintained. In the power sector, for instance, prices were used to cover only operation and maintenance costs before 1992 and investment costs were covered by the government through fiscal revenues. As a result, there was a lasting shortage of supply of power. Since then, electricity tariffs have been raised to reflect full costs. More precisely, the Chinese government has implemented the so-called "one-plant, one-price" policy, which is essentially meant to guarantee full cost recovery regardless of the financing structure. This has helped to attract investments in the power sector. Another important case is in telecommunications, in which the installation fee was introduced in the early 1990s. Indeed, about one-third of each year's capital investments in network expansion was covered by installation fees. While this policy was criticized and the installation fee was eventually eliminated in 2000, many argue that China would not have been able to develop its telecom infrastructure so fast without the installation fee policy. Still another example can be found in China's railways, where a special surcharge was levied on the top of tariffs to finance the huge investment costs which guaranteed the funds necessary for the rapid development of the railway networks in China. Before this policy was introduced in the late 1980s, however, all capital expenditures of the railway sector had to be allocated from general taxes.

Monitoring

The impact of monitoring on the power of incentives is quite different, depending on the type of monitoring adopted. Monitoring of *effort* generally enables the regulator to reduce the information rents and calls for higher-powered incentive schemes. A less efficient monitoring technology will call for relatively less powerful incentive schemes. Indeed, low incentives and monitoring are substitute instruments to extract the firm's rent. A decrease in the use of one instrument makes the other instrument more attractive. As a result, an increase in the cost of public funds induces low incentives both directly and indirectly (as explained above) through a decrease of the more costly monitoring approach.

We have emphasized so far the strong assumption of perfect observability of costs. In practice, however, costs are not perfectly observable and one must also take into account the possibility of *cost padding*, i.e. the many ways in which a firm can divert money. Cost can now be increased by undue charges, which benefit the management and the workers. The analysis (Laffont and Tirole, 1993) shows that the imperfect auditing of cost padding calls for a shift towards higher-power incentive schemes. In the extreme, if auditing did not exist, only fixed-price contracts would be possible. Indeed they would be the only ones preventing unlimited cost padding by making firms residual claimants of their costs. It is therefore obvious that weak auditing technologies, as can be expected in developing countries, will result in an even higher desire to shift towards fixed-price mechanisms. This effect is reinforced by the savings in auditing costs resulting from fixed-price mechanisms in countries with a high cost of public funds (see box 1.4). The impact of the lack of auditing cannot be overemphasized. It is a crucial point, which conflicts with the findings of the previous paragraphs but easily dominates the other effects. In the absence of reasonable accounting, price-cap regulation is the only way out. It is only through price-cap reviews that some cost elements can be brought in, leading to some cost-plus shift through the ratchet effect (see below).

Making cost information public may be a way for the regulator to improve the quality of accounting by fostering more truthful disclosure of information by the firm, establishing its credibility for honest behavior.

Box 1.4   Monitoring and auditing systems in China

A weak monitoring and auditing system has major impacts on regulatory policies in China. The Chinese government has chosen a kind of cost-of-service regulation, more precisely administered prices that have neither upward nor downward flexibility. Historical cost standards are adopted and cost disallowances are rare. In theory, such a pricing policy would need perfect observability of output or a good control system of monitoring and auditing, which are obviously not available in China. Constrained by such disadvantages, the government must ask enterprises to make price adjustment proposals and then approve their pricing policy. As can be expected, these regulatory policies provide no incentives for enterprises to cut cost. To appreciate the full impacts of such policies, one needs to realize that, like rate-of-return regulation, there are also lags between price adjustments. Moreover, these rigid prices have not been fully implemented due to the weak enforcement power of the government. A specific aspect of China is that competition takes place between public firms. The managers of these firms engage in excessive competition as their private benefits depend on the size of the firm more than on its profits. Because of these governance problems, price-cap regulation would not be effective, which explains the general use of rate-of-return regulation despite inappropriate accounting systems.

Hierarchical regulation and corruption

The next point to consider is the need to devolve regulation to the regulatory agencies or ministries. A main role of these institutions is to partially bridge the informational gap between public decision makers and the regulated firm. This gives rise to another issue, the possible capture of the regulatory agency by the firm. Such collusion will more probably occur if the stakes of collusion are high, if the cost of side-transfers between the firm and the regulator are low, and if no incentive mechanism is in place for the regulators.

The stake of collusion amounts to the information rent that an efficient firm obtains when the regulator hides the fact that it is efficient. It is the maximal bribe that a firm will be willing to offer to the agency. However, it should be discounted by the price of internal transfers, which includes the cost of being discovered as well as the need often to use indirect transfers that are less efficient than monetary transfers. Capture is avoided if the agency is paid an amount larger than the discounted value of the stake of collusion when it reveals that the firm is efficient (we will call this constraint the collusion-proof constraint).

In the simplest cases, the regulatory response to the fear of capture is to satisfy the collusion-proof constraint at the lowest possible cost. This includes shifting optimal regulation toward cost-plus schemes to decrease the stake of collusion, and improving monitoring to increase the cost of side transfers.

Three features of developing countries call for even higher shifts towards cost-plus mechanisms:

- First, we can expect a lower cost of internal transfers because of less stringent monitoring of illegal activities
- Second, incentive payments to the agency are more costly because of the higher cost of public funds
- Third, it may be politically more difficult to create such strong incentive payments.

So far, we have dealt with a case where the optimal regulatory response entails no corruption. If we extend the framework to a case where, for example, regulators are more or less susceptible to being corrupted (some requiring low bribes, others requiring higher bribes), it may be optimal to let some corruption occur if the proportion of regulators requiring low bribes is small enough. Creating incentive payments which suppress the corruption of this type of regulators would be too costly, because the high payments required to fight corruption would have to be incurred even for the other type of regulators (for whom it is not necessary). Then, the same features of developing countries which militate in favor of low-powered incentive schemes (high cost of public funds, poor auditing technologies) suggest that it is optimal to let more corruption happen at equilibrium.[8]

Therefore, the effect of corruption appears complex. If we consider corruption of cost auditing, it calls for higher-powered incentives, but if we consider corruption in information reporting, lower-powered incentives are required (see box 1.5).

Box 1.5   Hierarchical regulation and corruption in China

Regulation of public utilities has been substantially decentralized in China to both the regional agencies and the sectoral agencies. While no conclusions can be drawn as to whether

---

[8] See chapter 8 for an analysis of how the separation of regulatory powers may help fight corruption.

a centralized or decentralized agency is more susceptible to capture, there are some institutional factors that make regional regulation less robust to corruption.

On the one hand, the local regulatory agencies are subject to no effective control from the central government while the local governments can easily affect their policies. On the other hand, social networks are more developed and effective, implying that local regulators can be captured more easily than national ones. Such institutional arrangements will necessarily cause concerns about market segmentation or favoritism to local players.

A case in point is the development of many small-sized power stations. As a result of relaxed regulation on entry, small coal-fired plants and hydro plants have been built in many regions. These plants with below-efficient sizes are not only inefficient but also produce heavy pollution. Indeed, the sizes of these plants are in general below 5 MW and they produce on average three times more pollution than the more efficient plants with a minimal capacity of 30 MW. To solve this problem and to create a more efficient industrial structure, the government has issued strict regulations to close down these plants. Unfortunately, these regulations are not strictly implemented, on the contrary, the number and installed capacity of small generation plants continues to increase and crowds out more efficient generation capacity. The problem is that the local governments exert their influence on the local regulatory agencies to not implement the restructuring policies initiated by the central government. In some cases, the local governments simply collude with these plants against the central government through hiding information and false reporting. In other cases, when the central government checks the situation on site, the local government sends a warning in advance to the plants and they close temporarily to avoid being caught. When the inspections are over, business resumes as usual.

The local government's incentives to help local generation plants arise from the fact that local production increased employment and local tax revenues, which contribute to local officials' promotion.

However, there is another factor that may counter the argument that regional regulation is more prone to capture. This is related to the current division of labor between central and local regulatory agencies. Remember that in general the central regulatory agencies are in charge of controlling big projects in terms of investment size while the local regulatory agencies take care of small ones, which implies that there are higher stakes to bribe the central regulator. In this sense, one may argue that the probability of corruption may be smaller but the impacts are bigger with central regulation.

Commitment

Let us consider now the important issue of *commitment*, or, more specifically, the fact that governments in developing countries have even less credibility to commit to long-run regulatory rules than those in developed countries.[9]

A lack of commitment puts the ratchet effect into motion. Faced with incentives in the first period, firms fear that taking advantage of these incentives today (efficient firms make more money by having low costs) will lead to more demanding incentive schemes in the future. A way to commit credibly to not expropriating rents in the future is to learn nothing today about the firms' efficiency. Instead of offering, as in the static case, a menu of contracts with variable sharing of overruns, which induces self-selection, the extreme attitude is to offer a single contract which induces undereffort of the good type and higher-than-first-best effort of the bad type. The inefficiency created by the lack of commitment is an inappropriate provision of effort levels over the various periods and an incomplete self-selection of types in earlier periods, which has no simple interpretation in terms of the power of incentive schemes. In the case of linear schemes it can be shown (Freixas, Guesnerie, and Tirole, 1985) that the ratchet effect pushes towards high-powered schemes which create higher rents in the first period to induce the revelation

---

[9] Useful discussions include Heller and McCubbins (1996), Levy and Spiller (1996), and Henisz and Zelner (2001).

of types. More generally, the lower the commitment ability there is, the less the regulator should try to separate types, and the more so if the cost of public funds is high.

The lack of ability of regulators to commit can be mitigated by the repetition over time of their relationship with the firms and the building of a reputation for not expropriating the rents derived from future efficiency improvements.[10] It can be expected that this substitute for the commitment of institutions will be less easy to achieve in developing countries. No general analysis exists of how easy commitment is depending on the type of regulatory regime. Regulatory institutions must be particularly scrutinized in developing countries for their ability to provide long-run incentives through their power of commitment, since a major goal is to attract foreign investment. Price capping has been pushed in the Western world as a way to provide high-powered incentives. However, price caps are regularly renegotiated while a commitment to a fair rate of return might be less prone to costly renegotiations (Greenwald, 1984).[11]

Weakness of the rule of law

Enforcement of regulatory rules is poor in developing countries, for two reasons. First, enforcement is costly, and optimal enforcement decreases with the cost of public funds. Second, the principal–agent paradigm with full bargaining power attributed to the regulator does not fit the reality of developing countries. Note that weakness of the regulator in implementing the agreed-upon contract may call for less investment in enforcement. Finally, corruption of the enforcement mechanism itself, or of the regulatory mechanism, calls for less enforcement. Thus, the weakness of the rule of law in

[10] See Gilbert and Newbery (1988) for a model of infinitely repeated contracting in which some collusive equilibria do not exhibit the trading inefficiencies associated with shorter horizons.

[11] However, one can also commit to a fair renegotiation of price caps.

developing countries is not due only to poor human resources, it is also part of an optimal regulatory response (see chapter 4).

Box 1.6   Enforcement

Enforcement failures in telecommunications

In Ghana, the incumbent monopoly for fixed telephony, which was not allowed to enter the mobile business, did eventually enter the market and used all kinds of tactics to delay interconnection.

In Tanzania, the regulator attempted to enforce regional mobile licenses. However, the dominant operator, Mobitel, argued that its license was national and launched a service in an area where the regulator tried unsuccessfully to shut down the operator.

In Côte d'Ivoire, the incumbent monopolist priced access for competing public phones in a way that foreclosed entry. The regulator intervened in 1998 to set a minimum price for the incumbent's prices at its own call boxes to allow entry. However, until recently the incumbent refused to adjust its prices.

Enforcement failures in China

Lack of commitment is an important problem that plagues regulation in China. The most serious case comes from the enforcement of price regulations. In telecommunications, the regulatory officials openly admit that price regulation is not as effective as it used to be. Even though administered prices without any flexibility are officially imposed, price wars are common.

In China's mobile phone sectors, the receiver-pays principle (RPP) is currently adopted. But many cases have been reported where the caller-pays principle (CPP) is illegally adopted. While the government has punished and corrected some cases, the practice has not been eliminated completely. It is also the case in phone services by internet, where competitive pressures have led to dramatic price cuts in comparison to the official prices. It seems that the Ministry of Information Industry (MII) can do nothing but to let it happen. There are also indirect price cuts in the form of free calling time and subsidized handsets, etc., which are officially not allowed, but happen daily. The second case is related to the enforcement of concession contracts. Concessions have been introduced in power, toll roads, and water, etc. In many cases these innovative forms of regulation have contributed to the development of these sectors. But there are also some cases of enforcement failures due to change of market conditions, unsustainable terms in the contracts, or opportunistic behavior.

In the power sector, the government has allowed independent power producers (IPPs) to compete with the incumbent, the SPC. These IPPs enter into the market by signing power purchase agreements (PPAs) with the SPC which consist essentially of a load factor and a unit average price to recover both generation and capacity costs. When a shortage of energy prevails, the PPAs are enforced without much problem. But when the market conditions change and there is an excess supply of capacity, conflicts of interests occur and the PPAs may not be enforced. In particular, utilization of installed capacity is much lower than the specified load factor and the bulk power prices are also lower than the contracted prices.

The impacts on generators are different, depending on the vintage of the plants. The new plants suffer seriously because they still have a large part of cost to recover. To make things worse, the contract structure, with a unit price and a load factor, gives generators strong incentives to produce as much power as possible regardless of their economic costs, because the more they generate, the more profits they can earn. This only complicates the favoritism problem and makes economic dispatching of electricity more difficult to realize. It seems that the government can do nothing about this.

Enforcement failures of contracts have also taken place in water where concession contracts have been used to attract foreign investments. A typical example is the Sino-French Water Company which is a thirty-year joint venture for water production between the Shenyang Water Company (state-owned) and the Sino-French Hong Kong Water and Investment Company. The ownership structure was that each owned 50 percent of the joint venture. According to the agreement, the Shenyang Water Company would buy all the water produced by the joint venture. The purchase price would be negotiated each year between the Chinese parent company and the joint venture but the prices should guarantee a minimum rate of return of 18 percent for the joint venture. Since it began operation in 1996, the purchase price rose rapidly while the retail price did not catch up. This caused huge losses to the parent company which made the contract unsustainable. The contract was ended in 1999 when a listed company, the Shenyang Development Company, in which the parent company has 80 percent of ownership, bought out the joint venture with money raised from the capital market. The operation of the joint venture was taken over by a subsidiary 100 percent owned by the Shenyang Development Company. In the end, the initial build, operate, transfer contract (the so-called BOT contract) was changed into a management contract.

Another example which is related to the regulation of entry can be found in telecoms. A case in point is the so-called "Sino, Sino, Foreign (Zhong, Zhong, Wai)" controversy. When China Unicom was created in 1997, it needed huge amounts of capital to deploy its own network in both fixed-line and mobile services. At that time, raising a large amount of money through initial public offerings (IPOs) in either China or in foreign capital markets or from other channels seemed not immediately possible. On the other hand, foreign companies were eager to invest in China's huge telecoms markets. But, unfortunately, foreign investments were not allowed in basic telecom services, China Unicom overcame the legal barrier indirectly by establishing subsidiaries with 100 percent ownership. These subsidiaries then set up joint ventures with foreign companies. By heavy "closed-door" lobbying and, in the meantime, with the recognition that the government had to give China Unicom some favorable policy for competing with China Telecom, the Ministry of Post and Telecommunications (the forerunner of MII), tacitly accepted this practice. But later on, after huge investments had been sunk, the government announced that this practice was illegal and foreign capital had to exit. This has caused an outcry. Even though the government made some arrangements to compensate those foreign companies that had sunk investments, some problems have remained. While one can argue that the original practice was not legal so that it should not have been allowed in the first place, such practices are not uncommon in a country like China which still has a weak rule of law.

Financial constraints

Financial constraints compound the difficulties of asymmetric information in many circumstances. The basic intuition can be stated in simple moral hazard control problems with risk neutrality. Moral hazard in a delegated activity can be controlled without giving up a rent to the agent if penalties are possible even when the observation of the performance is noisy. However, if such penalties are not possible because of limited liability constraints, only rewards for good performance can induce appropriate effort levels – i.e. information rents must be given up.

The greater the financial constraints, the greater those rents. Both the strength of financial constraints and the high cost of public funds favor a shift towards less powerful incentive schemes in developing countries. The irony of the situation is that, even though these countries should make more effort to emerge from underdevelopment, inducing effort is much more difficult in developing countries.

Summing up

Section 1.3 has detailed many arguments that favor a move towards less powerful incentive schemes (and, therefore, a move towards less efficiency) in developing countries. However, the use of performance evaluation to improve the fundamental trade-offs between efficiency and rent extraction presumes a perfect, or at least unbiased, auditing of that performance. The main argument against such advice is the cost-padding effect and the corruption of the cost audits which favor fixed-price mechanisms that save all the auditing costs.

We may thus distinguish three stages of development concerning regulation. In stage (1), the auditing mechanisms are so poor that powerful incentive schemes should be advocated. They promote short-run efficiency in activities that are immune to ratchet effects, but they strongly favor *ex post* inequality (since the efficient types make more money than the inefficient ones), they encourage some types of corruption of regulatory and political institutions, and they are costly for the rest of the economy because they create a money drain towards the regulated monopolies. This first stage should be used to develop a good auditing system. Once it is in place, one can move rather discontinuously to stage (2) of development by promoting less powerful incentive schemes for the reasons explained above. Then, as development continues, the optimal solution is to move slowly towards more powerful incentive schemes in stage (3). The quality of regulation in each of these stages depends critically on the ability of the government to commit credibly to the implementation of the schemes.

1.4 Promoting competition by pricing access

Let us again distinguish between the three market structures considered in section 1.2 to discuss appropriate access pricing rules in developing countries.[12]

Vertical disintegration

Consider the simplest case where the final services are produced by competitive industries at constant marginal costs. Ramsey pricing tells us that the access price markup over the marginal cost of access for a given good relative to the access price for this good should be inversely proportional to its demand price elasticity. Such a pricing scheme can be decentralized; price caps can be applied to the regulated

---

[12] See chapter 5 for a more detailed analysis. See also Estache, Valletti, and Manacorda (2002).

firm in charge of the infrastructure, relying in this way on the firm's demand information. Of course, that information is the province of the users of the infrastructure. The utility can infer this demand information from the demand for access as long as the users report truthfully the type of final good for which they use the infrastructure.

It may be difficult to promote such truthful reporting in developing countries when inspection systems are easily corrupted. Moreover, price discrimination resulting from sophisticated Ramsey pricing may be manipulated by interest groups (see Laffont and Tirole, 1993, chapter 11). In the case of developing countries, Ramsey pricing should thus be based on broad categories of usage which do not raise complex inspection issues and should be decentralized by price caps.

The discretion surrounding the determination of price elasticities and the problem of capture is transferred to the choice of weights on individual prices when using price caps. A nondiscretionary method for choosing weights in the price cap, such as previous-year quantities (plus an exogenous change in the level) should be selected in developing countries.

Another concern in developing countries is the market power of users of the infrastructure. However, regulation should not attempt, via access pricing policy, to undo the monopoly power of the users of the infrastructure. Such a policy requires a lot of knowledge from the regulator and raises issues of favoritism. In the absence of long-term contracts, there is a potential for expropriation of some large users' investments, which is quite negative for attracting foreign capital. In this case, other policies should be used to foster the competitive use of the infrastructure (see section 1.5).

One-way access with vertical integration

We consider now the case of a vertically integrated utility which provides access to the infrastructure and also sells a service using the infrastructure (the incumbent), and we discuss two subcases.

Suppose, first, that the competitive users of the infrastructure provide an imperfect substitute for the service provided by the incumbent (e.g. mobile phones versus fixed-link telephony with a lot of unsatisfied demand). In this case, regulation of access should be treated just like regulation of an end-user service, because the incumbent will be willing to provide access that increases its business with little effect on its own service market. For example, global price caps including final goods as well as access goods can be used (see Laffont and Tirole, 2000, chapter 6).

The situation is more difficult when competitive users offer services that are very close substitutes of the services provided by the incumbent. Then, the Ramsey rule tells us that the access price should be high enough to avoid inefficient business stealing and to balance the budget of the incumbent. One is tempted to favor a generous (for the incumbent) access pricing rule, such as the efficient component pricing rule,[13] to avoid foreclosure and to focus regulatory resources on implementing quick and high-quality interconnection. Alternatively, one can use a global price cap supplemented by maximum prices determined by the efficient component pricing rule. It should be recognized that this is a very difficult case requiring a lot of regulatory expertise, making it difficult to implement good solutions in developing countries. Indeed, examples from Côte d'Ivoire, Ghana, Tanzania, China, and elsewhere show that incumbents in the telecommunications industry are using various strategies to avoid competition (foreclusion, delays, raising rivals' cost...) (see box 1.7).

Two-way access for competition in infrastructures

When there is competition in infrastructures, as in the case of telecommunications in particular, final prices are usually

[13] The ECPR sets a ceiling on the access charge equal to the infrastructure owner's opportunity cost, that is, the difference between the owner's price in the final market and his marginal cost in the competition segment.

Box 1.7   Access policies

Access policy in Colombia

A constitutional amendment prohibits monopolies in Colombia, even public ones. Several regional public companies offer local telephony (Bogota Telecom Company: 25 percent; Medellin: 10 percent; Cali: 7 percent), and there are four mobile companies. There appears to be no problem in setting interconnection charges for mobile and long-distance services. The services are sufficiently complementary so that both operators gain from fast interconnection. However, concern remains regarding high access charges.

When the Telecom and Medellin companies entered the local market in Bogota, Bogota Telecom refused them access. As a result, there were three fixed-link companies in Bogota that were not fully interconnected. Indeed, access charges were not included in the price cap on final prices and were determined by historical costs according to the fully distributed method. Since Bogota Telecom made no money on access, it had all the incentives to engage in exclusionary behavior.

Access policy in China

Under the current development of competition, access pricing policies are implemented differently in railways, electricity, and telecommunications. In railways, since competition in transport services has not been introduced, there is no separate access policy. Instead, tariffs are designed that integrate both transport and infrastructure services. However, there is a very complicated settlement system among different administrations which has been used to settle revenues, including access revenues among administrations.[1]

In telecommunications, access and interconnection prices are also to a large extent determined on a revenue-sharing basis. For instance, termination from mobile-to-mobile networks imposes no charge. But since China adopts the RPP in mobile networks, such a regime is equivalent to an equal sharing of revenues under the CPP. Indeed, such a revenue-sharing scheme is also explicitly implemented for the interconnection from fixed-line to fixed-line networks. More precisely, the interconnection charge is regulated to be equal to half of the rival's retail prices. The termination charges for a call between the mobile and fixed-line networks are somewhat more complicated. For a call from the fixed-line network to the mobile network, the former does not need to pay access charges. But remember that RPP is adopted in China's mobile services. So it is equivalent to a regime in which the calling party receives part of revenues, just covering termination costs. For a call from a mobile to a fixed-line network, the former will pay the latter an interconnection charge of 0.06 yuan/minute (the average marginal retail price is 0.1 yuan/minute).

To sum up, the current access and interconnection pricing is in general not cost-based. So one may ask what the main motivations are for adopting such pricing principles. First of all, access and interconnection pricing determined on a revenue-sharing basis alleviates the regulator's asymmetric information problem. Lack of information on cost and weak auditing systems are current features of the Chinese economy. Second, these policies have a flavor of asymmetric regulation, at least in the way that they are practiced. Indeed, one can argue that in price access and interconnection between asymmetric networks such as China Mobile, the dominant mobile player, and China Unicom (which have quite different calling patterns) an equal sharing of revenues basis has the obvious objective to facilitate the entry of the latter, because their access revenues are unequal. Indeed, some disputes have arisen between these two operators in the past when new services were introduced. For instance, when China Unicom negotiated termination charges for its new CDMA network with China Mobile and wanted to keep the current bill-and-keep policy, China Mobile strongly opposed it, arguing that China Unicom had now obtained enough market share, making asymmetric regulation unnecessary.

Note:
[1] To the extent that final prices are regulated, access prices have no efficiency role and only redistribute revenues between operators.

deregulated but the regulation of access prices remains an issue. For example, in the internet, the bill-and-keep doctrine amounts to a zero access charge, something that is currently being debated (see Laffont, Marcos, Rey, and Tirole, 2003).

According to the literature, access prices in telecommunications should be regulated because firms (at least for symmetric networks) can use access charges to collude against consumers (high access charges induce high final prices) and to block entry (see Armstrong, 1998; Laffont, Rey, and Tirole, 1998a, 1998b). One possible solution is to impose the bill-and-keep doctrine, because of its simplicity and because it encourages competition in final prices.

A more difficult situation occurs when networks are asymmetric in size or traffic. In particular, it is important to ensure that network competition does not interfere with network development.

The regulator may mandate negotiations for interconnection under the threat of arbitration by an international body. It is unlikely that he will often have the information to choose access prices himself. This is an area where it is particularly clear that it is not enough to declare that competition is possible, or even to sell licenses, for competition to really take place. The inability to ensure fair competition may even delay competition and lead to implementation of the alternative option – that is, of regulating the monopolist with a strict program for developing the network.

1.5 Competition policy

We have argued that competition policy is not appropriate to deal with the complex and rapidly evolving technical issues concerning the interface between the competitive and noncompetitive segments of infrastructure industries. It remains to be seen what kind of competition policy is appropriate for the potentially competitive segments.

Three ingredients are needed for competition. First, there must be a sufficient number of firms or potential entrants into the industry. Second, those firms must not enter into collusive side contracts. Furthermore, if a firm has developed a dominant position it should not abuse this position.

It should first be stressed that, in most developing countries, the major problem is the dearth of participants, particularly in infrastructures where investments are usually sunk for long periods. The major problem is how to attract local or foreign capital to those industries – that is, how to create the conditions that make investment attractive. The work required to favor entry is not the usual task of a competition agency; unfortunately, it concerns most of the characteristics of developing countries that were discussed earlier and which cannot be easily resolved: inefficient financial sectors, lack of credibility of institutions, lack of enforcement of laws, inefficient transportation and communications, lack of information available to consumers, etc. These are weaknesses that Carlin and Seabright (2000) refer to as "competitive infrastructure."

This is particularly the case in infrastructures where technologies favor high concentration, and international trade cannot be relied upon to create competitive pressures. The difficult question is: Which rate of return will attract the optimal level of investment? If this optimal rate were known, competition policy should ensure this rate and no more. This can probably be achieved more easily through concession contracts with regulated prices than through competition in infrastructures.

More traditional competition policy can be relied upon in the case of the competitive use of infrastructure. As observed by Rey (1997), collusion is facilitated by entry barriers, market concentration, and capacity constraints, and these factors are more likely to be present in developing countries. As already noted, the transaction costs of collusion are also likely to be lower in LDCs. Similarly, predatory strategies may be particularly dangerous in countries where credit markets are weak. Rey (1997) also argues that the high entry barriers often found in developing countries give more force to the market foreclosure argument when discussing the essential facility doctrine. He also recommends a more cautious attitude towards vertical restraints.

Competition policy during the liberalization process should apply to the competitive segments of the deregulated industry; namely, generation in electricity, long-distance service in telecommunications, and operating services in transportation. This is particularly difficult in developing countries where attracting capital for infrastructure investment generally requires giving sizeable market shares to investing firms.

In particular, merger and acquisition rules in developing countries must be designed with an emphasis on simplicity, nondiscretion, and adaptability to the rapidly changing market structures. One possibility is to establish explicit market share constraints (forgoing efficiency arguments), which are periodically revised.

Some industries may need more innovative combinations of regulation and competition. For example, under normal conditions, the electricity industry may be appropriately competitive and need only the oversight of competition authorities. However, when capacity constraints are binding, either under conditions of peak demand or because of supply shocks, generation firms may enjoy such power in local markets that price regulation becomes necessary.

More generally, the difficulty of attracting capital generates market structures that are imperfectly competitive and calls for a more frequent regulation of conduct than classical competition policy. It also creates conflicts between privatization committees or regulatory institutions (which are well aware of the constraints on competition imposed by the need to attract capital) and the competition authorities, which *ex post* tend to breach the explicit or implicit agreements that restrict competition.

In any case, it should be clear that US-style competition policy (with its armada of lawyers and economists) is neither

affordable nor achievable in developing countries. Designing simple and transparent rules for these countries, particularly to prevent horizontal collusion and abuse of dominant
position, remains a worthy task. Nevertheless, the benefits
that can be expected from competition policy in the fore-
seeable future are quite small, for several reasons. The lack
of adequately trained staff is particularly acute in view of
the complexities and ambiguities of the economic analysis of
such questions as predatory behavior and vertical restraints.
Emerging industries will necessarily be highly monopolistic and interest groups will have considerable potential for
interference (see box 1.8).

Yet, competition agencies should be developed. Their first
major goal is to play an *educational role* by advocating the
social benefits of fair competition and concentrating on specific goals. For example, competition is weak in developing
countries because transactions are localized as a result of
poor communications systems and inefficient trading organizations. Focusing attention on these areas should be particularly fruitful.

Box 1.8   Competition policy in China

It is argued in China that competition policy is less relevant in
developing economies because, on the one hand, natural monopolies are taken care of by regulation, and on the other, there is
no meaningful market power created by any enterprise's dominant position. Indeed, most Chinese firms are still small in comparison with the big-name multinationals. While the view may
underestimate the role of competition policy, it does highlight the
important fact that competition policy may have different dimensions in developing countries and one has to take into account
the institutional features in China. But since competition policy
includes the promotion of fair competition, let us focus on the
antitrust aspect of competition policy.

The most important problem of competition policy in the Chinese context is the so-called "administrative monopoly," which

means that market power is usually created by the abuse of administrative power. The undue exertion of administrative power, whether by ministries or local governments, is meant to create entry barriers which will segment the market, in particular local markets. Many cases have been reported on this, for instance, in the power sector, power exchanges are not actively transacted because of local governments' influence. The issue here is actually not a matter of competition policy but how to solve the conflict of interests and counter the abuse of power by local governments.

Another feature of competition policy is that it has to deal with price wars among socially owned enterprises (SOEs). In other words, predation strategy is more relevant in the Chinese case. For instance, price wars are so fierce in the airline industry that price regulation cannot be seriously implemented even though the government has tried various ways to curb them. In telecoms, price cuts, directly or indirectly, are often observed. While it may be difficult to judge whether it is a real competition policy problem or a "soft" budget problem typical of SOEs, these issues do raise an important question: To what extent can competition be introduced without ownership reform?

1.6 Universal service

Cross-subsidies between high-cost areas and low-cost areas are a major feature of public services provided by public or regulated private monopolies. The main motivations of these cross-subsidies are redistributional.[14] Even though economists favor targeted monetary subsidies rather than transfers through distorted pricing, motivations can be found for such a strategy in the imperfection of the tax system.[15]

---

[14] In addition to favoritism and rent seeking, cross-subsidies may induce inefficient bypass and create poor incentives for service-quality provision and proper coverage of underpriced consumers.

[15] See Laffont and Tirole (2000) for the various reasons why the Atkinson–Stiglitz theorem, according to which redistribution must be achieved only through income taxes, can be invalidated.

The introduction of competition in the low-cost areas (such as cities for telephony) destroys the profits which supported the cross-subsidies towards the high-cost areas. New ways of financing low prices in these areas must be found. Taxes on the industry or on a broader basis can be used, and should be preferred to increases in access charges which are more distortionary. Finally, auctions of universal service obligations (USOs) can be used to minimize their cost. This strategy is appropriate for developed countries,[16] but raises a number of issues in developing countries.[17]

The creation of a fund for universal service financed by taxation meets the high cost of public funds in these countries due to a very inefficient and often corrupt tax system (Laffont and N'Gbo, 2000; Gasmi, Kennet, Laffont, and Sharkey, 2002, chapter 8). Then, cross-subsidies may have lower deadweight losses. Furthermore, political events often lead governments to use these funds for other purposes. Cross-subsidies, despite their weaknesses, may then be the only way to fulfill USOs.

The major problem in LDCs is not how to subsidize the use of the network in high-cost areas. It is more fundamentally how to expand the network in these areas. This calls for huge investments with little profitability, which are often beyond the financial capacities of those countries. The issue of USOs in LDCs should be debated around this concern.

1.7 Conclusion

This chapter has highlighted the departures from developed countries practices that are required in developing countries on the basis of normative economic theory. However, a number of caveats must be borne in mind:

- First, more empirical work is needed to more precisely characterize the specific features of developing countries that

---

[16] See Cremer (2001) and Chisari, Estache, and Romero (1999).
[17] See Chisari, Estache, and Waddams-Price (2003).

are relevant for regulatory economics. Such work should naturally lead to distinguishing various stages of development and to obtaining a classification of countries requiring differentiated policies.

- Second, even though we have mentioned some characteristics of LDC governments, a broader political economy of reform, taking into account specific historical and political situations, is necessary.
- Third, liberalization, competition, and regulatory policies are very recent developments, especially in the very poor countries. The empirical evidence is limited and not easy of access. Moreover, it is never in a form that would allow rigorous econometric tests. Case studies and theory are often the only available tools that can be used under these circumstances, but these should be relied upon with a lot of caution, in particular because the economic theory relevant for developing countries is so far only sketchy.

In the following chapters, we will use both theoretical analysis and simple econometric tests to explore in more detail some of the major issues reviewed in this chapter.

2

The rent extraction–efficiency trade-off

2.1 Introduction

Following the pioneering application of incentive theory to regulation by Loeb and Magat (1979) and Baron and Myerson (1982), the 1980s witnessed the emergence of a new theory of regulation which emphasized the role of informational asymmetries between government, regulatory commissions, firms, and various interest groups. This work has been synthesized in particular in Laffont and Tirole (LT, Laffont and Tirole, 2000).

These theories have been developed at the same time as the large privatization–deregulation–liberalization movement was taking place in Europe, in the United States, and soon after in Latin America, and quite naturally focused on developed countries. Under the pressure of the International Monetary Fund (IMF) and the World Bank, this movement was imposed on LDCs in the 1990s with no attention paid to the specific circumstances of these countries.

In this chapter we recap in section 2.2 a canonical model of regulation built for developed countries. Then, in section 2.3 we examine the insights one can draw from this model in the light of the characteristics of LDCs. We use a unique data set of concession contracts in Latin America built by Guasch (2003) at the World Bank to test our theory. In section 2.4 we stress the weaknesses of this model for analyzing LDCs and make a list of the desirable extensions needed for a proper policy discussion of network industries in LDCs. Section 2.5 briefly concludes.

2.2 A simple model of regulation

Description

We consider a natural monopoly in charge of a public service such as water, electricity, telecommunications, or transportation. Let q be the level of production which brings to consumers a utility $S(q)$, $S' > 0$, $S'' < 0$. We also denote $P(q)$ the inverse demand function and $\eta(p)$ the price elasticity of demand. The net surplus of consumers is $S(q) - qP(q)$.

The cost function of the natural monopoly is

$$C = (\beta - e)q + K, \tag{2.1}$$

where K is a fixed cost which will be common knowledge, $\beta - e$ is the marginal cost composed of a firm-specific characteristic β which can be high $\bar{\beta}$ or low $\underline{\beta}$ and is private information of the firm, and of an effort level e which decreases the marginal cost for a disutility $\psi(e)$ ($\psi' > 0$, $\psi'' > 0$, $\psi''' \geq 0$) of the manager (see box 2.1).

β is an adverse selection parameter whose probability distribution is common knowledge with $\nu = \Pr(\beta = \underline{\beta})$. e is a moral hazard variable chosen by the firm which is also private information of the firm.

For the time being we aggregate the government and the regulator that we call the regulator and we assume that the regulator is benevolent and wishes to maximize social welfare. For so doing he can use transfers to the firm, say $\hat{t}$. These transfers are raised with distortive taxes which create a social cost $\lambda > 0$. In other words, the cost for consumers of the transfer $\hat{t}$ is $(1 + \lambda)\hat{t}$. Consumers' net welfare is then:

$$V = S(q) - qP(q) - (1 + \lambda)\hat{t}. \tag{2.2}$$

Box 2.1   A cost function for telecommunications

The cost function (2.1) has a specific form; in particular it is separable in β and e, i.e. such that $C = C(\xi(\beta, e), q)$. In Gasmi, Kennet, Laffont, and Sharkey (2002), we have approximated cost data simulated from an engineering cost model of telecommunications with a translog cost function:

$$\log C = 16.96 + 0.44 \log \beta + 0.44 \log(\bar{e} - e) + 0.15 \log q$$
$$+ 0.11(\log \beta)^2 + 0.12(\log(\bar{e} - e))^2 + 0.002(\log q)^2$$
$$- 0.18 \log \beta \cdot \log(\bar{e} - e) + 0.007 \log q \cdot \log(\bar{e} - e)$$
$$- 0.007 \log q \cdot \log \beta.$$

Next, we have shown that the separability restriction embodied in $C(\xi(\beta, e), q)$ is not rejected by the data, and we have obtained:

$$\log C = 16.39 + 0.80 \log(\beta - e) + 0.15 \log q$$
$$+ 0.05[\log(\beta - e)]^2 + 0.02(\log q)^2.$$

The major simplification brought about by such a specification is a dichotomy property that we will verify below, namely, that the optimal pricing formula is not perturbed by incentive considerations. This allows a simpler view of optimal regulation as composed of optimal Ramsey pricing on the one hand and a menu of cost-reimbursement rules on the other hand (see LT, chapter 3).

The natural monopoly's welfare is written:

$$U = \hat{t} + qP(q) - (\beta - e)q - K - \psi(e). \tag{2.3}$$

We also assume that cost C is *ex post* observable by the regulator as well as sales $qP(q)$, so that we can make the accounting convention that the regulator pays the cost, receives sales, and gives the firm a net transfer:

$$t = \hat{t} + qP(q) - (\beta - e)q - K,$$

so that the firm's utility level can be written simply as:

$$U = t - \psi(e),$$

and the consumers' utility level can be rewritten

$$V = S(q) + \lambda q P(q) - (1 + \lambda)\left((\beta - e)q + K + \psi(e)\right)$$
$$- (1 + \lambda)U.$$

We assume that the benevolent regulator is utilitarian so that social welfare is[1]

$$W = V + U = S(q) + \lambda q P(q) - (1 + \lambda)((\beta - e)q$$
$$+ K + \psi(e)) - \lambda U. \tag{2.4}$$

The writing of (2.4) emphasizes the fact that giving up a rent U to the firm is socially costly because it requires funding with taxes which create a deadweight loss.

The full information benchmark

If the regulator knows β and can observe e he is constrained only by the participation constraint of the firm which is normalized as

$$U \geq 0. \tag{2.5}$$

Maximizing social welfare under (2.5) we obtain immediately

$$U = 0, \tag{2.6}$$

i.e. no rent is given up to the firm;

$$\psi'(e) = q, \tag{2.7}$$

i.e. the marginal utility of effort is equated to the marginal cost saving; and

$$\frac{d}{dq}(S(q) + \lambda q P(q)) = (1 + \lambda)(\beta - e), \tag{2.8}$$

i.e. the social marginal utility of production is equated to the social marginal cost.

[1] Social welfare is concave in q and e if ψ'' is large enough and $P'' < 0$ or λ small enough.

Noting that $S'(q) = P(q) = p$, this last condition can be rewritten

$$\frac{p - (\beta - e)}{p} = \frac{\lambda}{1 + \lambda} \frac{1}{\eta(p)}, \tag{2.9}$$

i.e. the Ramsey pricing formula with respect to the marginal cost $(\beta - e)$ and with an exogenous cost of public funds λ.

p and q are determined simultaneously by (2.7) and (2.9). Let $e_1(p)$ be the solution of

$$\psi'(e) = q(p); \text{ with } \frac{de_1}{dp} < 0.$$

Assuming that the price elasticity η is constant from now on let $e_2(p)$ be the solution of

$$p - (\beta - e) = \frac{\lambda}{1 + \lambda} \frac{p}{\eta(p)}; \text{ with } \frac{de_2}{dp} < 0.$$

For ψ'' large enough, the curves cut as shown in figure 2.1.

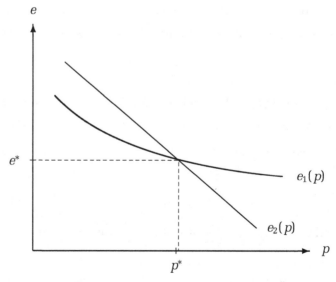

Figure 2.1   Optimal contract under complete information; e^* (resp. p^*) is the complete information effort (resp. price)

Optimal regulation under incomplete information

Now the regulator cannot observe the effort level e and knows only that β takes the values $\underline{\beta}$ (resp. $\bar{\beta}$) with probability ν (resp. $1 - \nu$). From incentive theory,[2] we know that optimal regulation can be obtained from the optimal truthful revelation mechanism.

Denoting

$$c = \frac{C - K}{q} = \beta - e$$

the marginal cost, a revelation mechanism is here a pair of contracts

$$\{(\underline{t}, \underline{q}, \underline{c}) ; \quad (\bar{t}, \bar{q}, \bar{c})\}, \tag{2.10}$$

designed respectively for type $\underline{\beta}$ and type $\bar{\beta}$.

Indeed, since $e = \beta - c$, the firm's objective function can be rewritten

$$U = t - \psi(\beta - c). \tag{2.11}$$

The incentive problem becomes a simple adverse selection problem with respect to the adverse selection parameter β, the marginal cost c, and the transfer t. Furthermore, the firm is indifferent to the level of q as long as t and c are unchanged. Such a revelation mechanism is truthful if it satisfies the incentive constraints:

$$\underline{U} = \underline{t} - \psi(\underline{\beta} - \underline{c}) \geq \bar{t} - \psi(\underline{\beta} - \bar{c}) \tag{2.12}$$

$$\bar{U} = \bar{t} - \psi(\bar{\beta} - \bar{c}) \geq \underline{t} - \psi(\bar{\beta} - \underline{c}). \tag{2.13}$$

Let $\Phi(e) = \psi(e) - \psi(e - \Delta\beta)$. It is an increasing convex function from our previous assumptions. The incentive constraints can be rewritten:

$$\underline{U} \geq \bar{U} + \Phi(\bar{e}) \tag{2.14}$$

$$\bar{U} \geq \underline{U} - \Phi(\underline{e} + \Delta\beta). \tag{2.15}$$

---

[2] See Laffont and Martimort (2002).

Optimal regulation is then obtained by maximizing expected social welfare under the incentive and participation constraints. This program can be rewritten as

$$\max_{(\underline{q},\underline{e},\underline{U};\bar{q},\bar{e},\bar{U})} \nu[S(\underline{q}) + \lambda\underline{q}P(\underline{q}) - (1+\lambda)((\underline{\beta} - \underline{e})\underline{q} + \psi(\underline{e}) + K)$$

$$- \lambda\underline{U}] + (1-\nu)[S(\bar{q}) + \lambda\bar{q}P(\bar{q}) - (1+\lambda)((\bar{\beta} - \bar{e})\bar{q}$$

$$+ \psi(\bar{e}) + K) - \lambda\bar{U}],$$

(2.14) (2.15) and the firm's participation constraints:

$$\underline{U} \geq 0 \qquad\qquad\qquad\qquad (2.16)$$

$$\bar{U} \geq 0. \qquad\qquad\qquad\qquad (2.17)$$

It is well known[3] that, in such a program, the participation constraint of the high-cost firm (2.16) and the incentive constraint of the low-cost firm (2.14) are the binding ones. Then $\bar{U} = 0$ and $\underline{U} = \Phi(\bar{e})$. Substituting these expressions in the regulator's objective function and maximizing with respect to $(\underline{q}, \underline{e})$ and $(\bar{q}, \bar{e})$ we obtain:

$$\psi'(\underline{e}) = \underline{q} \qquad\qquad\qquad\qquad (2.18)$$

$$\frac{\underline{p} - (\underline{\beta} - \underline{e})}{\underline{p}} = \frac{\lambda}{1+\lambda}\frac{1}{\eta} \qquad\qquad (2.19)$$

$$\psi'(\bar{e}) = \bar{q} - \frac{\lambda}{1+\lambda}\frac{\nu}{1-\nu}\Phi'(\bar{e}) \qquad (2.20)$$

$$\frac{\bar{p} - (\bar{\beta} - \bar{e})}{\bar{p}} = \frac{\lambda}{1+\lambda}\frac{1}{\eta}. \qquad\qquad (2.21)$$

We note first that the Ramsey pricing formulae are unchanged (this is due to the dichotomy property explained in box 2.1).

From (2.18) and (2.19), we see that for the low-cost firm we obtain the same effort level, production level (and therefore cost level) as under complete information.

---

[3] See LT or Laffont and Martimort (2002).

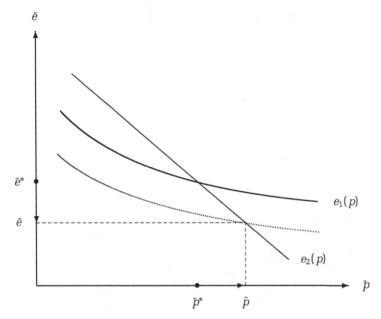

Figure 2.2   Impact of asymmetric information

On the contrary from (2.20) and (2.21), we see that the effort level and the production level of the high-cost firm are distorted downwards (see figure 2.2).

Also since $\bar{U} = 0$ the high-cost firm has no rent, while the low-cost firm has an *information rent* $\underline{U} = \Phi(\bar{e})$.

The intuition for the distortion in (2.20) is then clear. The ability of the low-cost firm to mimic the high-cost firm (due to the existence of asymmetric information) and to realize the same production level and the same cost with $\Delta\beta$ less effort, thereby obtaining a utility gain $\psi(\bar{e}) - \psi(\bar{e} - \Delta\beta) = \Phi(\bar{e})$, obliges the regulator to give up a rent to the low-cost firm. The best way to do that is to offer to that firm to produce more than a high-cost firm and exert more effort than when mimicking the high-cost firm, but to receive a higher transfer, a deal that is rejected by the low-cost firm.

However, such a rent is socially costly because of the social cost of public funds. At the second-best the regulator wishes to decrease this rent, which requires a decrease of $\bar{e}$ since $\underline{U} = \Phi(\bar{e})$ with $\Phi' > 0$.

Let us now interpret (2.18) and (2.20) in terms of cost-reimbursement rules.

Suppose that a share α of the cost is reimbursed to the firm. It then solves, for each q,

$$\min_e (1 - \alpha)(\beta - e)q + \psi(e)$$

and chooses a level of effort such that

$$\psi'(e) = (1 - \alpha)q.$$

So (2.18) can be interpreted as $\underline{\alpha} = 0$, i.e. no cost reimbursement. The contract chosen by the low-cost firm is a fixed-reimbursement scheme (which induces the firm to choose an effort level which is optimal conditionally on the level of production) complemented by the Ramsey pricing rule that the firm is willing to follow because it does not affect its rent. (2.20) instead corresponds to

$$\bar{\alpha} = \frac{\lambda}{1 + \lambda} \frac{\nu}{1 - \nu} \frac{\Phi'(\bar{e})}{\bar{q}}, \tag{2.22}$$

i.e. a share of cost is reimbursed to the firm (which induces the firm to choose an effort level which is too low with respect to the optimal level under complete information).

The higher $\bar{\alpha}$, the less powerful incentives are in the sense of a lower effort level being induced. This $\bar{\alpha}$ will characterize in our model the strength of incentives since the low-cost firm will always choose a fixed-reimbursement contract. Alternatively, $1 - \bar{\alpha}$ defines the power of incentives since the higher $1 - \bar{\alpha}$, the higher the level of effort $\bar{e}$.

Optimal regulation without auditing of cost

Suppose now that accounting is not well developed and that auditing of cost is too imperfect to be relied upon. Then the revelation mechanism can be based only on transfers and production levels, i.e. it is a pair $\{(\underline{t}, \underline{q}); (\bar{t}, \bar{q})\}$. The firm's utility level is then[4]

$$U = t - (\beta - e)q - \psi(e).$$

The incentive constraints are now:

$$\underline{U} = \max_e \left\{ \underline{t} - (\underline{\beta} - e)\underline{q} - \psi(e) \right\} \geq \max_e \left\{ \bar{t} - (\underline{\beta} - e)\bar{q} - \psi(e) \right\}$$

$$\bar{U} = \max_e \{ \bar{t} - (\bar{\beta} - e)\bar{q} - \psi(e) \} \geq \max_e \left\{ \underline{t} - (\bar{\beta} - e)\underline{q} - \psi(e) \right\}.$$

Effort is always conditionally optimal, i.e.

$$\psi'(\underline{e}) = \underline{q}$$
$$\psi'(\bar{e}) = \bar{q}.$$

Denoting $e^*(q)$ the solution of $\psi'(e) = q$ the low-cost incentive constraint becomes:

$$\underline{U} = \underline{t} - (\underline{\beta} - e^*(\underline{q}))\underline{q} - \psi(e^*(\underline{q}))$$
$$\geq \bar{t} - (\underline{\beta} - e^*(\bar{q}))\bar{q} - \psi(e^*(\bar{q}))$$
$$= \bar{t} - (\bar{\beta} - e^*(\bar{q}))\bar{q} - \psi(e^*(\bar{q})) + \Delta\beta\bar{q}$$
$$= \bar{U} + \Delta\beta\bar{q}.$$

As before, the participation constraint of the high-cost firm is binding ($\bar{U} = 0$) and the incentive constraint of the low-cost firm is binding ($\underline{U} = \Delta\beta\bar{q}$). Substituting in the regulator's objective function and maximizing, we obtain:

$$\frac{\underline{p} - (\underline{\beta} - e^*(\underline{q}))}{\underline{p}} = \frac{\lambda}{1 + \lambda} \frac{1}{\eta} \tag{2.23}$$

$$\frac{\bar{p} - (\bar{\beta} - e^*(\bar{q}))}{\bar{p}} = \frac{\lambda}{1 + \lambda} \frac{1}{\eta} + \frac{\lambda}{1 + \lambda} \frac{\nu}{1 - \nu} \frac{\Delta\beta}{\bar{p}}. \tag{2.24}$$

---

[4] We still simplify by assuming that $qP(q)$ (and K) is received (paid) by the regulator.

Contrary to the previous section, the marginal cost is now conditionally optimal, but a distortion occurs in the pricing formula of the high-cost firm. Indeed, we have lost one instrument of regulation, the (partial) reimbursement of cost. To decrease the information rent $\Delta\beta\bar{q}$ the regulator must now decrease $\bar{q}$ by increasing the price. This is the origin of the distortion

$$\frac{\lambda}{1+\lambda}\frac{\nu}{1-\nu}\frac{\Delta\beta}{\bar{p}}$$

in (2.24).

Optimal regulation without transfers

In some industries transfers from the government are not used or allowed (electricity, telecommunications). The revenues of the firm are then reduced to its sales. The firm utility level is then

$$U = qP(q) - (\beta - e)q - K - \psi(e). \tag{2.25}$$

If the marginal cost $c = \beta - e$ is observable the revelation mechanism is here a pair

$$\{(\underline{c}, \underline{q}); \qquad (\bar{c}, \bar{q})\}, \tag{2.26}$$

and the incentive constraints are

$$\underline{U} = \underline{q}P(\underline{q}) - \underline{c}\underline{q} - \psi(\underline{\beta} - \underline{c}) \geq \bar{q}P(\bar{q}) - \bar{c}\bar{q} - \psi(\underline{\beta} - \bar{c}), \tag{2.27}$$

or

$$\underline{U} \geq \bar{U} + \Phi(\bar{e}), \tag{2.28}$$

and similarly

$$\bar{U} \geq \underline{U} - \Phi(\underline{e} + \Delta\beta). \tag{2.29}$$

Therefore the incidence constraints are the same as on p. 45.
In the absence of transfers cancellation, social welfare is now

$$W = V + U = S(q) - P(q)q + P(q)q - (\beta - e)q - \psi(e) - K$$
$$= S(q) - (\beta - e)q - \psi(e) - K. \qquad (2.30)$$

The regulator's optimization program can then be written

$$\max_{(\underline{q}, \underline{e}, \bar{q}, \bar{e})} v \left[S(\underline{q}) - (\underline{\beta} - \underline{e})\underline{q} - \psi(\underline{e}) - K \right]$$
$$+ (1 - v) \left[S(\bar{q}) - (\bar{\beta} - \bar{e})\bar{q} - \psi(\bar{e}) - K \right]$$

s.t.

$$\underline{q}P(\underline{q}) - (\underline{\beta} - \underline{e})\underline{q} - \psi(\underline{e}) - K = \Phi(\bar{e}) \qquad (v\mu_1) \qquad (2.31)$$

$$\bar{q}P(\bar{q}) - (\bar{\beta} - \bar{e})\bar{q} - \psi(\bar{e}) - K = 0 \qquad ((1 - v)\mu_2), \qquad (2.32)$$

where $(v\mu_1)$ and $((1 - v)\mu_2)$ are the respective multipliers of
those constraints. Optimization yields

$$\frac{\underline{p} - (\underline{\beta} - \underline{e})}{\underline{p}} = \frac{\mu_1}{1 + \mu_1} \frac{1}{\eta} \qquad (2.33)$$

$$\psi'(\underline{e}) = \underline{q} \qquad (2.34)$$

$$\frac{\bar{p} - (\bar{\beta} - \bar{e})}{\bar{p}} = \frac{\mu_2}{1 + \mu_2} \frac{1}{\eta} \qquad (2.35)$$

$$\psi'(\bar{e}) = \bar{q} - \frac{\mu_1}{1 + \mu_2} \frac{v}{1 - v} \Phi'(\bar{e}). \qquad (2.36)$$

We obtain a distortion for the effort level of the high-cost
firm to decrease the information rent of the low-cost firm.
Ramsey pricing is adapted to ensure budget balance for the
high-cost firm and to provide the appropriate information
rent for the low-cost firm. The multipliers μ_1 and μ_2 are
adjusted for this purpose.

The major difference is that now pricing depends on the
level of fixed costs of the industry. For high (low) fixed costs,
prices will be scaled upwards (downwards) compared to the
case where available transfers make pricing related to the cost
of public funds in the whole economy.

(2.34) and (2.36) now have the following interpretation. The price allowed by the regulator is a function of the marginal cost, i.e. $p(\beta - e)$.[5]

The firm then solves

$$\max_{e} \; [p(\beta - e) - (\beta - e)]q(p(\beta - e)) - \psi(e) - K,$$

yielding:

$$\psi'(e) = q(p(\beta - e)) - p'(\beta - e)\left[q + (p - (\beta - e))\frac{dq}{dp}\right].$$

(2.34) is then interpreted as $p'(\underline{\beta} - \underline{e}) = 0$, i.e. a price independent of marginal cost, while (2.36) amounts to

$$p'(\bar{\beta} - \bar{e}) = \mu_1 \cdot \frac{\nu}{1 - \nu}\frac{\Phi'(\bar{e})}{q(p(\bar{\beta} - \bar{e}))}, \tag{2.37}$$

a price increasing with the marginal cost.[6] For the high-cost firm it is equivalent to average cost pricing (since (2.32) must hold):

$$p(\bar{\beta} - \bar{e}) = (\bar{\beta} - \bar{e}) + \frac{K + \psi(\bar{e})}{q(p(\bar{\beta} - \bar{e}))}. \tag{2.38}$$

To sum up, optimal regulation without transfers but with cost observability is equivalent to imposing a price as a function of the observed marginal cost to cover the cost of the high-cost firm and to leave an information rent to the low-cost firm.

Finally, suppose both that transfers are not allowed and costs are not observed *ex post*. Then the only instrument of the regulator is to constrain the prices of the firm in a set: $p \in P$.

An example is a price cap which, in our single-good example, is

$$p \le p^{\mathrm{sup}}. \tag{2.39}$$

---

[5] Indeed the revelation mechanism $(\underline{c}, \underline{q}); (\bar{c}, \bar{q})$ or $(\underline{c}, \underline{p}); (\bar{c}, \bar{p})$ is equivalent to a correspondence $p(c) = p(\beta - e)$.
[6] The solution obtained here must satisfy the incentive constraint of the high-cost firm. If it does not, then we have a solution with bunching.

Then we have two cases:

- Either only the high-cost firm is constrained at $\bar{p} = p^{\mathrm{sup}}$ and the low-cost firm can choose its monopoly price, defined by

$$\frac{\underline{p} - (\underline{\beta} - e^*(\underline{\beta}))}{\underline{p}} = \frac{1}{\eta}.$$

- Or both types are constrained at the price $\underline{p} = \bar{p} = p^{\mathrm{sup}}$.

Regulatory commission and capture

Let us continue to assume that the government is benevolent but that it uses a regulatory commission (RC) to attempt to bridge its information gap. More specifically, the role of the RC is to gather information about the cost parameter β of the firm. This is formalized by assuming that the RC observes a signal σ in $\{\underline{\beta}, \emptyset\}$. If $\beta = \underline{\beta}$ the RC observes $\sigma = \underline{\beta}$ with probability ξ and nothing with probability $1 - \xi$. If $\beta = \bar{\beta}$, it does not observe anything. Furthermore, the signal $\sigma = \underline{\beta}$ is verifiable.

With a benevolent RC, either $\sigma = \underline{\beta}$ and the government is informed and chooses the complete information regulation characterized by Ramsey pricing and

$$\psi'(\underline{e}^*) = \underline{q}^* \qquad (2.40)$$

or, $\sigma = \emptyset$ and the government updates its beliefs:

$$\Pr(\beta = \underline{\beta} | \sigma = \emptyset) = \frac{\nu(1 - \xi)}{(1 - \nu)} = \hat{\nu}, \qquad (2.41)$$

and chooses the optimal regulation under incomplete information with these updated beliefs, i.e.

$$\psi'(\underline{e}^*) = \underline{q}^* \qquad (2.42)$$

$$\psi'(\bar{e}) = \bar{q} - \frac{\lambda}{1+\lambda} \frac{\hat{\nu}}{1-\hat{\nu}} \Phi'(\bar{e}) = \bar{q} - \frac{\lambda}{1+\lambda} \frac{\nu(1-\xi)}{1-\nu} \Phi'(\bar{e}),$$

$$(2.43)$$

and Ramsey pricing.

The presence of the RC tilts the regulatory contract towards higher-powered incentives since from (2.43) $\bar{e}$ increases due to the term $1 - \xi$. Intuitively, when $\sigma = \emptyset$, the regulator believes that the firm is efficient with a lower probability, he fears less giving up an information rent, and affords a higher level of $\bar{e}$ (which increases the rent).

Suppose now that the regulator is not benevolent and has a utility function

$$R(s) = s$$

where $s \geq 0$ is his income.

When $\sigma = \underline{\beta}$, the regulator may offer to the agent to hide his signal in exchange for a bribe. This bribe is at most the information rent $\Phi(\bar{e})$ which is preserved by this action. However, for fear of being caught or because of the inefficiency of side contracting or because of some respect for norms of behavior, the regulator enjoys only a fraction k in $(0, 1)$ of this bribe.

To avoid collusion, it is then enough for the government to reward the regulator with an income[7] $\underline{s}$ when he reports the verifiable information $\underline{\beta}$ such that

$$\underline{s} \geq k\Phi(\bar{e}). \tag{2.44}$$

From incentive theory[8] we know that it is optimal for the government to offer a collusion-proof contract. However, the need to reward the regulator creates an additional expected cost of

$$\lambda \nu \xi \underline{s} = \lambda \nu \xi k\Phi(\bar{e}). \tag{2.45}$$

Indeed, the cost $k\Phi(\bar{e})$ occurs with probability $\nu\xi$, i.e. for an efficient firm which has been identified as such, multiplied by λ and not $1 + \lambda$, if the regulator's welfare is included in the utilitarian social welfare function.

---

[7] The reward can be of a different nature than monetary.
[8] See LT.

The government must then redesign his regulation to take into account this cost. He must solve

$$\max_{(\underline{q},\underline{e},\bar{q},\bar{e})} v\xi \left[S(\underline{q}^*) + \lambda \underline{q}^* P(\underline{q}^*) - (1+\lambda)\left((\underline{\beta} - \underline{e}^*)\underline{q}^* + \psi(\underline{e}^*) + K\right)\right]$$

$$+ v(1-\xi)\left[S(\underline{q}) + \lambda \underline{q} P(\underline{q}) - (1+\lambda)\left((\underline{\beta} - \underline{e})\underline{q} + \psi(\underline{e}) + K\right)\right]$$

$$+ (1-v)\left[S(\bar{q}) + \lambda \bar{q} P(\bar{q}) - (1+\lambda)\left((\bar{\beta} - \bar{e})\bar{q} + \psi(\bar{e}) + K\right)\right]$$

$$- v(1-\xi)\lambda \Phi(\bar{e}) - \lambda v\xi k\, \Phi(\bar{e}),$$

hence the Ramsey solution on the one hand and

$$\psi'(\underline{e}^*) = \underline{q}^* \tag{2.46}$$

$$\psi'(\bar{e}) = \bar{q} - \frac{\lambda}{1+\lambda}\frac{v}{1-v}\left[(1-\xi) + k\xi\right]\Phi'(\bar{e}). \tag{2.47}$$

If $k = 0$, we have the same solution as if the RC was benevolent.

If $k = 1$, we have the same solution as if there was no RC. The non-benevolence of the RC leads to a weakening of the power of incentives.

2.3 Optimal regulation and the characteristics of developing countries

High cost of public funds

Regulation with transfers

Under complete information an increase of λ calls for a higher price of the regulated good to cover more of the fixed cost with revenues of the sector or even extract revenue from the sector at the cost of decreasing the level of activity in the sector.

Asymmetric information requires giving up an information rent which has an expected social cost $\lambda v\Phi(\bar{e})$. The regulatory response is to decrease $\bar{e}$, i.e. to decrease incentives, and the more so the higher is λ (see appendix, p.62).

Proposition 2.1: *When costs are audited and transfers are used, the power of incentives in regulation decreases with the cost of public funds.*

The intuition is that giving up a rent is socially more costly. Note that the efficiency cost of the distortion $\bar{e}$ is also higher in a LDC, but the first effect increases with λ, and the second only with $1 + \lambda$. Also, as λ increases, the price increases according to Ramsey pricing; it decreases quantity, making effort less desirable.

In the absence of cost auditing, the regulator must leave the firm as residual claimant for its cost savings and therefore incentives are optimal conditionally on the level of production, independently of the cost of public funds. However, Ramsey pricing yields higher prices when the cost of public funds is higher. Quantities are therefore lower, and consequently the optimal effort level is lower despite being optimal conditionally on the level of production. The regulatory response to asymmetric information takes the form of a decrease in production because the information rent is then $\Delta\beta\bar{q}$.

Regulation without transfers
In the absence of transfers, but with cost observability, the solution appears independent of the cost of public funds ((2.33)–(2.36)). Revenues needed to cover fixed costs are obtained by increasing prices and contracting production to increase revenues. Incentives are also lowered to decrease the information rents. A more complete analysis would take into account the fact that high prices induce disconnection of some consumers from the services. Then, if social policy funds these consumers, a higher cost of funds makes the opportunity cost of the distortion higher. Accordingly, incentives will be lowered.

When only price constraints such as price caps are possible, effort is again optimal conditionally on the level of production. An increase in the cost of public funds will depress production, and therefore effort.

Incentives and stages of development
The results obtained in this section suggest the following synthesis in three levels of development:

(1) In stage (1) of development, auditing of cost is not available. Then there is no choice and firms must be left as residual claimants for their cost savings. Incentive schemes such as price caps or fixed-revenue contracts are used. They provide high incentives at the cost of high information rents.

(2) During stage (1), accounting and auditing are put in place opening for stage (2), the opportunity of using cost-reimbursement rules. One should then move rather discontinuously to low-powered incentive schemes of a cost-plus character.

(3) Finally, in stage (3), as the efficiency of the tax system improves one may return rather continuously towards higher-powered incentive schemes.

Note that these stages suggested by theory fit the historical evolution for the regulation of electricity in Western Europe. In the nineteenth century, electricity was regulated with price caps which became slowly more and more sophisticated (taking into account inflation, allowing some pass-throughs). Nationalizations in Europe or regulation of private firms in the United States then moved rather discontinuously to rate-of-return regulation, a cost-plus type of regulation. In the 1980s, the move to price caps was an attempt to reinstall high incentives in a world where better information and lower costs of public funds made information rents less problematic.

Higher propensity to corruption

From (2.47) we see immediately that an increase in the propensity to corruption, k, decreases incentives. Indeed, the higher the power of incentives, the higher the information rent of the low-cost firm, and the higher the stakes in capturing the regulator. In order to decrease the cost of providing incentives to regulators, the stakes of collusion are decreased by weakening incentives.

We reach a first result about corruption:

Proposition 2.2: *Under regulation with cost observability, an increase in the propensity for corruption calls for a reduction in the power of incentive schemes.*

However, this result presumes a perfect observability of cost. If auditing of cost is itself corrupted and allows cost padding, this creates a bias towards reimbursing less or no cost, and therefore a bias towards high-powered incentive schemes such as fixed-revenue contracts or price-cap regulation.[9]

Proposition 2.3: *Collusion in auditing calls for high-powered incentive schemes.*

Similarly, if supervision is the ability to observe with some probability the level of effort, we can show also that benevolent supervision permits high-power incentive schemes, but that the corruptibility of supervision calls for a weakening of those incentives.[10]

To sum up, when cost observability is available, a higher propensity to corruption calls for a weakening of incentives to decrease the stakes of corruption and for less investment in supervision because it is less valuable. However,

---

[9] See LT, chapter 12 for more on collusion in auditing.
[10] See LT, chapter 15.

if corruption affects the auditing of cost itself, it calls for using less or for neglecting cost observability, which precipates regulation in high-powered incentive schemes. So the end result of the effect of collusion on the power of incentives is ambiguous, as it depends largely on the type of collusion.

2.4 The rent extraction–efficiency trade-off in practice

Latin American countries are likely to be beyond stage (1) of development. Accordingly, our theory predicts that the probability of price-cap regulation should increase with the level of development – represented here by *per capita* GDP:PCGDP – and with everything that limits capture by politicians or by the industry. Three variables will play this role: the existence of a regulator (REG), its independence (IND), and the quality of institutions represented by the opposite of the level of corruption (NCORRUPTION). For testing the theory we use a data set of 852 concession contracts in Latin America assembled by L. Guasch at the World Bank.

A probit estimation confirms these conjectures (see table 2.1). The dependent variable *y* is 1 (resp. 0) if regulation is of a price-cap (not-price-cap) type.

In column (2) of table 2.1 we introduce an additional explanatory variable, the level of inflation (INFL) at the date of signing the concession contract. As expected, price-cap regulation appears as a protection against inflation.

In column (3) of table 2.1 we exclude the telecom sector.[11] Then the independence of regulator and inflation are no longer significant. Actually, looking at the same estimation for different sectors we find that the inflation variable has different signs according to the sector.

---

[11] Because many contracts in the sample are licenses rather than concession contracts.

Table 2.1. *Optimal contract under complete information*

	(1)	(2)	(3)	(4)	(5)
Constant	−7.38	−7.03	−11.15	−4.92	−10.76
	(−7.72)	(−7.29)	(−8.50)	(−5.56)	(−8.25)
Log (PCGDP)	0.74	0.68	1.31	0.47	1.24
	(6.26)	(5.62)	(7.91)	(4.20)	(7.53)
REG	1.59	1.76	1.45	0.44	1.14
	(11.66)	(12.14)	(7.06)	(2.61)	(5.65)
IND	0.82	0.98			
	(4.64)	(9.33)			
NCORRUPTION	0.11	0.11	0.06	0.20	0.08
	(4.47)	(4.55)	(2.22)	(7.41)	(2.93)
INFL		0.00077	0.001		
		(4.04)	(0.82)		
DTelecom				−0.92	2.39
				(−4.79)	(6.23)
DTransp				0.71	0.58
				(4.13)	(3.12)
DWater				0.42	0.24
				(1.87)	(0.98)
N	852	852	626	852	717
$Y = 1$	638	638	549	638	638
McFadden R^2	0.32	0.35	0.39	0.39	0.39

Note: t-statistics in parenthesis.

This is confirmed in column (4) where we introduce sector
dummies. The telecom and energy sectors have fewer price-
cap regulations than the water and transportation sectors. The
reason is that the telecom sector does not have any regulation
in many cases. In column (5) we exclude the cases of no regulation and find that the telecoms sector has more price-cap
than rate-of-return regulation.

Overall, the very robust explanatory variables are the
PCGDP, the existence of a regulator and the level of corruption. It would be desirable to look into the lengths of
the different types of price-cap regulation since we know

that price caps with short lags are close to rate-of-return regulation.

2.5 Conclusion

To conclude this chapter, now we want to stress a number of weaknesses of the model developed in this chapter to analyze regulation in LDCs. The first weakness of the model is its complete contracting nature which makes property rights irrelevant (Sappington and Stiglitz, 1987). The IMF and the World Bank always associate the deregulation of public services with privatization, but a debate about the pros and cons of privatization cannot be conducted within this model. In chapter 3, we will summarize the main arguments in favor of privatization and offer an extension of the model able to make predictions about when privatization occurs (positive theory) and should occur (normative theory).

An implicit assumption of the model developed in this chapter is the availability of a benevolent Court of Law which enforces at no cost any contract signed between the regulator and the firm. This assumption, which is debatable even in developed countries, is obviously not appropriate in developing countries as illustrated by several examples in chapter 1. The weakness and corruptibility of the rule of law, the lack of bargaining power of regulators facing large investors, the lack of checks and balances to avoid political opportunism – all these features explain why contracts often fail to be enforced. This fundamental feature of LDCs is incorporated in chapter 4 where a model with an endogenous level of enforcement is developed and tested on cross-country macrodata and microdata.

We have modeled in this chapter only the regulation of a natural monopoly. This is enough to discuss how incentive regulation must be adapted for LDCs when designing the regulation of the segments of the service industries which remain noncompetitive. However, a major issue of deregulation is how to price access to the monopoly segments for the segments opened to competition. Chapter 5 extends the model to discuss how the access pricing rules designed for different market structures must be reconsidered in view of the specific circumstances of LDCs.

The issue of universal service obligations (USOs) calls for the distinction between high-cost areas and low-cost areas. In chapter 6 we extend the model to account for this distinction. Moreover, we emphasize the major issue for LDCs, which is the investment decision in the network to define the optimal coverage of the country. Then, we study how interest groups affect the optimal provision of USOs, i.e. of pricing in high-cost areas and of the size of the network.

Finally, we extend the framework to discuss the design of regulatory institutions. We now consider many service industries and ask if regulation should be decentralized or centralized. We proceed in two steps. In chapter 7 we summarize for these questions the lessons from history in developed countries, from the recent experiences in developing countries, and from organization theory, and we offer a policy-oriented synthesis of this literature. Chapter 8 is more theoretical. It shows how the capture of regulators by interest groups bears on the issue of the design of regulation. Indeed, one or two regulators create different transaction costs of capture, and we discuss how the characteristics of LDCs affect the pros and cons of each regulatory structure. Chapter 9 draws some brief conclusions.

Appendix

The first-order conditions of the government's optimization problem with respect to $\bar{q}$ and $\bar{e}$ are:

$$(1 - v)\left[(1 + \lambda)P(\bar{q}) + \lambda\bar{q}P'(\bar{q}) - (1 + \lambda)(\bar{\beta} - \bar{e})\right] = 0 \quad \text{(A.1)}$$

$$-(1 - v)(1 + \lambda)(\psi'(\bar{e}) - \bar{q}) - \lambda v\Phi(\bar{e}) = 0. \quad \text{(A.2)}$$

Totally differentiating with respect to $\bar{q}$, $\bar{e}$ and λ

$$(1 - \nu)\left[(1 + 2\lambda)P'(\bar{q}) + \lambda\bar{q}P''(\bar{q})\right]d\bar{q} + (1 - \nu)(1 + \lambda)d\bar{e}$$
$$= -(1 - \nu)\left[P + \bar{q}P' - (\bar{\beta} - \bar{e})\right]d\lambda$$
$$(1 - \nu)(1 + \lambda)d\bar{q} - \left[(1 - \nu)(1 + \lambda)\psi''(\bar{e}) + \lambda\Phi'(\bar{e})\right]d\bar{e}$$
$$= \left[(1 - \nu)(\psi'(\bar{e}) - \bar{q}) + \nu\Phi(\bar{e})\right]d\lambda.$$

From these two equations, we can deduce $\frac{d\bar{e}}{d\lambda}$ using Cramer's rule. From Ramsey pricing we know that price is lower than monopoly price, hence $P + \bar{q}P' - (\bar{\beta} - \bar{e}) < 0$ and from (A.2) $(1 - \nu)(\psi'(\bar{e}) - \bar{q}) + \nu\Phi(\bar{e}) > 0$. Therefore,

$$\frac{d\bar{e}}{d\lambda} \propto \begin{vmatrix} - & + \\ + & + \end{vmatrix} < 0.$$

3

A positive theory of privatization

3.1 Introduction

> No region in the world is in greater need of new investment and more efficient operation of its infrastructure than Sub-Saharan Africa. The almost universally poor quality of the region's infrastructure directly impacts on the living standards of its people and constrains private investment in other activities.

This quote from the Foreword of Kerf and Smith (1996) raises two types of issues in relation to privatization. (1) Is infrastructure privatization a valuable option for very poor countries? This question will lead us to review the available theory about the role of property rights in the performance of public utilities. However, the main emphasis of this chapter will be on a more positive question which must be elucidated by a theory of reform if privatization appears to be the direction to go. (2) When does privatization occur in countries where governments clearly have private agendas?

Our starting point will be what appears currently as an internal contradiction of many theories of privatization. Public ownership is criticized for allowing excessive political interference by governments who are not benevolent. Privatization is supposed to curb this influence; however, privatization itself is decided by politicians. It is therefore important to understand why the governing bodies find it advantageous to choose the path of privatization.

We build a simple model which predicts the incentives for privatization as a function of various exogenous variables. We postulate that the rulers of the country derive private benefits in a rather inefficient way from public firms, which are poorly regulated, in particular because of corruption in the institutions of control. To obtain a more efficient operation of firms, the rulers must surrender the rights of control to (often foreign) private capital.[1] As a consequence, they lose most of their private benefits. They will accept privatization only if the privatization process enables them to fetch enough shares in those newly created firms providing revenues which compensate for their former benefits.[2]

Box 3.1   Privatization in Côte d'Ivoire and Guinea

Consider first the Compagnie Ivoirienne d'Electricité (CIE), which was created as a private management company with a fifteen-year concession, renewable to twenty years, for operating electricity generation, transmission, and distribution: 51 percent of the shares were attributed to the Société Internationale de Services Publics (SIPS), a joint venture between SAUR (a subsidiary of Groupe Bouygues) and Electricité de France. The remaining shares were distributed as follows: state 20 percent, private 24 percent, and a joint investment fund for staff 5 percent. One year after the concession, CIE registered a net profit of FCFA 700 million and in addition repaid a portion (FCFA 23 billion) of the 1990 FCFA 90 billion debt. The rights of control belonged to the foreign firm SIPS. The regulation of CIE through the concession seemed rather weak in view of the profits realized.

The previous state monopoly of telecommunications was sold as follows: 51 percent of the shares were sold through competitive bidding to France Télécom, with 35 percent to the state, 12 percent to Ivorians, and 2 percent to the personnel. Two regulatory

---

[1] See box 3.1.
[2] Direct side-transfers may also be used. They may enable the government to gain enough despite giving up control. However, they are in general politically more dangerous.

agencies were created, the Agence des Télécommunications de Côte d'Ivoire and the Conseil des Télécommunications.[1] In water supply, SODECI is an Ivorian Company owned 48 percent by local interests, 48 percent by SAUR, and 4 percent by a government investment fund. The lack of control by the foreign investor may not be unrelated to the problems remaining even after the new 1987 contract. Public users do not pay their bills and, as a result, SODECI seeks compensation by keeping the share of the tariff which should be allocated to debt payments.

Similarly, in Guinea, non-payment by public users remains a major problem, and lack of monitoring on the part of authorities results in excessive profits for the operator on the construction work which is carried out (as it happens, also for SODECI).

Note:
[1] See Laffont and N'Guessan (2000) for more details.

Results vary according to the level of corruption of governments, the pressure of democratic forces, the parameters of inefficiency of public regulation, as well as the expected revenues from the operation of the privatized firm.

The review of the literature is presented in section 3.2. Section 3.3 describes the basic model. The conditions for privatization are derived in section 3.4. Their empirical implications are tested in section 3.5.

3.2 Literature review

The reference point of any theory of privatization should be the Sappington–Stiglitz (1987) irrelevance result which shows that, even with asymmetric information, ownership does not matter for a benevolent government unrestricted in contracting. Anything a private firm can achieve can be mimicked by an appropriately designed public firm. To give any substance to privatization requires us to relax either the complete contracting assumption, or the benevolence assumption, or both.

Incomplete contracts with benevolent governments

Schmidt's (1996a) model has two building blocks. First, he assumes that privatization is a commitment not to learn some information about the firm and, therefore, that it is a credible commitment to give an information rent to the firm in the future. On the contrary, under public ownership the government is informed and expropriates the rent. Second, managers of the firm can make, or not, noncontractible investments which increase efficiency. By providing incentives for investment through the potential information rent, privatization may improve efficiency.

The government's inability to commit sounds like an appropriate assumption for the weak governments of developing countries with the associated underinvestment effect. It is conceivable that private owners are better able to commit not to expropriate private benefits of managers. However, the crucial assumption, according to which the government is better informed when the firm is private, remains unexplained.

In Laffont and Tirole (1991), the cost of privatization is due to the multiprincipal structure, since both the regulator of the private monopoly and the owners of the firm attempt to control the managers who have private information about the firm's efficiency. The result of this dual control is that each principal fails to internalize the effects of his own contract on the other principal and provides socially too few incentives for the firm's managers. Contrary to Schmidt (1996a), privatization is here associated with lower rents. As in Schmidt, managers can realize noncontractible investments which yield noncontractible private benefits. The government can not commit not to expropriate managers' investments in order to maximize the *ex post* public use of investment. This is because the government has often *ex post* incentives to reallocate the benefits of the investments to other parties – for example, if the firm becomes more efficient, it can force the firm to keep more employees than needed. Given the greater congruence of objectives between managers and stockholders, this reallocation of benefits to outsiders seems less likely in a privatized firm, at least if privatization has a strong content of noninterference in the internal management of the firm. The multiprincipal nature of privatization is true, but can be argued also for a government structured with different ministries or regulators.

A major common assumption of these models is that governments, despite being benevolent, have weak commitment abilities. This is certainly a correct positive observation about our institutions. Such limits rest implicitly on arguments of incomplete contracting, which themselves are related to complexity, bounded rationality, nonbenevolence of judges, etc. The assumption that ownership is associated with private information (needed in Schmidt) has been given some foundations in Aghion and Tirole (1997) by again appealing to *ex post* bargaining justified by incomplete contracts. The multiprincipal control of private firms is also an expression of the incompleteness of the regulation.

By postulating various implications of incomplete contracts, for both private and public firms, those papers are able to escape the Sappington–Stiglitz irrelevance result and exhibit interesting trade-offs. However, predictions may be quite limited if several of these incomplete contracting features are combined. Furthermore, the weakness of those approaches is that it is not clear that we are permitted to make several independent shortcuts implied by the same fundamental reasons behind incomplete contracts.

An alternative explanation of the restrictions on commitment of governments imposed by our institutions is the fear of nonbenevolent politicians.[3] But, then, this should be taken into account in the objectives pursued by the governments in both managing public firms and in regulating private firms.

---

[3] See LT, chapter 16.

Common sense suggests that political interference by governments with private agendas is a major driving force of privatization. The above incomplete information and incomplete contracting arguments must certainly be combined with a more cynical view of government.

Governments with private agendas

Shapiro and Willig (1990) were the first to build a model concerning privatization with an explicit assumption of private agendas for the government. Such an assumption can be traced to the simplicity of the constitutional–judicial rules which make the control of politicians quite imperfect. The second major hypothesis is that, as in Schmidt (1996a), privatization is a commitment not to learn all the private information of the firm.[4]

If we accept that public firms are more controllable by politicians than private firms, an argument in favor of privatization may appear. Less control means some inefficiencies and in particular higher information rents for the firm, but it also limits the ability of government to pursue its private agenda. Privatization is a costly instrument to prevent, or at least decrease, political interference.

In Boycko, Shleifer, and Vishny (1996), the starting point of the analysis is the observation that public enterprises are inefficient because they address the objectives of politicians rather than maximize efficiency. The argument in favor of privatization is based on the hypothesis that it may be politically less costly for the politician to spend the profits of the firm on labor without remitting them to the Treasury (a policy possible with a public firm) than to generate new subsidies for the firm as necessitated for interference in a private firm

---

[4] Note that in some sense the analysis relies on incomplete contracts. Private agendas are implied by incomplete constitutions, and the link between ownership and information by incomplete contracts. (See Laffont, 2000 for more details.)

(such as obliging it to keep excessive labor). Privatization is good because it makes political interference more costly. The reason is that the public is less aware of the wasting of profits in public firms than of inappropriate use of tax revenues obtained from private firms.

This theory rests on misperceptions by the public of the cost to them of alternative taxation schemes, which are neither theoretically explained nor empirically substantiated. There is also an internal inconsistency, in a static model, in claiming that privatization controls political discretion when privatization is decided by politicians themselves. Even though we are sympathetic with the basic idea that governments have private agendas and that privatization alters the way political interference occurs, the modeling of these ideas lacks foundations. A secondary theme of Boycko, Shleifer and Vishny (1996) is that corruption of politicians by managers is socially beneficial, since it may substitute the political benefits of labor employment by monetary benefits, a more efficient way to provide benefits to politicians.

Shleifer and Vishny (1994) consider a more precise game describing bargaining between politicians and managers and study the influence of the allocation of cash flows (to the private shareholders or to the Treasury: corporatization or not) and the influence of the allocation of control rights (to shareholders or to the politicians: privatization or not) on the outcome of bargaining. With efficient bribes between politicians and managers, the outcome is unaffected by these allocations. Without bribes, corporatization but not privatization may improve welfare. To have an effect of privatization the authors must invoke an ad hoc decency constraint, which limits transfers to profitable firms, but maintains the puzzle that politicians do not want to privatize.

Bennedsen (1996) constructs a model with a government controlled by the labor union, with imperfect taxation, and with market failure.[5] Ownership matters because under state ownership the government has more resources to correct the market failure but also to pursue nonprofit-generating activities, while with private ownership it has fewer resources for such goals. In a world where the constitution protects the rights of private firms, clearly the loss of control of the firm's rent by the government affects the outcome. What is not explained is why privatization limits the ability of the government to extract rents in such a complete information world. Again, no positive explanation of privatization is provided.

Laffont (1996) considers a privately owned natural monopoly in an economy where the majority rule gives alternatively the control of government, and therefore of regulation, to a group of citizens who share the rent of the private monopoly or not (majority 2 and 1, respectively). Regulation takes place under incomplete information and majority 2 selects a regulation with (excessively) high-powered incentives which leaves a high rent to efficient firms; majority 1 selects instead a regulation with too low-powered incentives which leaves a small rent to the efficient firms. The low incentives imposed by majority 1 translate into lower informational costs and therefore into smalles tax payments for citizens. Moving to public ownership means for majority 1 the appropriation of the firm's rent when they control the government,[6] and therefore more, and even excessive, rents and efficiency. Depending on the parameters, private or public ownership dominates for an *ex ante* utilitarian social welfare function. Here also, ownership affects the ability of governments to extract rents but the rents have an informational explanation and are influenced by economic policy.

---

[5] This creates scope for public intervention.
[6] Here again ownership affects information and interferes with the political game. The model delivers a positive theory of privatization in a democratic country in the sense that it can be the outcome of constitutional bargaining between majorities.

Table 3.1. *Descriptive statistics*

	Benevolent government with limited commitment	Nonbenevolent government
Ownership affects information structures	Schmidt (1996a)	Shapiro and Willig (1990)
Different ownerships yield different multiprincipal structures	Laffont and Tirole (1991b)	
Ownership directly affects the ability of governments to extract rents		Shleifer, and Vishny (1994) Bennedsen (1996) Boycko, Shleifer, and Vishny (1996) Laffont (1996)

Clearly, the theories of privatization will remain a difficult exercise in incomplete contracting for a long time, with no completely satisfactory theoretical foundations, and more an art than a science. The best we can do is to try, through a deep knowledge of the specific situations we are interested in, to make relevant sets of assumptions which appear reasonably compatible and confront the comparative statics properties of the models obtained with our stylized facts. In the following sections we will propose such a model for studying privatization in developing countries. We summarize the literature in table 3.1.

Remark: The main normative theories of privatization available are shown in table 3.1. For democratic countries there also exists an interesting literature which takes into account election constraints in the privatization process (see Dewatripont and Roland, 1992; Perotti, 1995; Schmidt, 1996b; and Biais and Perotti, 1997). ■

3.3 The model

We consider the same model as in chapter 2 except that we take a public project of size normalized at one to simplify the exposition. The natural monopoly can realize a project of social value S at a cost

$$C = \beta - e,$$

where $\beta \in \{\underline{\beta}, \bar{\beta}\}$ is a cost characteristic which is private knowledge of the monopoly and e is a cost-reducing effort variable with disutility $\psi(e)$ ($\psi' > 0, \psi'' > 0, \psi''' \geq 0$) for the monopoly.

The probability distribution of β is common knowledge. Let $\nu = \Pr(\beta = \underline{\beta})$. Cost is observable *ex post* by the government – the principal – so that the firm's utility can be written

$$U = t - \psi(e),$$

where t is the net transfer received by the firm from the principal.

Ex post social welfare is

$$S - (1 + \lambda)(t + C) + U = S - (1 + \lambda)\Big(\beta - e + \psi(e)\Big) - \lambda U,$$

where $1 + \lambda$ is the social cost of public funds.

Under complete information, a benevolent principal would request an effort level e^* such that

$$\psi'(e^*) = 1$$

and would give to the firm a transfer to extract the firm's rent ($U = 0$)

$$t^* = \psi(e^*).$$

However, we want to allow for a nonbenevolent principal who extracts private benefits from public ownership. We assume that the principal can extract private benefits b which create a cost increase of $b + \frac{b^2}{2}$. It is a particular case of cost padding. The principal maximizes a weighted sum of his private benefit and of social welfare. Social welfare is here a surrogate for the future private benefits he can hope for, if his constituency is well off. Such a principal maximizes

$$\delta b + \left[S - (1 + \lambda)\left(\beta - e + b + \frac{b^2}{2} + \psi(e) \right) - \lambda U \right] \qquad (3.1)$$

with respect to $b, e,$ and U with the constraint $U \geq 0$. δ measures the degree of corruption of the principal, for $\delta \geq 1$. Note that δ depends on the principal's moral standards, but also on the strength of the political constraints which align more or less his own interest with those of the community. A high δ can also be interpreted as a highly nondemocratic country. Optimizing yields

$$e = e^* \qquad (3.2)$$

$$t = \psi(e^*) \qquad (3.3)$$

$$b = \max\left\{0, \frac{\delta}{1 + \lambda} - 1\right\}. \qquad (3.4)$$

As long as $\delta \leq 1 + \lambda$, no private benefits are extracted. When $b > 1 + \lambda$, the principal extracts private benefits.[7]

Under asymmetric information, the principal has two instruments to mitigate his informational gap. First, he can send an inspector who has a technology enabling him to discover, with probability one, verifiable information about the true value[8] of β. If the inspector is sent with probability p,

---

[7] This extraction of private benefits is socially inefficient since for a utilitarian social welfare ($\delta = 1$) it yields

$$b - (1 + \lambda)\left(b + \frac{b^2}{2}\right) = -\lambda b - (1 + \lambda)\frac{b^2}{2} < 0.$$

Monetary transfers would be more efficient, but they are politically too costly.

[8] However, such an inspector can be sent only after the realization of the project. Note that the inspector has no discretion since the principal knows that he will discover, with probability one, verifiable information about the true value of β.

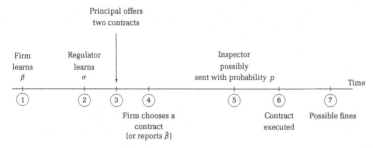

Figure 3.1 The timing of the model

the cost is $p^2 H$ where H is a normalization parameter. Second, he can use *ex ante* a regulator who entails no fixed cost, but who finds with probability ξ only verifiable evidence that $\beta = \underline{\beta}$ or otherwise nothing. In other words the supervisor's information is

$$\sigma = \underline{\beta} \text{ with probability } \nu\xi$$
$$= \phi \text{ otherwise.}$$

Let us first assume that the regulator is benevolent. The optimal strategy is to wait for the regulator's report and if $\sigma = \phi$, to send the inspector with some probability p if the agent selects the contract designed for the inefficient agent (or announces that he is inefficient).

The timing of the model is summarized in figure 3.1.

If the inspector is not sent, the contract chosen at time ④ is executed.

If the inspector is sent, the contract chosen at time ④ is unaltered if the firm has not lied. If it has lied, in addition, a penalty is imposed on the firm. As the firm is protected by limited liability, the maximal penalty[9] is the payment received in the execution of the contract.

Since the regulator is benevolent, with probability $\nu\xi$, the principal is informed that $\beta = \underline{\beta}$ and can impose the complete

---

[9] Note that the inspector does not find out anything on the level of cost padding b. It amounts to saying that cost padding (corruption) acts as a nondetectable fixed cost on the firm.

information regulation. With probability $1 - \nu\xi$, he remains uninformed but has posterior beliefs:

$$\Pr(\beta = \underline{\beta}|\sigma = \phi) = \frac{(1 - \xi)\nu}{1 - \nu\xi}.$$

From the revelation principle, we know that the optimal use of the inspector is associated with a truthful revelation mechanism, i.e. a pair of contracts $\{(\underline{t}, \underline{C}); (\bar{t}, \bar{C})\}$ or with a different notation $(\underline{U}, \underline{e})$, $(\bar{U}, \bar{e})$ with $\underline{e} = \underline{\beta} - \underline{C}$, $\bar{e} = \bar{\beta} - \bar{C}$, $\underline{U} = \underline{t} - \psi(\underline{e})$, $\bar{U} = \bar{t} - \psi(\bar{e})$. The efficient type's incentive constraint is:[10]

$$\underline{t} - \psi(\underline{e}) \geq (1 - p)(\bar{t} - \psi(\bar{e} - \Delta\beta)) - p\psi(\bar{c} - \Delta\beta),$$

or equivalently

$$\underline{U} \geq (1 - p)(\bar{U} + \Phi(\bar{e})) - p\psi(\bar{e} - \Delta\beta).$$

Since the principal dislikes giving up rents we have:

$$\bar{U} = 0.$$

The low-cost firm's incentive and participation constraints are written, respectively, as:

$$\underline{U} \geq (1 - p)\Phi(\bar{e}) - p\psi(\bar{e} - \Delta\beta) \geq \Phi(\bar{e}) - p\psi(\bar{e}) \quad \underline{U} \geq 0.$$

Of course, the most costly of these constraints will be binding. The optimal contract if $\sigma = \phi$ is determined by:

$$\max_{(\underline{e}, \bar{e}, p)} (1 - \xi)\nu \left[S - (1 + \lambda)\left(\underline{\beta} - \underline{e} + \psi(\underline{e})\right) \right.$$
$$\left. - \lambda\left(\max\left\{0, \Phi(\bar{e}) - p\psi(\bar{e})\right\}\right) \right]$$
$$+ (1 - \nu)\left[S - (1 + \lambda)(\bar{\beta} - \bar{e} + \psi(\bar{e})) \right] - (1 + \lambda)p^2(1 - \nu)H.$$

$$(3.5)$$

Two cases must be distinguished. With probability $(1 - \xi)\nu$ the firm is efficient but not identified by the regulator. A menu of contracts is offered and a rent $\underline{U} = \max\{0, \Phi(\bar{e}) - p\psi(\bar{e})\}$

---

[10] The other incentive constraint is irrelevant.

is given up to the firm. With probability $1 - \nu$ the firm is inefficient, and the contract with the effort level $\bar{e}$ and zero rent is chosen. An inspector is then sent with probability p for an expected cost

$$(1 + \lambda)p^2(1 - \nu)H.$$

The solution is characterized by[11]

$$\psi'(\underline{e}^+) = 1 \tag{3.6}$$

$$\psi'(\bar{e}^+) = 1 - \frac{\lambda}{1+\lambda} \frac{(1-\xi)\nu}{1-\nu}\left[\Phi'(\bar{e}^+) - p\psi'(\bar{e}^+)\right] \tag{3.7}$$

$$p = \frac{1}{2} \frac{\lambda(1-\xi)\nu}{(1+\lambda)(1-\nu)H}\psi(\bar{e}^+). \tag{3.8}$$

Proposition 3.1: *With a benevolent regulator, the principal uses his two instruments to reduce the efficient firm's rent:*

(i) The inspector is sent with probability

$$p = \frac{1}{2} \frac{\lambda(1-\xi)\nu}{(1+\lambda)(1-\nu)H}\psi(\bar{e}^+).$$

(ii) Low-powered incentives for the inefficient firm, which exerts an effort characterized by

$$\psi'(\bar{e}^+) = \frac{1 - \frac{\lambda}{1+\lambda}\frac{(1-\xi)\nu}{1-\nu}\Phi'(\bar{e}^+)}{1 - \frac{\lambda}{1+\lambda}\frac{(1-\xi)\nu}{1-\nu}p}.$$

The principal has two substitutable instruments to extract the firm's rent. He can either offer a low-powered incentive scheme which induces a low level of effort but decreases the rent – the cost here is an efficiency cost – or can send the inspector – the cost here is the cost of the inspector – or both instruments. Sending the inspector more often (higher p) decreases the rent needed for a given effort level

---

[11] We focus on an interior solution for p such that $\Phi(\bar{e}) - p\psi(\bar{e}) > 0$. The concavity of the problem is ensured for H large enough and ν not too large.

$(\underline{U} = \Phi(\bar{e}) - p\psi(\bar{e}))$. Accepting lower incentives (a low $\bar{e}^{+}$) makes less useful the sending of the inspector ((3.8)).

The comparative statics of the model can be easily derived in the quadratic case where $\psi(e) = \frac{1}{2}e^2$. Then (3.8) is equivalent to

$$p = \frac{1}{4}\frac{\lambda(1 - \xi)v}{(1 + \lambda)(1 - v)H}e^2 \equiv p_1(e)$$

and (3.7) is equivalent to

$$p = \frac{(1 + \lambda)(1 - v)}{\lambda(1 - \xi)v} - \frac{1}{e}\left(-\Delta\beta + \frac{(1 + \lambda)(1 - v)}{\lambda(1 - \xi)v}\right) \equiv p_2(e).$$

If $e = 1$ $p_2(1) = \Delta\beta$

$$p_1(1) = \frac{1}{4}\frac{\lambda(1 - \xi)v}{(1 + \lambda)(1 - v)H}.$$

H large ensures the concavity of the problem and gives $p_1(1) < p_2(1)$, identifying A in figure 3.2 as the solution. As the cost of the inspector H decreases or the size of the asymmetric information $\Delta\beta$ decreases, the inspector is used more often but incentives are higher. As the efficiency of the regulator decreases or the cost of public funds increases, incentives are decreased, and the inspector is used less often (see appendix 1, p.93). In a developing country where H is large, $\Delta\beta$ high, ξ low, and λ high we can expect lower incentives and less use of the inspector.

If the regulator is not benevolent, he must be motivated not to collude with the firm when his signal is informative.

For collusion-proofness,[12] the payment to the regulator who has the utility function

$$R(s) = s   s \geq 0$$

must be, when he reports $r = \underline{\beta}$, such that:

$$\underline{s} \geq k(\Phi(\bar{e}) - p\psi(\bar{e}))$$

---

[12] See p. 54.

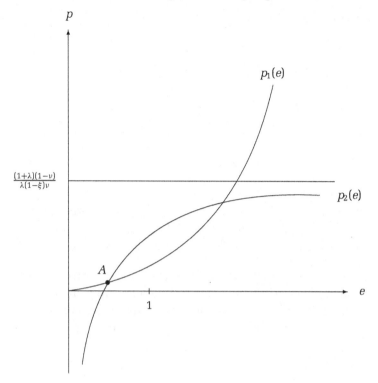

Figure 3.2   The optimal contract

hence an additional cost for the principal of

$$\lambda v \xi k \left(\Phi(\bar{e}) - p\psi(\bar{e}) \right).$$

Expected social welfare is now (up to the terms in b which are the same as before):

$$v\xi \left[S - (1+\lambda)(\underline{\beta} - e^* + \psi(e^*)) - \lambda k \left(\Phi(\bar{e}) - p\psi(\bar{e}) \right) \right]$$
$$+ (1 - \xi)v \left[S - (1+\lambda)(\underline{\beta} - \underline{e} + \psi(\underline{e})) - \lambda \left(\Phi(\bar{e}) - p\psi(\bar{e}) \right) \right]$$
$$+ (1 - v) \left[S - (1+\lambda)(\bar{\beta} - \bar{e} + \psi(\bar{e})) \right] - (1+\lambda)p^2(1 - v)H$$

$$(3.9)$$

with the solution

$$\psi'(\underline{e}^{++}) = 1 \tag{3.10}$$

$$\psi'(\bar{e}^{++}(p)) = 1 - \frac{\lambda}{1+\lambda}\frac{v}{1-v}[1 - (1-k)\xi]$$
$$\times \left[\Phi'(\bar{e}^{++}) - p\psi'(\bar{e}^{++})\right] \tag{3.11}$$

$$p = \frac{1}{2}\frac{\lambda v[1 - \xi(1-k)]\psi(\bar{e}^{++})}{(1+\lambda)(1-v)H}. \tag{3.12}$$

The nonbenevolence is equivalent to a decrease of efficiency for the regulator (ξ smaller).

Proposition 3.2: *In the quadratic case, for H large enough, the nonbenevolence of the regulator implies that the inspector is used less often and incentives are decreased.*

A major assumption of the above analysis concerns the commitment ability of the principal. When he claims he is going to use the inspector, the agent does not lie. *Ex post* the principal could save the cost of the inspector. We restrict our analysis to the case of principals who have the reputation of really carrying out the task of sending *ex post* the inspectors.[13]

3.4 Privatization

When the firm is public, expected social welfare is[14]

$$S + b - \bar{C} - (1+\lambda)\left(b + \frac{b^2}{2}\right)$$

with

$$\bar{C} = v\xi\Big[(1+\lambda)(\underline{\beta} - e^* + \psi(e^*)) + \lambda k\,(\Phi(\bar{e}) - p\psi(\bar{e}))\Big]$$
$$+ (1-\xi)v\Big[(1+\lambda)(\underline{\beta} - e^* + \psi(e^*)) + \lambda(\Phi(\bar{e}) - p\psi(\bar{e}))\Big]$$
$$+ (1-v)\Big[(1+\lambda)(\bar{\beta} - \bar{e} + \psi(\bar{e}))\Big]$$
$$+ (1+\lambda)p^2(1-v)H,$$

---

[13] Without such a commitment, the firm uses a mixed strategy.
[14] For a utilitarian social welfare function which includes the principal's private benefit with a weight of one.

where $\bar{e}$ and p are characterized in (3.10), (3.11), and (3.12) and b by (3.4).

The principal's welfare is then

$$\delta b + S - \bar{C} - (1 + \lambda)\left(b + \frac{b^2}{2}\right).$$

Privatization is defined by the loss of private benefits, the appropriation of a maximal share $\alpha = 49$ percent of profits compatible with the commitment of leaving the control rights in the hands of the private shareholder and by the efficiency of production, i.e. $e = e^*$, which can be interpreted as a move towards fixed price regulation (high-powered incentives).[15] The *ex post* information rent is then $\Phi(e^*)$.[16]

The sale value of 51 percent of the shares is approximately equal to the social value of the associated information rent if the sale occurs through an auction and this is already taken into account in the expected cost after privatization[17] denoted C^*. It can have a higher social value if the country has short-run financial problems. To capture this effect, we introduce a weight $\tilde{\tau}$ on the sale value of a share $1 - \alpha$ of the firm's profit in the social welfare function. If the principal is able to capture some of the proceeds of privatization, he overvalues them (and gives a weight τ higher than $\tilde{\tau}$ in the principal's objective function below).

Ex post social expected welfare is then

$$S - C^* + \tilde{\tau}(1 - \alpha)\lambda v \Phi(e^*)$$

where

$$C^* = (1 + \lambda)(E(\beta) - e^* + \psi(e^*)) + \lambda v \Phi(e^*)$$

[15] We simplify the presentation by assuming this extremely high-powered incentives. The ownership of shares by members of the government leads *ex post* the principal towards a rent extraction–efficiency trade-off which is too favorable to high rents.

[16] Here we simplify somewhat a more detailed model. We could consider a two-period model with independently drawn type β and one-period commitment for the regulator. Having financial stakes in the firm's profits, politicians favor a high-powered regulation which creates large profits. We take here the extreme case of a fixed price contract.

[17] The point here is that the information rent was previously captured by the management. Now, some of this rent is sold, but the management must be compensated for its loss of rent.

is the expected cost and $\tilde{\tau}(1 - \alpha)\lambda\nu\Phi(e^*)$ is the additional social value of the privatization proceeds that the public treasury captures if the country has serious financial problems. The principal's welfare is proportional to

$$(\delta - 1)\alpha\nu\Phi(e^*) + S - C^* + \tau(1 - \alpha)\lambda\nu\Phi(e^*).$$

Privatization occurs if

$$(\delta - 1)\alpha\nu\Phi(e^*) + S - C^* + \tau(1 - \alpha)\lambda\nu\Phi(e^*)$$
$$\geq \delta b + S - \bar{C} - (1 + \lambda)\left(b + \frac{b^2}{2}\right)$$

or

$$J(\delta) = (\delta - 1)[\alpha\nu\Phi(e^*) - b] - b + (1 + \lambda)\left(b + \frac{b^2}{2}\right)$$
$$+ \tau(1 - \alpha)\lambda\nu\Phi(e^*) \geq C^* - \bar{C}. \tag{3.13}$$

By definition of $\bar{e}$, $C^* > \bar{C}$. The social cost of efficient production is higher than the social cost of optimal regulation. From (3.13) we derive immediately.

Proposition 3.3: *When privatization occurs for some values of δ, there exists δ_0, δ_1 such that*

(a) for $\delta < \delta_0$ and $\delta > \delta_1$ privatization does not happen. For $\delta_1 > \delta > \delta_0$ privatization occurs.
(b) For $\tau = 0$, $\delta_0 > 0$. For $\tau > 0$, δ_0 may be zero.

δ_0 decreases with k and with H and δ_1 increases with k and with H.

Proof: See appendix 2 and figure 3.3.   ∎

If the proceeds of privatization are not taken into account, privatization occurs only with governments at an intermediary level of corruption and more often when regulation is more prone to corruption and when inspectors are costly. We should not see privatization in countries with strong governments and little or extreme corruption of the government. The intuition is as follows. For δ low, private benefits derived from

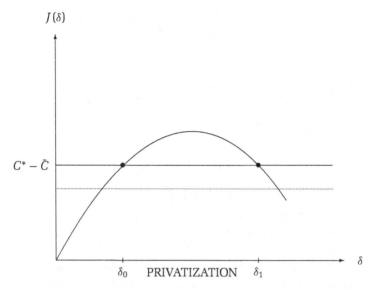

Figure 3.3   Privatization and corruption. The dotted line corresponds to higher H and higher k.

the public firm do not matter much and the choice of the principal is close to optimal regulation. This dominates privatization which gives up too much rent. As δ becomes larger, the private gains of the principal made possible in privatization are larger than those obtained with a public firm and dominate the greater social costs associated with privatization.

For δ very large, it may happen that the private gains associated with public firms (which are quadratic in δ) cannot be compensated by the appropriation of the rent under privatization because of the necessity to leave control to the private shareholder.[18]

For a given δ, in a society where transaction costs of corruption of regulators are low and the cost of uncorrupted inspectors (H) is high (features we may associate with underdevelopment), privatization is more likely.

[18] As δ becomes larger, the government should lose credibility and might have to surrender more than 51 percent of the shares. α decreasing may also justify the domination of nonprivatization for δ large.

For $\tau > 0$, and λ large enough, privatization may be justified even for a benevolent principal by the tax value of the privatization proceeds, and even more clearly for a nonbenevolent principal.

From a social welfare point of view, privatization should occur if and only if the social cost of extraction of private benefits exceeds the excess cost of privatization, i.e. (for $\tilde{\tau} = \tau = 0$)

$$W(\delta) = -b^* + (1 + \lambda)\left(b^* + \frac{b^{*2}}{2}\right) \geq C^* - \bar{C}. \qquad (3.14)$$

This condition can be viewed as the condition for normative desirability of privatization found in Shapiro and Willig (1990). Privatization results in higher rents but lower private agendas.

From (3.13), we note that when privatization is desirable by a noncorrupt principal, it is of course socially desirable. But, it may be socially desirable with (3.14) holding and may not happen because the principal is not benevolent. Figure 3.4

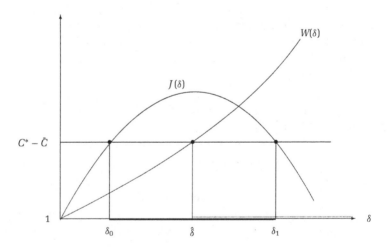

Figure 3.4   Social and optimal privatization
·············· δ such that privatization should happen.
———— δ such that privatization happens.

summarizes the differences between the normative and positive analyses. Privatization should happen for $\delta \geq \hat{\delta}$, when it occurs for δ in $[\delta_0, \delta_1]$. Clearly privatization may occur for good or bad reasons.

3.5 Testing the theory

Empirical implications

Taking a positive point of view towards privatization leads to two main conclusions.

- The occurrence of privatization may be the expression of inefficient regulation, corruption, or financial problems.
- Privatizations may happen when they should not because of corruption. The well-documented fact that efficiency increases with privatization should not make us forget that untaxed profits often increase even more. This second phenomenon should not be viewed as an imperfection of privatization but as the necessary price to buy corrupt principals. Sometimes this price is worth it because social welfare also increases. At other times it is not.

We have neglected a large number of factors which are important. Let us briefly comment on the way they would affect the analysis.

We have not taken into account the fact that foreign investors are often the only ones who can run the firms efficiently. This may entail an additional loss of welfare as part of the profits will leave the country. Privatization is then slowed down both positively and normatively.

To give control to foreign firms also has various political costs as it may upset the population or create the hostility of local capital. A nonbenevolent government may then give up privatization because of these expected negative effects. At the opposite end, privatizations may disappoint by not inducing efficient behavior. One reason may be that not enough shares are awarded to agents having the right incentives for efficiency or that the principals still manage to extract private benefits after privatization. Note that the second case may be compatible with our positive theory. The main gain for the principal is then to get rid of an inefficient regulatory institution. The outcome is still poor as private benefits are still extracted inefficiently. Again, the privatization decision is taken less often.

We have assumed the extreme case where the privatized monopoly has given up large rents to emphasize the weakness of the regulatory institutions in developing countries. Note, however, that good regulation would improve the privatization case from the normative viewpoint. But, since it is decided by principals who derive benefits from the rent (i.e. who overvalue the rent of the firm), we can expect a bias[19] towards too high-powered incentives which give up large rents, as we have postulated.

We have subsumed all the democratic constraints in the principal's objective function which partially take into account social welfare; more complex effects appear if the privatization process affects the future elections, as is recognized in England, or Slovakia. For developing countries, the shortcut of our modeling may not be too problematic. Democratic pressure can be interpreted as a decrease of δ.

The positive theory of privatization developed in this chapter suggests a demand for privatization if

Principal's welfare under privatization > Principal's welfare under public regime.

Hence, in the econometric model the probability of privatization will be a function of the difference Δ between these two terms. Δ is a nonlinear function of the level of corruption

---

[19] This bias is higher, the higher is δ.

E, an increasing function of the level of debt of public firms DEBTPE. To account for the dynamics of privatization we may want to make it dependent on the stock of public firms at the beginning of the period (normalized, for example, by the GDP of the beginning of the period) STOCK. It is also a function of the "price" of privatization which corresponds to the privatization revenues. We can specify a demand for privatization:

$$Y^D = a_0 + a_1 E + a_2 E^2 + a_3 \text{DEBTPE} + a_4 \text{STOCK} + a_5 P.$$

We can similarly define a supply function which will decrease with the political risk (R) in the country, decrease with the level of public deficit (which undermines credibility), maybe increase with the dynamism of the country (represented by the growth rate), and increase as well if the country is offered aid and of course decrease with the price

$$Y^S = b_0 + b_1 R + b_2 \text{DEFICIT} + b_3 \text{RGDP} + b_4 \text{AID} + b_5 P.$$

Unfortunately it is not possible to construct a price index for our data set. The value of privatization sales is available for only a few countries and this public data is probably far from the real price. So we will follow two paths. First, we will assume that the demand for privatization is price insensitive since the decision makers are more concerned with the long-run value of privatization than with the sales proceeds. Therefore we will estimate a demand function Y^D with $a_5 = 0$. In a second step we will assume that the demand function is price sensitive and we will look only for an estimation of the reduced form:

$$Y = c_0 + c_1 E + c_2 E^2 + c_3 \text{DEBTPE} + c_4 \text{STOCK} + c_5 R$$
$$+ c_6 \text{DEFICIT} + c_7 \text{RGDP} + c_8 \text{AID}.$$

The data

The data we use are obtained from several sources. Most economic data are from *African Development Indicators* (1997) for the following countries: Burkina Faso, Cameroon, Congo, Côte d'Ivoire, Ethiopia, Gabon, Gambia, Ghana, Guinea, Guinea-Bissau, Kenya, Liberia, Madagascar, Malawi, Mali, Mozambique, Namibia, Niger, Nigeria, Senegal, Sierra Leone, Somalia, South Africa, Sudan, Tanzania, Togo, Uganda, Zaire, Zambia, and Zimbabwe:

GDP(t):	Real gross domestic product of date t in constant prices (1987).
RGDP:	Average annual percentage growth between 1990 and 1996.
RGDP89:	Average annual percentage growth between 1985 and 1989.
DEFICIT90:	Government deficit in 1990 as a percentage of GNP.
DEBTPE(t):	External debt of public enterprises as a percentage of GNP at date t.
AID:	Annual average of net official development assistance from all donors as share of recipient GNP from 1990 to 1996.
STOCK:	Number of public firms in 1990.
Y:	Proportion of 1990 public firms subject to privatization operations up to 1995.
ILLITERACY:	Percentage of population fifteen years of age and above that is illiterate (average of 1990 and 1995).
WB:	World Bank lending operations supporting privatization up to end-1995 as a proportion of GDP, drawn from Campbell, White, and Bhatia (1998).

The political risk variables are obtained from the World Bank. A political risk variable, RATE, is obtained from twelve

Table 3.2. *Descriptive statistics*

| | Economic variables | | | | | |
	Mean	Median	Maximum	Minimum	Std dev.	Obs.
AID	18.56	13.00	84.80	0.10	18.10	29
DEBTPE90	5.81	3.20	28.00	0.00	7.02	29
DEBTPE95	4.21	1.90	25.70	0.00	5.61	27
PRIVATIZATION	0.30	0.24	0.79	0.00	0.23	30
STOCK	163.33	95.00	1200.00	16.00	227.41	30
WB	0.07	0.04	0.31	0.00	0.08	29
GDP95	8684.55	2823.00	90156.00	229.00	17565.91	27
GDP90	8159.62	2849.00	86869.00	197.00	16296.77	29
RGDP	1.90	2.50	6.90	−7.00	2.81	28
RGDP89	2.57	2.80	6.00	−3.80	2.19	30
DEFICIT90	4.02	3.35	12.30	−6.10	4.28	30
ILLITERACY	50.76	52.50	81.50	18.00	19.54	30

| | Political variables | | | | | |
	Mean	Median	Maximum	Minimum	Std dev.	Obs.
E95	2.83	3.00	5.00	0.00	1.23	30
E90	2.86	3.00	5.00	0.00	1.13	30
MM95	2.56	2.00	5.00	1.00	1.10	30
MM90	2.53	2.00	6.00	1.00	1.25	30
RATE95	54.20	56.50	77.00	28.00	13.05	30
RATE90	45.03	47.00	61.00	9.00	12.54	30

indicators, including government stability, corruption, law and order, bureaucracy development, etc. We use the global index for 1995 and 1990, denoted RATE 95, RATE 90, respectively. We will also use the corruption index E (E95, E90, and the average EM) and an index of bureaucratic quality MM90, MM95.

Table 3.2 presents some descriptive statistics about the data.

Determinants of the rate of privatization

In addition to the nonlinear relationship with the corruption variable we expect the rate of privatization to be higher if the

Table 3.3. *Least squares*

| Dependent variable: | Privatization rate | |
	(1)	(2)
Cte	0.26	−0.04
	(1.61)	(−0.53)
E90	0.14	0.21
	(1.37)	(4.22)
E902	−0.04	−0.04
	(−2.03)	(−3.70)
STOCK/GDP90	0.77	0.15
	(2.19)	(1.20)
DEBTPE90	−0.009	0.006
	(−1.10)	(1.49)
LSSZ	−	−0.18
	−	(−2.44)
GGGGM	−	0.44
	−	(6.77)
	$R^2 = 0.26$	$R^2 = 0.76$

stock of public firms (relative to GDP) is high and if the public firms have a lot of debt. We obtain the data in table 3.3.

In all cases, we use White heteroskedasticity consistent standard errors and covariance.

Column (2) of table 3.2 shows that even if we use dummy variables for the extreme observations (those with very low privatization rate, LSSZ, and those with very high privatization rate, GGGGM), the quadratic relationship remains. However, the sign of DEBTPE90 seems satisfactory only when they are included. The stock variable is no longer significant when dummy variables are introduced.

We obtain similar results for other measures of corruption (E95 corruption index for 1995 and EM average of E95 and E90) and then with variables related to the quality of the administration (MM90) with more general political risk

Table 3.4. *Two-stage least squares*

	Dependent variable: PRIVATIZATION					
Cte	0.10	−0.06	0.30	−0.04	−1.01	−0.41
	(0.81)	(−0.70)	(1.55)	(−0.61)	(−1.23)	(−0.70)
E95	0.23	0.25				
	(−2.34)	(−5.37)				
E95^2	−0.04	−0.04				
	(−2.34)	(−5.37)				
EM			0.13	0.20		
			(1.40)	(4.50)		
EM^2			−0.03	−0.03		
			(−1.81)	(−3.67)		
RATEM					0.06	0.02
					(1.57)	(0.94)
RATE M^2					−0.0001	−0.00006
					(−1.51)	(−0.85)
STOCKGDP90	0.64	0.13	0.71	0.12	0.53	0.17
	(1.85)	(1.56)	(1.97)	(1.13)	(1.57)	(1.08)
DEBTPE90	−0.009	0.004	−0.009	0.006	−0.009	0.002
	(−1.02)	(1.66)	(−0.97)	(1.66)	(0.23)	(0.52)
LSSZ	−	−0.20	−	−0.18	−	0.18
	−	(−3.63)	−	(−2.81)	−	0.18
GGGGM	−	0.44	−	0.45	−	0.41
	−	(8.21)	−	(7.16)	−	(5.46)
	$R^2 = 0.23$	$R^2 = 0.83$	$R^2 = 0.20$	$R^2 = 0.76$	$R^2 = 0.23$	$R^2 = 0.73$

variables (RATE90 for 1990 and RATEM for an average of 1990 and 1995 (table 3.4)).

We also deal in table 3.3 with the endogeneity of E95, EM, RATE by using two-stage least squares.

Clearly the corruption variables are the only ones which maintain the statistical significance of the nonlinear relationship, throughout the various estimation methods, a property which is not perturbed by the LSSZ and GGGGM variables.

There is a supply for privatization with which the theory we have referred to is concerned. However, developing countries may lack the capital willing to invest in privatized firms: there is a demand for privatization. Accordingly, we estimate

Table 3.5. *Different measures of corruption*

	Dependent variable: PRIVATIZATION RATE				
	LS	TSLS	TSLS	TSLS	TSLS
Cte	−0.02	−0.01	−0.03	0.009	−0.11
	(−0.27)	(−0.10)	(−0.23)	(0.07)	(−0.74)
E90	0.12	0.11	0.12	0.15	0.13
	(2.17)	(1.50)	(1.59)	(0.62)	(1.69)
$E90^2$	−0.04	−0.04	−0.04	−0.04	−0.04
	(−3.51)	(−2.00)	(−2.11)	(1.11)	(−2.14)
STOCKGDP90	1.05	0.95	1.02	0.08	1.01
	(7.41)	(4.13)	(2.14)	(3.56)	(6.24)
DEB	−0.02	−0.02	−0.02	−0.02	−0.02
	(−5.88)	(−5.16)	(−4.97)	(−3.35)	(−6.27)
RATE90	0.009	0.009	0.010	0.008	0.01
	(5.21)	(4.13)	(4.15)	(1.55)	(4.29)
WB		0.35			
		(0.53)			
AID			0.003		
			(0.07)		
RGDP				−0.006	
				(−0.16)	
ILLITERACY					0.001
					(0.67)
Adjusted R^2	$R^2 = 0.48$	$R^2 = 0.45$	$R^2 = 0.43$	$R^2 = 0.40$	$R^2 = 0.56$

in table 3.5 the reduced form yielding the privatization rate.

The first regression leads to a fairly good fit and a Wald test rejects (at 1 percent level) the hypothesis that corruption does not affect privatization ($c_2 = c_3 = 0$).[20]

At the 10 percent significance level, the World Bank operations, aid, the rate of growth, and the illiteracy rate are not significant.

---

[20] The DEB variable is obtained by adding the government deficit rate in 1990 and the public enterprise debt rate in 1990.

We see that the quadratic effect of corruption is rather stable and that the stock variable becomes quite significant in the reduced form equation, suggesting its appearance in the supply equation. Also, we were not able to exhibit the positive effect of debt on the desired privatization, and it seems also here that the supply effect dominates (investors are reluctant to invest in countries with very high debt). Maybe debt should be viewed as a substitute for the lack of credibility.

The main conclusion is that the nonlinear relationship in the corruption variable is robust to these various specifications.

Appendix 1

When $\psi(e) = \frac{1}{2}e^2$, social welfare equals, up to a constant and terms in $\underline{e}$:

$$-(1 - \xi)v\lambda \left(\bar{e}\Delta\beta - p\frac{\bar{e}^2}{2} \right) - (1 - v)(1 + \lambda)\left(\frac{\bar{e}^2}{2} - 1 \right)$$

$$-(1 + \lambda)(1 - v)p^2 H.$$

The first-order conditions are

$$-(1 - \xi)v\lambda(\Delta\beta - p\bar{e}) - (1 - v)(1 + \lambda)\bar{e} = 0$$

$$(1 - \xi)v\lambda\frac{\bar{e}^2}{2} - 2(1 + \lambda)(1 - v)pH = 0.$$

The Jacobian is:

$$[- (1 - v)(1 + \lambda) + (1 - \xi)v\lambda p \quad (1 - \xi)v\lambda\bar{e}$$
$$(1 - \xi)v\lambda\bar{e} \quad -2(1 + \lambda)(1 - v)H].$$

When v is not too large $(1 - \xi)v\lambda p - (1 - v)(1 + \lambda) < 0$ and when H is large enough, the matrix is definitely negative.

Differentiating the first-order conditions we have

$$[(1 - \xi)v\lambda p - (1 - v)(1 + \lambda)]\,d\bar{e} + (1 - \xi)v\lambda\bar{e}dp$$
$$= [(1 - v)\bar{e} + (1 - \xi)v\Delta\beta]\,d\lambda - v\lambda(\Delta\beta - p\bar{e})d\xi$$
$$+ (1 - \xi)v\lambda d\Delta\beta$$

$$(1 - \xi)v\lambda\bar{e}d\bar{e} - 2(1 + \lambda)(1 - v)Hdp$$
$$= \left[2(1 - v)(1 + \lambda)H - (1 - \xi)v\frac{\bar{e}^2}{2}\right]d\lambda + v\lambda\frac{\bar{e}^2}{2}d\xi$$
$$+ 2(1 + \lambda)(1 - v)pdH.$$

Using H large we have immediately

$$\frac{d\bar{e}}{d\lambda} < 0 \quad \frac{dp}{d\lambda} < 0 \quad \frac{d\bar{e}}{d\xi} > 0 \quad \frac{d\bar{e}}{d\Delta\beta} < 0 \quad \frac{dp}{d\Delta\beta} < 0$$

$$\frac{d\bar{e}}{dH} < 0 \quad \frac{dp}{dH} < 0.$$

$$\frac{dp}{d\xi} \propto [(1 - \xi)v\lambda p - (1 - v)(1 + \lambda)]\frac{\bar{e}}{2} + v\lambda(\Delta\beta - p\bar{e})(1 - \xi).$$

From the first-order condition

$$[(1 - \xi)v\lambda p - (1 - v)(1 + \lambda)]\bar{e} = (1 - \xi)v\lambda\Delta\beta$$

$$\frac{dp}{d\xi} \propto v\lambda\left(\frac{3\Delta\beta}{2} - p\bar{e}\right)(1 - \xi) > 0 \quad \text{if} \quad H \quad \text{is large.}$$

Appendix 2   Proof of proposition 3.3

Let

$$J(\delta) = (\delta - 1)[\alpha v\Phi(e^*) - b] - b + (1 + \lambda)\left(b + \frac{b^2}{2}\right) \quad \text{for} \quad \tau = 0.$$

From the Envelope Theorem

$$\frac{dJ}{d\delta} = \alpha v\Phi(e^*) - b.$$

At $\delta = 1$, $b = 0$ and $\frac{dJ}{d\delta} > 0$. However, $J(0) = 0 < C^* - \bar{C}$.

As δ increases, $\frac{dJ}{d\delta}$ decreases and becomes negative for $\hat{\delta}$ such that $\alpha\nu\Phi(e^*) = \frac{\delta}{1+\lambda} - 1$.

Therefore two cases may occur.

In case (1), $J(\hat{\delta}) < C^* - \bar{C}$ and privatization never occurs whatever the level of corruption, because the private gains from privatization do not compensate the greater social cost of privatization.

In case (2), $J(\hat{\delta}) > C^* - \bar{C}$. Then there exists δ_0 and δ_1 such that

$$J(\delta_0) = C^* - \bar{C} \quad \text{with} \quad \delta_0 < \hat{\delta}$$
$$J(\delta_1) = C^* - \bar{C} \quad \text{with} \quad \delta_1 > \hat{\delta}.$$

Privatization takes place for $\delta \in [\delta_0, \delta_1]$.

Note that there should be a limit $\bar{b}$ to the private benefits that the principal can extract from the firm. Then it may be that $\delta_1 = +\infty$.

As $\bar{C}$ decreases with k and increases with H, δ_0 and δ_1 decrease with k and with H. ∎

4

Enforcement, regulation, and development

There is a growing international consensus...that regulation, particularly in poor countries, must be designed with an appreciation of both information asymmetries and difficulties of enforcement.

(*World Bank Development Report 2001/2*)

4.1 Introduction

Regulatory contracts, like any other contractual relationships, suffer in developing countries from a severe lack of enforcement. Good laws and rules are rather straightforward to import from the developed world. A good set of lawyers can transfer this institutional knowledge quite easily (if not cheaply). It is much more difficult to enforce them,[1] because of the lack of financial and technical resources, because of the corruption of enforcement institutions, and because of the weak bargaining power of regulators.

The vital role of enforcement for laws, rules, and contracts was first stressed by the Chicago School (Becker, 1968; Stigler, 1970; Becker and Stigler, 1974). They modeled economic agents as performing a cost–benefit analysis when breaching the law and they reflected on the role of punishments and their limitations due to corruption and limited liability.

---

[1] See box 4.1 for examples of enforcement failures in regulation.

In the law and economics literature (Posner, 1972; Polinsky, 1983), a lot of work has been done on breach of contracts and on the types of remedies which can be offered by the law. However, the emphasis is not on how to react to renegations of contracts in fully anticipated states of nature, but rather on how laws can deal simply with circumstances arising from unexpected states of nature. It is about how the law can be an efficient substitute for the excessive transaction costs resulting from an attempt to include all possible contingencies in contracts.

The contract literature has developed initially without worrying about the verifiability and contractibility of the actions specified in the contracts. More recently, attention has shifted towards those issues. For example, the income taxation literature started with Mirrlees (1971) by assuming that incomes are observable. It was only much later (Border and Sobel, 1987; Mookherjee and Png, 1989; Cremer, Marchand, and Pestieau, 1990) that taxpayers' lies about their incomes and the need for auditing incomes were taken into account. Actually, many LDCs are still unable to implement income taxes because of enforcement issues.

Similarly, the costly state-verification literature in loan contracting with asymmetric information (Townsend, 1979; Gale and Hellwig, 1985) arose from the difficulties of indexing the repayment of a loan on the firm's revenue, because of the firm's ability to hide its revenue. This transaction cost was used to motivate debt contracts, which specify payments which are not conditional on the firm's revenue.

In the procurement literature, the need for auditing costs was also taken into account (Baron and Besanko, 1984) with attention given to imperfect commitment of auditing procedures (Khalil, 1992) and to the corruption of auditors (Laffont and Tirole, 1992). In this work, the verification of states of nature is costly, but the enforcement is assumed to be perfect when auditing is successful. Krasa and Villamil (2000) is an exception, where costly enforcement is a decision variable and where it is shown that imperfect commitment makes debt contracts optimal.[2] In contrast, we assume in this chapter that the enforcement of contracts does not solve the asymmetric information problem, but simply forces the regulated firm to select an outcome in the set of allocations contractually agreed upon *ex ante*. This description of enforcement seems particularly adapted to LDCs and to regulation where solving the asymmetric information problem following a dispute seems much too costly to be realistic and too much open to manipulation.

Section 4.2 reconsiders the basic regulation model of chapter 2. Now the regulatory contract is written before the firm discovers its type (for simplicity, only two types are considered), and contrary to chapter 2 the firm's participation constraint is an *ex ante* constraint. Consequently, with perfect enforcement of contracts, optimal regulation achieves the full information optimum. However, the *ex post* utility of an inefficient type is negative. If the regulator cannot enforce such negative utility levels for the firm, it must resort to self-enforcing contracts which ensure *ex post* nonnegative levels of utility. Optimal regulation is then identical to that obtained when the regulator offers a contract after the firm discovers its type. It entails downward distortions of production to achieve the optimal rent-extraction–efficiency trade-off. Against these benchmarks, we develop in section 4.3 a model with imperfect enforcement. The regulator offers a menu of contracts from which the firm must select. With some probability, which depends on enforcement expenditures, the firm is indeed forced to choose one contract in the menu. With the complementary probability, the contract is renegotiated. Then we characterize the optimal menu of contracts and the optimal enforcement expenditures. In particular, we find that the optimal level of enforcement expenditures, and therefore

---

[2] The Townsend–Gale–Hellwig result justifying debt contracts was criticized because they ignored stochastic contracts.

the quality of the rule of law, decreases with the cost of public funds and with corruption. In section 4.4, we extend the model to account for reputation effects in the regulatory process and we argue that these effects should strengthen the previous one on the quality of the rule of law, but introduce a countervailing effect for the level of enforcement expenditures as a function of the level of development. Cross-country regressions provide some support to these conjectures in section 4.5.

Box 4.1   Enforcement failures

Ghana's telecommunications

The intended design of the Ghanaian telecommunications industry was unusually competitive for Africa, with three mobile operators and two fixed-link networks. However, the regulator turned out to be particularly weak and "despite Ghana's well-intentioned law, the weakness of enforcement has left telecommunication consumers at the mercy of a battle of influence between the champions of the various players. One serious casualty may be Ghana's credibility with investors" (Haggarty and Shirley, 1999).

A spectacular example of lack of enforcement is the fact that the incumbent monopoly for fixed telephony,[1] Ghanaian Telecom (GT), which was not allowed to enter the mobile business, did enter, and furthermore used all kinds of tactics to delay interconnection.[2] Furthermore, interconnection disputes with GT until recently also prevented the second fixed-link operator from entering.

Tanzania's telecommunications

In Tanzania, the regulator attempted to enforce regional mobile licenses. However, the dominant mobile operator, Mobitel, argued that its license was national, and launched services in an area where the regulator tried to shut down the operator. After a crisis involving the court and the president, all cellular licenses were declared national in scope.

At the opposite end, governments and regulators also break contracts. In Tanzania, the initial two cellular operators complained that the government's commitment to having only two or three operators in the market was reneged on with impunity.[3]

Côte d'Ivoire's telecommunications

The concession contract of CItelecom specified quality levels and an expansion program of fixed lines which have repeatedly not been satisfied. Despite the existence of penalties in the contract, the regulator has not enforced these penalties and has not succeeded in implementing the contract.

CItelecom has priced access for public phones built by the competitor Publicom at a price of FCFA 65 per impulse, while the price in its own public phones was FCFA 73. The margin of FCFA 8 was too small to allow entry. In August 1998 the regulator intervened to set a minimum price of FCFA 85 for CItelecom's own callboxes. However, CItelecom refused[4] to adjust its prices until very recently, and since then has imposed long delays for connecting competitors' callboxes.

Notes:
[1] It was bought by Telekom Malaysia through a competitive tender.
[2] GT charged cellular companies more than its local retail tariff.
[3] We will not develop this dimension of renegotiation. See Aubert and Laffont (2001) for a model of political renegotiation.
[4] The reason put forward by CItelecom to justify their behavior is that they consider that public phones belong to the fixed network and therefore fall into their monopoly license.

4.2 Optimal regulation

We consider a natural monopoly which, in addition to a fixed cost F which is common knowledge, has a variable cost function:

$$C = (\beta - e)q, \tag{4.1}$$

where q is the production level, β is an adverse selection parameter in $\{\underline{\beta}, \bar{\beta}\}$ with $v = \Pr(\beta = \underline{\beta})$, and e is a moral hazard variable which decreases cost, but creates for the manager a disutility $\psi(e)$ with $\psi'(\cdot) > 0$, $\psi'' > 0$, $\psi''' \geq 0$.

Consumers derive a utility $S(q)$ $(S' > 0$, $S'' < 0)$ from the consumption of the natural monopoly's good. Let $P(\cdot)$ be the inverse demand function and $\hat{t}$ the transfer to the firm from the regulator. The firm's net utility is written:

$$U = \hat{t} + P(q)q - (\beta - e)q - F - \psi(e). \tag{4.2}$$

We assume that cost is *ex post* observable by the regulator, as well as the price and the quantity. So we can make the accounting assumption that revenues and cost are incurred by the regulator, who pays a net transfer $t = \hat{t} + P(q)q - (\beta - e)q - F$. Accordingly, the participation constraint of the firm can be written:

$$U = t - \psi(e) \geq 0. \tag{4.3}$$

To finance the transfer t, the government must raise taxes with a cost of public funds $1 + \lambda$, $\lambda > 0$. Hence, consumers' net utility is

$$V = S(q) - P(q)q - (1 + \lambda)t. \tag{4.4}$$

Utilitarian social welfare is then written:

$$W = U + V = S(q) + \lambda P(q)q - (1 + \lambda)((\beta - e)q + F + \psi(e)) - \lambda U. \tag{4.5}$$

Under complete information, the maximization of social welfare would lead to:

$$S'(q^*) + \lambda(P'(q^*)q^* + P(q^*)) = (1 + \lambda)(\beta - e^*) \tag{4.6}$$

$$\psi'(e^*) = q^* \tag{4.7}$$

$$U = 0. \tag{4.8}$$

Let us denote for $\underline{\beta}$ and $\bar{\beta}$, respectively the solutions of (4.6), (4.7), and (4.8) as $\underline{q}^*$, $\underline{e}^*$, $\underline{U}^*$ and $\bar{q}^*$, $\bar{e}^*$, $\bar{U}^*$.

Since consumers equate their marginal utility to the price $(S'(q) = p)$ (4.8), which says that social marginal utility

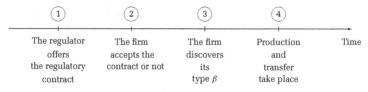

Figure 4.1   Timing of the model

equals social marginal cost, this can be rewritten as a Lerner index formula:

$$\frac{p - (\beta - e)}{p} = \frac{\lambda}{1 + \lambda}\frac{1}{\eta(p)},$$

where $\eta(p)$ is the price elasticity of demand. The price is between the marginal cost $(\beta - e)$ and the monopoly price p^M defined by

$$\frac{p^M - (\beta - e)}{p^M} = \frac{1}{\eta(p)}.$$

The marginal disutility of effort $\psi'(e)$ is equated to its marginal social gain q, and no rent is given up to the firm because funds are socially costly $(\lambda > 0)$.

Suppose now that the regulator can not observe the effort level e and does not know β. However, he can offer a contract to the firm before the latter discovers its type (see figure 4.1 for the timing).

In addition to the participation constraint, the regulator's contract must now satisfy the firm's incentive constraints because of incomplete information. The firm's utility level can be rewritten by substitution of (4.1) in (4.3):

$$U = t - \psi(\beta - c), \tag{4.9}$$

where $c = \frac{C}{q}$ is average cost. From the revelation principle, there is no loss of generality in restricting the analysis to direct revelation mechanisms $\{(\underline{t}, \underline{c}); (\bar{t}, \bar{c})\}$ which specify for each message $\tilde{\beta} = \underline{\beta}$ or $\tilde{\beta} = \bar{\beta}$ an average cost to achieve and a net transfer from the regulator.

The regulatory contract also recommends a production level $\underline{q}$ (or $\bar{q}$) and a total cost $\underline{C}$ (or $\bar{C}$), compatible with $\underline{c}$ (or $\bar{c}$) which maximizes expected social welfare. The direct revelation mechanism must be truthful, i.e. must satisfy the incentive constraints

$$\underline{U} = \underline{t} - \psi(\underline{\beta} - \underline{c}) \geq \bar{t} - \psi(\underline{\beta} - \bar{c}) \tag{4.10}$$

$$\bar{U} = \bar{t} - \psi(\bar{\beta} - \bar{c}) \geq \underline{t} - \psi(\bar{\beta} - \underline{c}). \tag{4.11}$$

Since the firm must accept or reject the contract before it knows its type, its participation constraint must be written *ex ante*:

$$\nu\underline{U} + (1 - \nu)\bar{U} \geq 0. \tag{4.12}$$

The incentive constraints (4.12) and (4.13) can be rewritten:

$$\underline{U} \geq \bar{U} + \Phi(\bar{e}) \tag{4.13}$$

$$\bar{U} \geq \underline{U} - \Phi(\underline{e} + \Delta\beta), \tag{4.14}$$

where $\Phi(e) = \psi(e) - \psi(e - \Delta\beta)$, (where $\Phi' > 0$, $\Phi'' > 0$).

Finally, the regulator's maximization program is written:

$$(P): \max_{\{q,c,U,\bar{q},\bar{c},\bar{f}\}} \left[S(\underline{q}) + \lambda P(\underline{q})\underline{q} - (1 + \lambda)(\underline{c}\underline{q} + \psi(\underline{\beta} - \underline{c})) - \lambda\underline{U} \right]$$

$$+ (1 - \nu)\left[S(\bar{q}) + \lambda P(\bar{q})\bar{q} - (1 + \lambda)(\bar{c}\bar{q} + \psi(\bar{\beta} - \bar{c})) - \lambda\bar{U} \right],$$

s.t. (4.12) (4.13), and (4.14).

It is more transparent to rewrite this program in terms of the variables (q, e, U) rather than (q, c, U). Let us also denote $W(q, e, \beta)$ the complete information *ex post* social welfare for a production level q and an effort level e when the efficiency parameter is β, i.e.:

$$W(q, e, \beta) = S(q) + \lambda P(q)q - (1 + \lambda)\left((\beta - e)q + F + \psi(e)\right). \tag{4.15}$$

The regulator's program is rewritten:

$$(P): \max_{\{q,c,U,\bar{q},\bar{c},\bar{f}\}} \nu\left[W(\underline{q}, \underline{e}, \underline{\beta}) - \lambda\underline{U} \right] + (1 - \nu)\left[W(\bar{q}, \bar{e}, \bar{\beta}) - \lambda\bar{U} \right]$$

s.t.

$$\underline{U} \geq \bar{U} + \Phi(\bar{e}), \qquad (4.16)$$

$$\bar{U} \geq \underline{U} - \Phi(\underline{e} + \Delta\beta), \qquad (4.17)$$

$$\nu\underline{U} + (1 - \nu)\bar{U} \geq 0. \qquad (4.18)$$

The regulator will make the participation constraint binding to maximize social welfare. For each value of β he finds the complete information optimum. It remains to check if one can find values of rents (or net transfers) such that (4.16) and (4.17) are satisfied. There are many such transfers. If we make (4.16) binding, we get:

$$\bar{U} = -\nu\Phi(\bar{e}) \qquad (4.19)$$

or

$$\bar{t} = \psi(\bar{e}) - \nu\Phi(\bar{e}). \qquad (4.20)$$

If we make (4.17) binding, we get instead:

$$\bar{U} = -\nu\Phi(\underline{e} + \Delta\beta)$$

or

$$\bar{t} = \psi(\bar{e}) - \nu\Phi(\underline{e} + \Delta\beta). \qquad (4.21)$$

Any value of $\bar{t}$ between those obtained in (4.20) and (4.21) would work. Adding (4.16) and (4.17) we obtain:

$$\Phi(\underline{e} + \Delta\beta) \geq \Phi(\bar{e}). \qquad (4.22)$$

The main point to notice is that the inefficient type $\bar{\beta}$'s *ex post* utility is always negative and, from (4.22), the largest *ex post* utility is obtained when (4.16) is binding.

This negative *ex post* utility raises the issue of enforcement. Indeed, once it discovers its type $\bar{\beta}$ the firm would like to renege on the regulatory contract. In a country with strong institutions, the contract is enforced in both states of nature $\underline{\beta}$ and $\bar{\beta}$. As a consequence, asymmetric information does not create any transaction cost for society and the complete information optimal allocation is achieved despite the setting of incomplete information.

At the other extreme, suppose that the regulator anticipates that he will not be able to enforce a negative *ex post* utility level for the firm. He will then choose a regulatory contract which maximizes expected social welfare under the incentive constraints, but also under the *ex post* participation constraints:

$$\underline{U} \geq 0 \tag{4.23}$$

$$\bar{U} \geq 0. \tag{4.24}$$

The set of constraints is then the same as if the contract was offered to the firm at the interim stage, i.e. once it knows its type. We can then anticipate that the efficient type's incentive constraint (4.16) and the inefficient type's participation constraint (4.24) will be the binding ones. Substituting into the objective function of the regulator, we obtain:

$$\psi'(\bar{e}^{SB}) = \bar{q}^{SB} - \frac{\lambda}{1+\lambda} \cdot \frac{\nu}{1-\nu} \Phi'(\bar{e}^{SB}) \tag{4.25}$$

$$\psi'(\underline{e}^{SB}) = \underline{q}^{SB} = \underline{q}^* \tag{4.26}$$

$$\underline{U} = \Phi(\bar{e}^{SB}) > 0, \tag{4.27}$$

and the same pricing equations as under complete information.[3]

Now, the efficient type captures a positive rent, and to decrease somewhat this socially costly rent, the regulator decreases the effort level in the case $\beta = \bar{\beta}$. However, the efficient type's effort level is not distorted.

Then, the loss in expected social welfare due to the extreme weakness of enforcement institutions and the need to rely on

---

[3] This is due to the fact that the cost function we have chosen satisfies the separability assumption $C(q, h(\beta, e))$ which implies the dichotomy property (see chapter 2).

self-enforcing contracts is:

$$\Delta W^{SB} = \underbrace{\lambda v \Phi(\bar{e}^{SB})}_{\text{Rent loss}} + (1-v) \underbrace{\left[W(\bar{q}^*, \bar{e}^*, \bar{\beta}) - W(\bar{q}^{SB}, \bar{e}^{SB}, \bar{\beta}) \right]}_{\text{Efficiency loss}}.$$

(4.28)

4.3 Regulation and enforcement

We now want to model more precisely what happens when institutions ensure only an imperfect enforcement of regulatory contracts.

We will assume that when the firm obtains an *ex post* negative utility, it attempts to renegotiate its regulatory contract. However, with a probability $\pi(x)$, the regulator is able nevertheless to impose the implementation of the agreed-upon contract.[4] This probability depends on the expenses x incurred to set up an efficient enforcement mechanism.[5] We assume that $\pi(0) = 0$, $\pi' > 0$, $\pi'' < 0$ with the Inada conditions $\pi'(0) = \infty$ and $\lim_{x\to\infty} \pi(x) = 1$.

With probability $1 - \pi(x)$, the regulator is forced to accept a renegotiation. To model this renegotiation we use the Nash bargaining solution, but assume that renegotiation is costly (say, because it takes time). The status quo payoffs, which obtain if the negotiation fails, are determined as follows: The firm loses its fixed cost and gets the utility level $U_0 = -F$. The regulator obtains the utility level $W_0 = -H$.

We can choose rents in the original contract so that the efficient type firm never wants to renege on its contract.

---

[4] We do not allow for penalties when enforcement is successful. This seems more descriptive of real practice in regulation, probably because regulatory agencies are often not allowed to impose penalties and do not want to go to court if they manage to enforce the contract. When enforcement is not successful, costly renegotiation is *ex post* better than enforcing penalties.

[5] Of course, these expenses are raised through distortionary taxation.

Therefore, costly bargaining takes place under complete information only when $\beta = \bar{\beta}$. Its outcome solves:

$$\max_{\{\bar{q},\bar{e},\bar{U}^E\}} \{(\bar{U}^E - U_0)(\delta W(\bar{q}, \bar{e}, \bar{\beta}) - \lambda \bar{U}^E - W_0)$$

$$= (\bar{U}^E + F)(\delta W(\bar{q}, \bar{e}, \bar{\beta}) - \lambda \bar{U}^E + H)\},$$

with δ in $(0, 1)$ to model the cost of renegotiation. This yields the complete information production and effort levels $\bar{q}^*$, $\bar{e}^*$ and the rent level

$$\bar{U}^E = \frac{\delta W(\bar{q}^*, \bar{e}^*, \bar{\beta}) + H}{2\lambda} - \frac{F}{2}, \tag{4.29}$$

i.e. the firm and the regulator share the social surplus equally. Social welfare is then

$$\bar{W}^E = \frac{\delta W(\bar{q}^*, \bar{e}^*, \bar{\beta}) - H + \lambda F}{2}. \tag{4.30}$$

The higher the fixed cost, the lower the firm's rent from renegotiation and the higher social welfare will be despite renegotiation. The weaker the regulator's position in case of unsuccessful renegotiation (the higher H), the lower is social welfare.

We still need the offer of contracts to be incentive compatible (conditions (4.16), (4.17)).

The new *ex ante* participation constraint is written:

$$v\underline{U}_1 + (1 - v)\pi(x)\bar{U}_1 + (1 - v)(1 - \pi(x))\bar{U}^E \geq 0, \tag{4.31}$$

where $\underline{U}_1$ and $\bar{U}_1$ are the new rents allocated in the initial contract.

Substituting the outcome of renegotiation into the regulator's objective function, it becomes

$$v[W(\underline{q}, \underline{e}, \underline{\beta}) - \lambda \underline{U}_1] + (1 - v)\pi(x)[W(\bar{q}, \bar{e}, \bar{\beta}) - \lambda \bar{U}_1]$$

$$+ (1 - v)(1 - \pi(x))[\delta W(\bar{q}^*, \bar{e}^*, \bar{\beta}) - \lambda \bar{U}^E] - (1 + \lambda)x. \tag{4.32}$$

Maximizing by making the participation constraint[6] binding, we obtain:

$$\underline{q}^E = \underline{q}^* \; ; \quad \underline{e}^E = \underline{e}^* \tag{4.33}$$

$$\bar{q}^E = \bar{q}^* \; ; \quad \bar{e}^E = \bar{e}^* \tag{4.34}$$

$$(1 - \nu)\pi'(x^E) = \frac{1 + \lambda}{(1 - \delta)W(\bar{q}^*, \bar{e}^*, \bar{\beta})}. \tag{4.35}$$

Clearly, it is valuable to build an enforcement institution since the social welfare obtained by the initial contract for $\beta = \bar{\beta}$ is higher than what would result from renegotiation ($W(\bar{q}^*, \bar{e}^*, \bar{\beta}) > \delta W(\bar{q}^*, \bar{e}^*, \bar{\beta})$). The more efficient is renegotiation (δ higher), the smaller is x^E. More efficient renegotiation and more enforcement are substitute instruments.

What are the main features of the solution obtained above? First, an enforcement mechanism is financed. It is imperfect and its quality is determined by (4.35). The quality of enforcement decreases (and therefore the probability of renegotiation increases) with the cost of public funds and with the efficiency of *ex post* bargaining. Second, the power of incentives is not intermediary between those which will be obtained with perfect enforcement (high-powered) and self-enforcing contracts (low-powered). This is because any rent obtained *ex post* through renegotiation is captured *ex ante* in the contract offered by the government. Third, the status quo payoffs of the two players who bargain do not affect the outcome, because again the rent given up in the bargaining is recaptured *ex ante* as bargaining is anticipated. If these payoffs affected the efficiency (δ) of renegotiation, of course, they would matter.

Remark: Another interpretation of δ could be some ability of the regulator to commit not to renegotiate. As an extreme case, the regulator might be able to end the relationship if the

---

[6] $\tilde{U}_1$ and $\underline{U}_1$ can be chosen so that the β-incentive constraint is satisfied and the β-firm does not want to attempt to renegotiate. For this, it must be that:

$$\underline{U}_1 \geq \max\left\{\tilde{U}_1 + \Phi(\bar{e}^*), \pi(x^E)[\tilde{U}_1 + \Phi(\bar{e}^*)] + (1 - \pi(x^E))[\tilde{U}^E + \Phi(\bar{e}^*)]\right\}.$$

enforcement mechanism was not successful. Then (4.35) is replaced by

$$(1 - v)\pi'(x^E) = \frac{1 + \lambda}{W(\bar{q}^*, \bar{e}^*, \bar{\beta}) + H + F}.$$

The more the regulator would suffer from the failure to enforce the contract (H high) and the higher the lost fixed cost F, the higher the investment in enforcement.   ■

If the enforcement mechanism is not very efficient, it could be that (due to the loss of trade when enforcement fails) the optimal solution obtained above is dominated by self-enforcing contracts.

Indeed, the welfare loss with respect to the first best can now be written:

$$\Delta W^E = (1 - v)(1 - \pi(x^E))(1 - \delta)$$
$$\times W(\bar{q}^*, \bar{e}^*, \bar{\beta}) \qquad \text{Bargaining costs}$$
$$+ (1 + \lambda)x^E \qquad \text{Enforcement costs.}$$

However, it may be a little misleading to include the enforcement costs in the welfare loss, since it suggests that the enforcement institutions which yield the first-best in developed countries are costless. Actually, they are not really comparable. In some sense these costs have been partly sunk in the past in developed countries so that they are relatively small in comparison with the enforcement needed today in a developing country to eradicate opportunistic behavior.

Still, ΔW^E is the right expression to compare to ΔW^{SE} obtained in (4.28) to know if it is worthwhile in the short run setting up an (imperfect) enforcement institution rather than relying only on self-enforcing contracts.

4.4 Predictions of the model

Countries differ by the level of development, the level of corruption, and the credibility of their institutions. As the level of development increases, the efficiency of the tax system increases and λ decreases, inducing from (4.35) an increasing trend for the level of enforcement.[7] Intuitively, enforcement expenditures increase because they are less costly.

So far, we have assumed that the $\bar{\beta}$-firm is not penalized when it attempts to renegotiate and then fails. Suppose instead that it suffers a loss of reputation R in such circumstances. Then, it will not attempt to renegotiate if

$$\bar{t} - \psi(\bar{\beta} - \bar{c}) \geq \pi(x^E)(\bar{t} - \psi(\bar{\beta} - \bar{c}) - R) + (1 - \pi(x^E))\bar{U}^E.$$

For R large enough, any modest expense x^E will make this penalty credible and even though enforcement expenditures are low, an outstanding quality of rule of law is achieved.

Only a dynamic model explaining reputation could do justice to this argument. However, we can argue that as *per capita* GNP increases these reputation arguments become stronger. This has two effects on the predictions of the model. First, it will induce a decline of enforcement expenditures after some level of *per capita* GNP. Second, it will strengthen the prediction that the quality of the rule of law increases with *per capita* GNP.

So a reasonable prediction is then that even though enforcement expenditures normalized by GNP first increase and then decrease with *per capita* GNP, the quality of the rule of law increases with *per capita* GNP.

The level of corruption may affect the results in various ways. Corruption at the renegotiation stage may increase the cost of renegotiation (i.e. decrease δ), making renegotiation less profitable for the government and the firm. From (4.35), this implies a higher level of enforcement expenditure. However, corruption may more directly affect the outcome through the corruption of the enforcement system itself and lead to a lower probability of enforcement for given expenses.[8] This second effect is intuitively potentially

---

[7] W should also increase with development.
[8] This can be formalized with a parameter θ in the $\pi(\cdot)$ function which becomes $\pi(x, \theta)$. This result requires $\pi_{c\theta} < 0$.

stronger, so that higher corruption should lead to less enforcement since it makes enforcement expenses less valuable.[9] Furthermore, the level of corruption itself should then be related to the level of enforcement expenditures and therefore be inversely U-shaped with *per capita* GNP.

It is difficult to find appropriate data to test our theory. We will proceed in two steps, first with cross-country regressions on macroeconomic variables, second by probit regressions on the Guasch microeconomic data set already used in chapter 2.

For cross-country regressions, we measure enforcement with two variables:

- The level of expenses in public order and safety expenses as a percentage of GNP, which is an input measure of enforcement and corresponds to our variable x.
- The quality of the rule of law as measured by the index from Kaufmann, Kraay, and Zoido-Lobaton (1999a, 1999b), which is a measure of the result of enforcement expenditures.

With these two measures, we will explore the conjectures with cross-country regressions.

Let us first consider[10] the expenses in public order and safety (POS) as a percentage of GNP 98, which is an input measure of enforcement (but clearly not the most appropriate proxy for our purpose). We use the Kaufmann, Kraay, and Zoido-Lobaton (1999a, 1999b) index of corruption. We obtain table 4.1 with a sample of 40 observations.

Indeed, we find that the enforcement expenses are increasing and then decreasing in GNP, and decrease with the level of corruption COR. Lesotho and Tunisia have an unusually high level of public order and safety expenses while Chile and Denmark have an unusually low level.

---

[9] Other factors reinforce this effect: The difficulty of punishing economic agents in LDCs, and their greater limited liability constraints.

[10] See the appendix (p. 116) for more on the variables.

Table 4.1. *Enforcement expenses*

Dependent variable(:) POS			
C	−7.69	−8.46	−7.57
	(−2.22)	(−1.98)	(−1.67)
COR		−0.18	−0.23
		(−2.78)	(−2.24)
Log (GNP)	2.26	3.02	2.94
	(2.69)	(2.78)	(2.78)
[Log (GNP)]^2	−0.14	−0.21	−0.21
	(2.78)	(−3.06)	(−3.22)
LESOTHO	3.81	3.34	3.40
	(6.85)	(12.24)	(12.75)
TUNISIA	1.21	1.02	1.06
	(2.27)	(8.77)	(8.97)
NEGATIVE	−1.05	−1.61	−1.64
	(−1.96)	(−5.07)	(−4.33)
Hausman residual			0.08
			(0.65)
R^2	0.66	0.73	0.73

Note: The dummy variable "NEGATIVE" corresponds
to Chile and Denmark.[11]

Taking the imports–GDP ratio and the news circulation as
instruments for the level of corruption, a Hausman test does
not reject the endogeneity of the corruption variable.[12]

Finally, note that the turning point for the effect of GNP on
enforcement expenditures occurs at US$3,000 which corre-
sponds to a country like Panama.

Now, we consider the endogenous variable RUL (Rule of
Law in the data bank of Kaufmann, Kraay, and Zoido-Lobaton

[11] In tables 4.1 and 4.2 we provide *t*-statistics with the White correction for
heteroskedasticity.
[12] One can argue that these two instruments are correlated with the level
of corruption, but not with the enforcement expenses, and are therefore
valid instruments.

Table 4.2. *Lack of rule-of-law enforcement*

	Dependent variable (:) NRULE[1]					
C	15.34	16.02	3.40	4.59	7.64	8.88
	(13.46)	(19.22)	(2.31)	(2.41)	(5.61)	(5.28)
Log (GNP)	−1.40	−1.47	−0.31	−0.42	−0.71	−0.81
	(−10.77)	(−15.17)	(−2.19)	(−2.33)	(−5.37)	(−5.06)
POSITIVE		2.16			1.54	1.49
		(13.21)			(7.68)	(6.87)
NEGATIVE		−2.76			−1.59	−1.63
		(−7.73)			(−4.54)	(−4.93)
COR			0.63	0.56	0.42	0.36
			(8.36)	(5.76)	(5.94)	(4.17)
Hausman residual				0.10		0.10
				(0.72)		(0.87)
R^2	0.68	0.86	0.87	0.87	0.92	0.92

Note: [1]Note that NRULE is measured here in such a way that quality decreases with the index and COR increases with corruption.

POSITIVE is a dummy variable for   Belarus and Colombia.
NEGATIVE is a dummy variable for   Denmark, Mauritius, Dominican
                                   Republic, Tunisia.

(1999a, 1999b)), which is a measure of the quality of enforcement.

We obtain table 4.2 for a sample of forty observations. As expected, higher *per capita* GNP is positively correlated with better rule of law, and corruption diminishes the quality of the rule of law. The Hausman test does not reject the exogeneity of COR.

Note finally that if corruption is largely associated with enforcement, then as *per capita* GNP increases, corruption should increase and then decrease. Indeed, we obtain this result, summarized in table 4.3.

For well-known reasons, the results of these cross-country regressions are very fragile. We pursue the testing with micro-data.

Table 4.3. *Corruption and development*

	Dependent variable (:) COR			
C	7.51	7.70	8.00	8.19
	(23.68)	(20.15)	(20.59)	(21.47)
GNP	−0.00051	−0.00049	−0.00055	−0.00050
	(−7.57)	(−7.18)	(−8.79)	(−9.20)
(GNP)^2	$9.92.10^{-9}$	$9.62.10^{-9}$	$1.10.10^{-8}$	$1.07.10^{-8}$
	(4.65)	(4.61)	(5.51)	(6.45)
DENMARK	−5.81	−4.99	−5.95	−5.11
	(−26.44)	(16.49)	(−25.49)	(−16.59)
NEWS		−0.0032		−0.003
		(−2.63)		(−2.89)
$\frac{\text{IMPORTS}}{\text{GDP}}$			−0.008	−0.008
			(−1.25)	(−1.30)
N	40	38	39	37
R^2	0.82	0.84	0.83	0.85

Guasch (2001) has assembled a data set on the renegotiation of concessions for telecommunications, energy, water,
and transportation in Latin America which is rather appropriate to test our theory. Indeed the probability of renegotiation
is $(1 - v)(1 - \pi(x^E))$, so that (4.35) provides the input for a
structural form explaining renegotiation.

In table 4.4 we provide probit regressions which explain
renegotiation as a function of the environment. The existence
of a regulation (ER) at the time of signing the concession
decreases the probability of renegotiation, while price-cap
regulation (PC) (which is more risky than rate-of-return
regulation) increases it. Then corruption increases the probability of renegotiation, as expected. This appears through
the corruption variable COR, taken as before from Kaufmann,
Kraay, and Zoido-Lobaton (1999a, 1999b), and through the
variable which mentions that the concession is awarded
to a concession-holder who has a local partner (LP). The

Table 4.4. *Endogenous variable: dummy variable (0,1) for renegotiation*

C	1.67	−2.05	−36.77	22.53	22.15
	(4.13)	(−3.16)	(−2.31)	(1.14)	(1.09)
ER	−1.81	−0.69	−1.81	−0.58	−0.55
	(−8.24)	(−2.67)	(−8.14)	(−2.11)	(−2.05)
PC	0.89	0.87	0.88	0.75	
	(4.05)	(3.19)	(3.77)	(2.56)	
COR	0.15	0.10	0.16	0.10	0.09
	(7.45)	(4.13)	(−7.82)	(3.93)	(−3.82)
LP	0.82	1.22	0.77	1.11	1.05
	(3.20)	(4.03)	(3.03)	(3.57)	(3.41)
EXP	−0.18	−0.20	−0.17	−0.22	−0.21
	(−7.64)	(−6.88)	(−7.23)	(−6.94)	(−6.87)
Log (GDP)			9.37	−6.34	−6.33
			(2.38)	(1.34)	(1.35)
D Water		3.44		3.53	3.44
		(7.73)		(7.68)	(7.76)
D Trans		2.63		2.77	2.77
		(7.68)		(7.68)	(7.79)
McFadden R^2	0.33	0.57	0.34	0.57	0.56
Number of observations with renegotiation	180	180	180	180	180
Number of observations without renegotiation	453	453	453	453	453

probability is also quadratic in the logarithm of *per capita* GDP (Log GDP), first increasing and then decreasing. Adding a variable expressing the experience of the regulator (EXP) weakens this last effect. However, when sector dummies are introduced, the corruption variables remain stable and significant, and the GDP effect becomes insignificant and even reverses, first decreasing and then increasing. Note that our theory is ambiguous about the impact of the level of development since if x^E is first increasing and then decreasing, we have to account for the fact that enforcement is more efficient as development occurs.[13]

4.5 Conclusion

In this chapter, we have started to integrate regulation theory and enforcement issues using a canonical model of regulation. One outcome of this modeling is that it renders endogenous institutional features such as the enforcement system or the quality of the rule of law. Indeed, they become regulatory responses which vary with the level of development of the country, as well as with other sociological phenomena such as corruption.

Even though we have not developed a dynamic model which would be needed to analyse these institutional phenomena, we have argued that transaction costs derived from informational asymmetries suggest that enforcement expenditures increase and then decrease, while the rule of law increases with *per capita* GNP. Also, corruption should both call for smaller enforcement expenditures[14] and yield a lower quality of the rule of law.

With cross-section regressions for 1997 and probit regressions on microdata, we have shown that those predictions are not rejected by the data.

Appendix

The endogenous public order and safety variable (POS), as well as the instruments index of price distortion (PD), news circulation (news), openness (which is the ratio of imports

---

[13] See Guasch, Laffont, and Straub (2002) for a more detailed analysis.

[14] Exceptional measures against corruption may temporarily induce a large increase in enforcement expenditures, as has been witnessed in some countries (see Klitgaard, 1988).

over GNP) and GNP 98 (GNP), are taken from the World Bank Development Indicators.

The index of corruption (COR or NCOR) and the measure of the rule of law (RUL or NRUL) are taken from Kaufmann, Kraay, and Zoido-Lobaton (1999a, 1999b). They are based on indices for 1997–8.

List of countries: Argentina, Australia, Belarus, Bolivia, Bulgaria, Cameroon, Chile, Colombia, Costa Rica, Czech Republic, Denmark, Dominican Republic, El Salvador, Estonia, Finland, Greece, Hungary, Indonesia, Iran, Israel, Kazakstan, Latvia, Lesotho, Mauritius, Mongolia, Norway, Panama, Poland, Singapore, Slovak Republic, Slovenia, Sri Lanka, Sweden, Tajikistan, Thailand, Turkey, United Kingdom, United States, Uruguay.

Descriptive statistics:

Series:	COR	RUL	GNP
Sample	1 40	1 40	1 40
Observations	40	40	40
Mean	4.907500	3.900000	7562.850
Median	5.450000	3.850000	3232.000
Maximum	9.300000	8.000000	34310.00
Minimum	0.100000	0.100000	370.0000
Std dev.	2.629165	2.134215	9586.401
Skewness	−0.416273	−0.083344	1.537724
Kurtosis	2.081089	2.097929	3.981838
Jarque–Bera	2.562548	1.402527	17.37064
Probability	0.277683	0.495958	0.000169

5

Access pricing rules for developing countries

5.1 Introduction

Parts of the former natural monopolies for public services in telecommunications, electricity, gas, transportation, etc. are now viewed as potentially competitive, such as long-distance services in telecommunications, and generation in electricity or gas, and consequently open to competition. Conversely some elements, such as the transmission grid in electricity and the tracks in railways are still considered natural monopolies, and remain regulated, possibly with new forms of regulation like incentive regulation.

The management of the *interface between the competitive and regulated sectors* is crucial for the success of liberalization. The conditions under which competitors can access the regulated sector, which is an essential input for their activities, determine the profitability of entry and therefore the level of competition in the sectors opened to competition. They also dictate the efficiency of the utilization of the natural monopoly elements.

Despite its vital role for the success of liberalization, which is regarded as a key institutional change for development, no specific proposals of desirable access pricing rules for developing economies are currently available. The purpose of this chapter is to start to fill this gap. All along, we will keep in mind the main features of developing countries which may call for specific rules: high cost of public funds, poor auditing and monitoring facilities, low transaction costs of corruption, weak counterpowers, weak ability to commit, and inefficient tax systems.

Section 5.2 considers market structure. Section 5.3 deals with structural separation and the pricing of access. Sections 5.4 and 5.5 examine one-way and two-way access, respectively. Section 5.6 concludes.

5.2 About the optimality of the market structure

The pricing of interconnection is highly dependent on the market structure. We will distinguish three different situations.

In case (1), vertical disintegration prevails. The firm controlling the bottleneck (the natural monopoly) is not allowed to compete in the provision of services using the bottleneck as an input. In case (2), the firm controlling the bottleneck is one competitor among many providing services using the bottleneck as an input. Finally, in case (3), competition takes place between vertically integrated firms which each control a bottleneck and provide services.

A first question to ask is whether the characteristics of developing countries favor one or the other market structure.

The comparison between cases (1) and (2) rests essentially on a comparison between the economies of scope that vertical integration makes possible and the problems of favoritism it raises. Since the economies of scope are likely to be independent of the characteristics of developing countries (at least for given technologies), while on the contrary favoritism is more difficult to fight in LDCs, there should be a bias towards vertical disintegration in these countries.

However, the comparison between case (2) and case (3) rests on a comparison of the fixed costs which will be associated with competition in the provision of the bottleneck, as in local telephony, and the gains one may expect from this competition. The comparison here is difficult for the LDCs, where the high cost of public funds makes more expensive both the duplication of fixed costs and the information rents of a monopolistic provision of the bottleneck.

These comparisons are further complicated by the dynamics of the industry which may be moving towards case (3), as in the telecommunications industry. Vertical disintegration may then in fact slow down the emergence of competition among vertically integrated firms providing both local and long-distance telephony. Advising vertical disintegration may then be particularly inappropriate. However, for railways, gas, or electricity, vertical disintegration of the track, the pipelines, or the transmission grid from transportation or generation can be strongly advised if competition in services is introduced.

In all these cases one has the choice between a single regulated entity owning the tracks, the pipelines, or the grid and a shared ownership of the bottleneck by the users who agree on rules for using it. The comparison is here between the inefficiency of regulation and the free-rider problems of joint ownership. In a country where regulation is easily captured one may favor the second scenario.

Currently, the main difference between telecommunications and the other industries is that the local network which is a bottleneck for long-distance services is providing a service of its own. For gas, electricity, and railroads, consumers have no separate interest in the service provided by the bottleneck. A piece of the pipeline, of the electricity grid, or of the track that is of interest to the consumer will not in general be provided by different firms. This is not necessarily so in railways, when there are several roughly equivalent itineraries, or more rarely in the gas industry. At the opposite extreme, one could imagine that the last copper line or fiber optic to the consumer would be provided by a different company than the incumbent in local telephony and that this bottleneck would be rented to different users, including the local telephony companies.

5.3 Structural separation and pricing of access to an independently owned infrastructure

The utility owning the infrastructure sells wholesale services to other firms, who market final services to the consumers.

Competitive usage

The simplest case arises when the n final services are produced by competitive industries at some constant marginal cost. Then it is as if the utility produced the final services itself at a unit cost equal to its own cost of providing access to the competitive downstream firms plus the latter's unit cost of producing the final services.

The Ramsey formulae can be applied to the prices charged for access to the utility's infrastructure and they can be decentralized through a price cap on access charges:

c_k = long-run marginal cost of producers of the final
     service k

c_{0k} = long-run marginal cost of access to supply
     service k

$\hat{\eta}_k$ = price superelasticity of good k

a_k = access price for service k.

Ramsey pricing entails:

$$\frac{p_k - c_{0k} - c_k}{p_k} = \frac{\lambda}{1 + \lambda} \frac{1}{\hat{\eta}_k} \qquad k = 1, \ldots, n,$$

where λ is the shadow price of the utility's budget constraint.

Since from competition, $p_k = a_k + c_k$ Ramsey pricing yields the Access Pricing Rules:

$$\frac{a_k - c_{0k}}{p_k} = \frac{\lambda}{1 + \lambda} \frac{1}{\hat{\eta}_k} \qquad \text{for} \quad k = 1, \ldots, n.$$

Alternatively, we can define the demand for access for good k (access k) as:

$$\tilde{D}_k(a_1, \ldots, a_n) = D_k(p_1, \ldots, p_n).$$

Then, it is easily seen that the price superelasticity of the demand for access k is:

$$\tilde{\eta}_k = \frac{a_k}{p_k} \cdot \hat{\eta}_k.$$

Then, we obtain a classic Ramsey type of pricing for access:

$$\frac{a_k - c_{0k}}{a_k} = \frac{\lambda}{1 + \lambda} \cdot \frac{1}{\tilde{\eta}_k} \qquad k = 1, \ldots, n.$$

Proposition 5.1: *The excess of the access price over the marginal cost of access for good k relative to the access price for good k should be inversely proportional to its demand price superelasticity.*[1]

The decentralization of Ramsey pricing by price caps enables the regulator to rely on the demand information of the regulated firm (even if we still have the difficult choice of weights in the price cap).

The typical market structure is illustrated in figure 5.1. It raises the following new informational issues.

The demand information is naturally located with the users of the infrastructure. The utility can infer this demand information from the demand for access as long as the users report truthfully the type of final good for which they use the infrastructure.

Examples
• For railways, this requires each shipper to specify truthfully the content of their cargos. This additional agency problem may be a serious issue in countries where one cannot expect

---

[1] See Laffont and Tirole (2000) for the general theory.

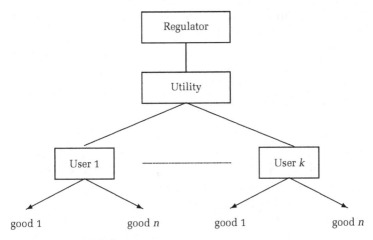

Figure 5.1 *Market structure*

a noncorrupt inspection system of cargos to be workable. This is particularly problematic with a very large number of users, as we have implicitly assumed in this section.

- For the use of the backbones of the internet, pricing independent of usage is still necessary because of the technical difficulties in identifying the type of usage.
- In telecommunications, long-distance carriers who face a higher access price to the final consumers than local carriers may bypass their interconnection by sending their traffic directly to a local carrier who then benefits from lower access prices.
- In electricity, the pricing of transmission should depend on the demand elasticity or supply elasticity at each node of the network. This creates a lot of discretion for the system operator and one typically favors a single injection price and a single extraction price, i.e. prices based on easily observable characteristics. With congestion one has the further difficulty of having to rely on nodal pricing which accounts for the Kirchoff laws. Here again one may prefer a uniform price completed by the local treatment of congestion.

Technical limits exist for the best possible use of Ramsey pricing, but also institutional limits due to the need to curb corruption activities. Laffont and Tirole (LT, Chapter 11) show that optimal regulation may require no price discrimination and therefore may entail "political" cross-subsidization. We can then derive our first warning for LDCs.

Corollary 5.1: *In LDCs, and if one insists on a very competitive usage of the infrastructure, Ramsey pricing of the infrastructure should be based on broad categories of usage which do not raise complex inspection issues and should be decentralized by price caps.*

Note that decentralization is partial only in the sense that the regulator will still have to make sure that the firms use the correct classification of services into the different categories. Ramsey pricing is often criticized for its informational requirements. Note that price-cap regulation does not require the regulator to know the price elasticities; it uses the knowledge firms have of these elasticities. Of course, the calculation of the optimal weights in the price-cap formula requires the same type of information (see below).

Remark: For a very competitive usage of the infrastructure, two-part tariffs cannot be used since competition would drive prices to marginal cost and bankrupt providers. ∎

Market power of users

Consider the simple case where each user is a monopoly in one independent market. It will charge a monopoly price computed according to the usual formula:

$$\frac{p_k - (a_k + c_0 k)}{p_k} = \frac{1}{\eta_k},$$

where η_k is the price elasticity of good k.

Since Ramsey pricing requires:

$$\frac{p_k - c_{0k} - c_k}{p_k} = \frac{\lambda}{1 + \lambda} \frac{1}{\eta_k},$$

one could undo the monopolistic markup of the user by a discount on the access price defined by:

$$\frac{a_k - c_k}{p_k} = -\frac{\lambda}{1 + \lambda} \frac{1}{\eta_k}.$$

These marginal access charges can be supplemented by a fixed payment to form a two-part tariff

$$a_k q_k + A_k,$$

which ideally can extract the monopolist's profit. More generally, one can use nonlinear pricing.

Proposition 5.2: *With market power of users, the marginal access charges should subsidize access, and excess profits of users should be recovered by fixed charges, and more generally by nonlinear pricing.*

Such a policy requires a lot of knowledge from the regulator and raises issues of favoritism in price discrimination. In the absence of long-term contracts, there is a potential for expropriation of some large users' investments. The complexity and potential discretion involved, in countries with little technical expertise and low transaction costs of collusion, leads us to:

Corollary 5.2: *In LDCs the regulator should not attempt to undo with access prices the monopoly power of users of the infrastructure. Alternative policies should be used to foster the competitive use of the infrastructure.*

For example, the control of monopoly power of user k, say, can be undertaken by the competition agency or by an appropriate policy of marginal subsidization-cum-profit tax. The regulator can as before use a simple price-cap regulation. What is really needed is more instruments but in general the regulator is not given tax instruments and can achieve multiple objectives only very imperfectly with the single instrument of access prices.

Additional problems with Ramsey pricing

Regulatory capture
When the regulator designs the tariffs, the discretion surrounding the determination of elasticities raises the problem of capture (when a price cap is used, the problem is transferred to the choice of weights for prices in the price-cap formula).

Corollary 5.3: *A nondiscretionary method for choosing weights in the price cap should be selected (for example, last year's quantities and an exogenous change in the level).*

In practice, the choice of a good starting point is difficult and is generally based on past prices. This is a crucial area where benchmarking made by good experts would be crucial, and LDCs should be helped in this task.

Risk of expropriation
Price-cap regulation with reviews is considered as the best and simplest way to strike a balance between rent extraction and incentives for cost minimization. However, in countries with little credibility one may argue that rate-of-return regulation offers a more reassuring environment.

First, in addition to the traditional problems of rate-of-return regulation, the specific circumstances of LDCs (lack of reliable accounting, lack of regulatory expertise) favor price-cap regulation. The drawback of giving up too much rent is weakened by the urgent need to attract capital. Second, rate-of-return regulation is not necessarily more effective in committing to a fair treatment when the government has little credibility in fulfilling its promises.

5.4 One-way access with vertical integration

We consider now the case of a vertically integrated utility (the incumbent) which provides access to the infrastructure and which also sells a service using the infrastructure. The problem is to price access for other providers of services using the infrastructure.

Competitive users

We consider first the case of competitive users with constant marginal cost providing a service which is an imperfect substitute for the service provided by the incumbent.

Let good 1 refer to the service offered by the incumbent with:

c_{01} long-run marginal cost of access for good 1,
c_1 long-run marginal cost of producing good 1.

Let good 2 refer to the service offered by the competitors with:

c_{02} long-run marginal cost of access for good 2,
c_2 long-run marginal cost of production.

There is no fixed cost in the production of services.
Let a be the access price to be charged to competitors.
Ramsey pricing of access leads to:

$$a = c_{02} + \frac{\lambda}{1 + \lambda} \frac{p_2}{\hat{\eta}_2},$$

with $p_2 = a + c_2$ from perfect competition.

Alternatively we can write:

$$a = c_{02} + \delta[p_1 - c_{02} - c_1] + \frac{\lambda}{1 + \lambda} \frac{p_2}{\eta_2}, \qquad (5.1)$$

where

$$\delta = \frac{\partial q_1 / \partial p_2}{\partial q_2 / \partial p_2}$$

is the displacement ratio (change in incumbent retail sales divided by the change in its sales to rivals as the access price varies).

Case a
Competitors are providing new products that are not (or can not) be provided by the incumbent $\Leftrightarrow \delta \approx 0$.

Example
Mobile phones when the incumbent provides local and long-distance services by fixed link (δ small).

In this case a global price cap appears particularly promising. Here it takes the following form:

$$\bar{q}_1 p_1 + \bar{q}_2 a \leq \Pi,$$

where $\bar{q}_1$ and $\bar{q}_2$ are the equilibrium quantities of goods 1 and 2.

Proposition 5.3: *If the services provided by users of access to the incumbent do not compete seriously with the services sold by the incumbent, a global price cap should be favored or, more generally, regulation of such access should be treated just like regulation of an end-user service.*[2]

The owner of the infrastructure then has good incentives to favor interconnection, which will increase its business. However, there may be problems if there is congestion and pricing is not flexible enough to allocate the infrastructure through

---

[2] See Laffont and Tirole (1994, 1996) for the general theory.

prices. If rationing occurs, then favoritism of the incumbent may happen, and this problem may be particularly serious in LDCs.

Example
Incumbent railways do only freight and the entrant passenger cars (see examples in Argentina and Mexico). See also box 1.6 on electricity in China.

It is important to allow peak-load pricing of access and end-user service symmetrically to avoid favoritism.

Note that the arrival of new users leads the incumbent to lower the access price, since there are more users, and this decreases the shadow price of the budget constraint.

Case b
We now consider the case where competitive users offer services that are very close substitutes for the services provided by the incumbent.

Formula (5.1) shows that the access price should be higher than in case a in order to avoid inefficient business stealing and balance the budget of the incumbent.

Proposition 5.4: *When entry leads to business stealing, the access price should be higher than the marginal cost corrected by the Ramsey own elasticity term.*[3]

Regulation which does not allow this "competitive" response of the incumbent will create incentives for exclusionary behavior.

Examples include telecommunications in Argentina, Côte d'Ivoire, Ghana, and Colombia (see box 5.1).

A good policy would be to allow an access pricing rule generous for the incumbent and to focus regulatory resources on implementing fast and high-quality interconnection. One

---

[3] See Laffont and Tirole (1994, 1996) for the general theory.

Box 5.1   Access pricing in developing countries

Côte d'Ivoire

Competition has been introduced only in the mobile market where prices are unregulated. The operator of the fixed link (CItelcom) has been a monopoly for years and its final prices are regulated.

Consider, for example, the interconnection agreement between CItelcom and the mobile operator Comstar Cellular which was accepted by the regulator.

The tariffs[1] committed to by CItelcom are:

Local	$p_1 = 25 + a_1$	where a_1 is the access price of Comstar,
Long-distance	$p_L = 130 + a_2$	where a_2 is the access price of Comstar.

For Comstar to CItelcom, the access prices are:

Local	$a_1^l = 25,$
Long-distance	$a_1^L = 130.$

CItelcom uses a kind of "ECPR-type rule" if we interpret (a_1, a_2) as the avoided costs of CItelcom. Since its access price equals then its opportunity cost of losing a customer:

$$p_l - a_1 = 25 \quad \text{for local,}$$
$$p_L - a_2 = 130 \quad \text{for long-distance.}$$

The final price and access price of Comstar are unregulated, but the idea is that the mobile market is competitive and the avoided costs of CItelcom are approached by the costs of the mobile competitors.

These prices must be contrasted with the tariffs of CItelcom for:

Local calls	10,
Long-distance calls	180.

But, given that tariffs are very unbalanced, it is not possible to relate the prices of access to CItelcom's costs.

A danger of this rule for CItelcom is that mobile operators collude in choosing high access prices which reduce CItelcom's revenues on the outgoing calls of its own subscribers. However, CItelcom has a subsidiary in mobile telephony which could maintain a downward pressure on prices. But this is not really the case because competition to attract consumers of mobile telephony has no effect on the high charges that consumers of the fixed-link network have to pay to access the mobile network. Note also that we have focused only on marginal prices. There are also fixed parts both in consumers' tariffs and in interconnection pricing.

Finally, the mobile companies have a zero reciprocal access price, but must pay CItelcom's 25 local access price for intermediating the calls.

Ghana

Competition was introduced from 1992. The three mobile operators entered developed interconnection agreements with the incumbent Ghana Telecom (GT), largely through bilateral negotiations.

However, as one may fear from theory, access charges are very high. GT charges cellular companies for interconnection more than its local tariff (note, however, that tariffs are unbalanced). Disputes occur around the sharing of revenues from access.

A second license for fixed-linked telephony was sold to Westel, which has not started its activities.

The weakness of the regulator is extreme and the future of competition not assured.

Colombia

A constitutional amendment prohibits monopolies, even public ones. Several regional public companies offer local telephony, with the following percentage market shares:

Bogota Telecom Company	25
Medellin	10
Cali	7

and four mobile companies.

There appeared to be no problem in setting interconnection charges for mobile, as well as for long-distance. The services were sufficiently complementary, so that both operators gained from quick interconnection. But, when the Telecom and Medellin companies entered Bogota's local market, access was refused by Bogota Telecom. Now, there are three fixed-linked companies in Bogota that are not fully interconnected. Indeed, access charges are not included in the price cap on final prices and are determined by historical costs according to the fully distributed method. Bogota Telecom, making no money on access, has all the incentives for exclusionary behavior.

Argentina

Argentina was divided into two territories of approximately equal size, each one allocated to a monopoly regulated by price caps. The North of the country and Buenos Aires was awarded to France Télécom and the South to Telefónica. As regulated tariffs between the two regions were balanced, interconnection charges washed out and the pricing of interconnection did not matter for efficiency.

Since the autumn of 1999, competition has been open to many operators with the two incumbents regulated with price caps on their initial territory until "competition is a fact." Interconnection charges are negotiated, but the regulator can intervene if deviations from forward-looking incremental costs (FLICs) are important. Also, if operators do not agree, the regulator will impose a price with reference to the FLIC.

Given the uncertainty surrounding the FLIC, one may fear that the two incumbents will set high interconnection charges to blockade further entry.

Note:
[1] We neglect some taxes and some factors taking account of unpaid invoices.

option is to use the efficient component pricing rule (ECPR):

$a = p_1 - c_1$.

If accounting is not available for calculating the incumbent's cost c_1 one may, in the competitive context considered here, use the marginal cost of the entrants unless the incumbent can demonstrate that his cost is higher.

Corollary 5.4: *When the competitive entrants offer services which are highly substitutable with the incumbent's services, the ECPR rule supplemented by active regulatory oversight to favor nondiscriminatory interconnection can be used. Alternatively, one can use a global price cap supplemented by maximal access prices defined by ECPR.*

A noncompetitive entrant

When entry is durably noncompetitive, regulation of prices of services must be envisaged.

5.5 Two-way access

When network competition develops, reciprocal access charges between networks must be determined. This situation of network duplication is not very common in the LDCs we are considering, but it may arise in telecommunications and in railways.

When the final prices are regulated (access prices play no allocative role but only a distributional one), one can let the networks negotiate interconnection charges and use the regulatory resources to facilitate interconnection and the reaching of agreements, especially when the networks are asymmetric in size.

When the final prices are unregulated, reciprocal access prices should be regulated. Two dangers must be avoided.

The first is the collusion of networks for agreeing on high reciprocal access charges which may induce monopolistic final prices. The second is that access prices can be used to blockade further entry.

Proposition 5.5: *When symmetric networks compete in linear prices, the optimal access charges should be below marginal cost of access to undo the monopolistic competition of networks on final prices.*[4]

Given that we can expect weak competition of networks, we favor the bill-and-keep doctrine because of its simplicity.

Corollary 5.5: *For symmetric networks competing in linear prices, we favor the bill-and-keep doctrine of zero access charges.*

Indeed for such situations, the access payments wash out whatever the access price, and a low access price encourages competition in the final prices. A danger is that networks choose not to be interconnected. Again regulatory resources should focus on ensuring good interconnection. Theory shows that, if networks compete in nonlinear tariffs, the collusion effect disappears, and access should be priced at marginal cost. The bill-and-keep doctrine leads to marginal prices which are too low and to fixed charges too high with high levels of exclusion for consumers.[5] However, such a situation is likely to be uncommon in LDCs.

A more difficult situation occurs when networks are quite asymmetric in their marginal costs of access (fixed and mobile networks) and in size. When networks are of mature sizes, regulatory resources are likely to be on the high side, and

---

[4] This assumes that the fixed costs of the network are recovered. Otherwise one must combine proposition 5.5 with recovery of such cost. See Laffont, Rey, and Tirole (1998a, 1998b) for the general theory.

[5] A menu of tariffs including linear prices might then emerge.

negotiated access tariffs under the threat of competition policy are a reasonable option. The most difficult case corresponding to the second danger is when a small network tries to enter. Then the incumbent network is likely to use access charges to blockade entry. One must be sure that network competition does not interfere with network development in areas of interest. If network competition – in an urban area, say – is still desired it must be because large unsatisfied demand exists and the networks may develop without interconnection (telecoms in Colombia) and there will come a point when the regulator can mandate negotiated access prices with a fallback option using international benchmarking.

Corollary 5.6: *In the cases where network competition is desirable, mandated negotiations under the threat of arbitration by an international body are an interesting option.*

5.6 Conclusion

Recommendations about access pricing depend on many factors. In this chapter we have focused mainly on the optimal use of the network when cost recovery is a constraint. In practice, four further considerations must be kept in mind:

- First, the type of accounting information available is crucial to assess the workability of cost-based access-pricing rules. In the absence of such data, price-cap regulation or international benchmarking are the only possible options.
- Second, the rules should depend on the type of other instruments available. Often access-pricing rules are also used to accommodate entry. We believe that with fixed costs of entry there is no simple solution to this problem and one should not use access prices for this purpose. Multiple objectives are detrimental to good governance; other

instruments should be used if entry in the industry is to be encouraged.

- Third, one should remember that the main problem in LDCs is entry in the infrastructures, and access rules should make sure and credible that investors in infrastructures can recover their costs. This is why we have pointed out on several occasions that generous access rules may be needed. From this point of view, restricting the access prices to long-run incremental costs goes in the wrong direction.

Finally, nonprice conditions for interconnection are as important as pricing for efficient liberalization. Regulatory attention to these issues by independent technical staff is essential.

6

Universal service obligations in LDCs

6.1 Introduction

Universal service obligations (USOs) have been largely debated in the arena of public policy in most public utility sectors.[1] In the United States, for instance, USOs were one of the major issues that were dealt with in the reform of the telecommunications sector. Indeed, the Telecommunications Act of 1996 devoted a large section to the reform of USOs and its regulatory agency, the Federal Communications Commission (FCC), has expended great efforts to implement the reforms. In other reforming countries, governments have also taken USOs seriously as a social commitment and implemented universal service policies in their regulatory reforms.

Even though most governments have committed to universal service policies to various degrees, the issue of USOs has also created considerable controversy in the reform process. Indeed, universal service policies raise many important practical as well as theoretical issues. Two important issues in the central debate of public policies are most relevant to developing countries.[2] One is how the *expansion of the network* can best be promoted. Unlike industrialized economies, where penetration of basic infrastructure services is no longer an

---

[1] For a recent contribution, see Cremer, Gasmi, Grimaud, and Laffont (2001).
[2] There is almost no literature on USOs in LDCs. See Laffont and N'Gbo (2000) and Gasmi, Laffont, and Sharkey (1999).

issue, developing countries have not yet created the infrastructures that are necessary for the provision of services to most people, particularly in rural areas. Expansion of the network therefore remains an essential dimension of universal service policies in LDCs. The other important issue in LDCs is the design of the *pricing policy* to implement USOs. In practice, since the necessary fiscal instruments are not available, policy makers often use pricing to achieve not only allocative efficiency but also a redistributive goal. In addition, new challenges arise after the infrastructure sectors have been liberalized. Universal services used to be financed by cross-subsidization within the firm, which was made feasible by the firm's monopoly position. But this method of financing is not possible after competition has been introduced, and a new avenue has to be found to implement USOs. This problem becomes more serious in LDCs, which have less experience in managing the regulation of infrastructures in a competitive environment.

In addition to the classical motivations of USOs (see Laffont and Tirole, 2000), the issue of USOs is viewed more broadly in LDCs as a development problem. Policy-makers in LDCs often believe that universal service policies are an important instrument for the promotion of economic development.

We develop a simple model in which the government has asymmetric information about a monopolistic firm's marginal cost of providing services in rural areas in the context of LDCs. The model is used to analyze in the context of developing countries the impact of asymmetric information and the threat of collusion on optimal universal service policies in their public utility sectors. Here the optimal universal service policy is implemented by two regulatory instruments – i.e. pricing in the rural network and network investment. We conduct our analysis under both discriminatory pricing (between the urban and rural sectors) and uniform pricing.

Our results show that under both pricing regimes, asymmetric information induces a higher price and a smaller network in the rural area than those under complete information. We also find that while uniform pricing may indeed induce a lower price in the rural area, it is achieved at the cost of a smaller network in the rural area.

When considering the issue of collusion, we introduce the hard information structure as in Tirole (1986) and LT. An important feature in our model is that there are multiple interest groups which have incentives to collude with the regulator. As usual, the firm, which will obtain an information rent when its private information is not revealed by the regulator, has incentives to collude with him when it is endowed with a low cost technology. In addition, the interest group of taxpayers, which will finance any deficit, may also benefit from information-hiding by the regulator by paying less tax when the firm has a highcost technology. While collusion between the interest group of taxpayers and the regulator raises the critical issue that the former may not be well organized, our analysis does point out the potential stakes that the taxpayers may have in a specific universal service policy.

In our model, the prevention of collusion between the regulator and the firm calls for an increase in the price and a decrease in the size of the network for the rural area. But preventing collusion between the regulator and the interest group of taxpayers calls for an opposite reaction. Therefore, the existence of the interest group of taxpayers hardens the collusion-proofness constraint for the firm.

The main contribution of this chapter is to apply incentive theory to analyze a specific public policy issue in a LDC. We observe that the USO issue often puzzles governments in LDCs when they form their universal service policies, and it seems that they have little opportunity to learn not only from the theory but also from the experiences of other countries. Indeed, even though the USO issue has been discussed as an important public policy, there is still a lack of theoretical analysis. This chapter is a first step towards understanding the theoretical foundations of universal service policies from a normative point of view, and the associated features of political economy in LDCs.

This chapter is organized as follows: section 6.2 establishes the basic setting. Then we obtain the optimal regulation of pricing under discriminatory pricing (section 6.3) and under uniform pricing (section 6.4). Section 6.5 shows how regulation must be modified to deal with various threats of collusion. Finally, section 6.6 concludes. We collect the proofs of all the propositions in the appendix (p. 164).

6.2 The basic setting

Let us consider a simple principal–agent relationship between a benevolent government and a monopolistic firm which is regulated when providing, for instance, telecommunications services in a territory. The territory is divided into two areas – i.e. a low-cost, or urban, area and a high-cost, or rural, area. Let α_1 and α_2 be the share of population in the urban and rural area, respectively, with $\alpha_1 + \alpha_2 = 1$.

Assume that the marginal cost of providing services in the urban area is c_1 which is common knowledge. One can think of this assumption as a reduced form of competition in the urban sector. However, the government has asymmetric information about the marginal cost c_2 in the rural area. For simplicity, assume there are only two types – i.e. $c_2 \in \{\underline{c}_2, \bar{c}_2\}$, with probability distribution $\Pr(c_2 = \underline{c}_2) = \nu$ and $\Pr(c_2 = \bar{c}_2) = 1 - \nu$. Let $\Delta c_2 \equiv \bar{c}_2 - \underline{c}_2 > 0$.

We assume that full coverage has been achieved in the urban area but that the rural area is only partially connected. Denote $\mu < 1$ the proportion of population that is served in the rural area. Since there are still people in the rural area who are not connected, the government imposes on the monopoly universal service obligations in the form of a specified expansion of the network and pricing in the rural area. We assume that the cost of network investment $C(\mu)$ is a convex function satisfying $C'(\cdot) > 0$ and $C''(\cdot) > 0$.

Let $S(q)$ be the gross social surplus for subscribers derived from consumption of the service in both the low-cost and high-cost areas, and $P(q)$ the corresponding inverse demand function. To simplify our analysis we do not consider consumers' connection decisions, which means that consumers derive all the surplus from consumption of services and all capacities are utilized immediately. We also assume for simplicity that consumers have a demand with constant absolute elasticity $\eta > 1$.

The timing of events is as follows: After the firm learns its private information about c_2, the government determines the regulatory policy for the size of network and the prices of services in both the urban and rural areas. Then, the monopolist invests to expand the network in the rural area and consumers make their decisions about consumption.

6.3 Optimal regulation under price discrimination

In this section, we first consider the case in which price discrimination is permitted so that the regulator sets different prices p_1 and p_2 for each area and consumers accordingly consume q_1 and q_2. Then, the firm's utility function is as follows:

$$U = t + \alpha_1 P(q_1)q_1 + \alpha_2 \mu P(q_2)q_2 - [\alpha_1 c_1 q(p_1) + \alpha_2 \mu c_2 q(p_2)] - C(\mu), \tag{6.1}$$

where t is the monetary transfer obtained from the government since we do not constrain the firm to balance its budget.

We assume that the benevolent regulator has a utilitarian social welfare function. Then,

$$W = \alpha_1 [S(q(p_1)) - p_1 q(p_1)] + \alpha_2 \mu [S(q(p_2)) - p_2 q(p_2)] - (1 + \lambda)t + U, \tag{6.2}$$

where $\lambda > 0$ is the shadow cost of public funds, which is exogenous. Substituting from (6.1) the transfer t, we can rewrite the objective function as:

$$W = \alpha_1[S(q(p_1)) + \lambda p_1 q(p_1)] + \alpha_2 \mu[S(q(p_2)) + \lambda p_2 q(p_2)]$$
$$- (1+\lambda)[\alpha_1 c_1 q(p_1) + \alpha_2 \mu c_2 q(p_2) + C(\mu)] - \lambda U. \quad (6.3)$$

For expositional simplicity, the following notations are introduced:

$$(\bar{p}_i, \bar{q}_i) \quad \text{and} \quad (\underline{p}_i, \underline{q}_i)$$

are the price and quantity when c_2 is, respectively, $\bar{c}_2$ and $\underline{c}_2$;

$$\bar{t} = t(\bar{c}_2) \underline{t} = t(\underline{c}_2)$$
$$\bar{\mu} = \mu(\bar{c}_2) \underline{\mu} = \mu(\underline{c}_2).$$

are the transfers and share of rural area served when c_2 is, respectively, $\bar{c}_2$ and $\underline{c}_2$.

Before proceeding further, we derive the benchmark under full information. The following participation constraints have to be satisfied to induce voluntary participation of the firm: for the high-cost (or bad-type) firm

$$\bar{t} + \alpha_1 \bar{p}_1 \bar{q}_1 + \alpha_2 \bar{\mu} \bar{p}_2 \bar{q}_2 - (\alpha_1 c_1 \bar{q}_1 + \alpha_2 \bar{\mu} \bar{c}_2 \bar{q}_2) - C(\bar{\mu}) \geq 0,$$

$$(6.4)$$

and for the low-cost (or good-type) firm

$$\underline{t} + \alpha_1 \underline{p}_1 \underline{q}_1 + \alpha_2 \underline{\mu} \underline{p}_2 \underline{q}_2 - (\alpha_1 c_1 \underline{q}_1 + \alpha_2 \underline{\mu} \underline{c}_2 \underline{q}_2) - C(\underline{\mu}) \geq 0.$$

$$(6.5)$$

So the government's optimal regulatory policy under complete information can be obtained by solving the following program:

$$\max_{\{\underline{q}_1, \underline{q}_2, \underline{\mu}, \underline{U}, \bar{q}_1, \bar{q}_2, \bar{\mu}, \bar{U}\}} v\{\alpha_1(S(\underline{q}_1) + \lambda \underline{p}_1 \underline{q}_1) + \alpha_2 \underline{\mu}(S(\underline{q}_2) + \lambda \underline{p}_2 \underline{q}_2)$$

$$- (1+\lambda)(\alpha_1 c_1 \underline{q}_1 + \alpha_2 \underline{\mu} \underline{c}_2 \underline{q}_2 + C(\underline{\mu})) - \lambda \underline{U}\}$$

$$+ (1-v)\{\alpha_1(S(\bar{q}_1 + \lambda \bar{p}_1 \bar{q}_1)$$

$$+ \alpha_2 \bar{\mu}(S(\bar{q}_2) + \lambda \bar{p}_2 \bar{q}_2) - (1+\lambda)(\alpha_1 c_1 \bar{q}_1$$

$$+ \alpha_2 \bar{\mu} \bar{c}_2 \bar{q}_2 + C(\bar{\mu})) - \lambda \bar{U}\}$$

s.t. (6.4) and (6.5).

Then, optimal regulation entails:

Proposition 6.1: *If $|S''|$ is large enough, then under complete information and discriminatory pricing, the optimal prices follow the Ramsey rule and the optimal size of the network is such that the social marginal cost of network expansion is equal to the social marginal gain. More precisely,*

$$\frac{\underline{p}_1^* - c_1}{\underline{p}_1^*} = \frac{\bar{p}_1^* - c_1}{\bar{p}_1^*} = \frac{\lambda}{1 + \lambda}\frac{1}{\eta}$$

$$\frac{\underline{p}_2^* - \underline{c}_2}{\underline{p}_2^*} = \frac{\bar{p}_2^* - \bar{c}_2}{\bar{p}_2^*} = \frac{\lambda}{1 + \lambda}\frac{1}{\eta}$$

$$(1 + \lambda)C'(\underline{\mu}^*) = \alpha_2 \left[S(\underline{q}_2^*) + \lambda \underline{p}_2^* \underline{q}_2^* - (1 + \lambda)\underline{c}_2 \underline{q}_2^* \right]$$

$$(1 + \lambda)C'(\bar{\mu}^*) = \alpha_2 [S(\bar{q}_2^*) + \lambda \bar{p}_2^* \bar{q}_2^* - (1 + \lambda)\bar{c}_2 \bar{q}_2^*].$$

Proof: See the appendix. ∎

Under complete information the regulator needs only to satisfy the participation constraints of the monopolistic firm so that no information rent is left to the firm. The optimal prices are set according to the Ramsey principles. The markups above the marginal costs are due to the social cost of public funds.

To determine the optimal size of the network, one needs to take into account two types of benefits from providing services in the rural area: the net surplus effect, $S(\bar{q}_2) - (1 + \lambda)\bar{c}_2\bar{q}_2$, represents the net benefits from consumption obtained by those connected to the network in the rural area; and the revenue effect, $\lambda \bar{p}_2 \bar{q}_2$, is the social gain of revenues from those same consumers. One can show that $\underline{p}_1^* = \bar{p}_1^* = p_1^*$ and $\underline{p}_2^* < \bar{p}_2^*$. Moreover, $\underline{\mu}^* > \bar{\mu}^*$. In words, a higher marginal cost leads to a higher price and a smaller network for the rural area.

By differentiating the network investment equation with respect to λ, we find that the optimal size of network is a decreasing function of the social cost of public funds, i.e. $\frac{d\mu^*}{d\lambda} < 0$. So in a typical developing country where λ is larger than in the developed economies, the size of network should be smaller from a normative point of view.

Now let us assume that the regulator has asymmetric information about c_2. From the revelation principle, we can without loss of generality restrict our attention to regulatory rules which are direct revelation mechanisms. A direct revelation mechanism is here characterized by

$$\{p_1(\tilde{c}_2), \ p_2(\tilde{c}_2), \ \mu(\tilde{c}_2), \ t(\tilde{c}_2)\} \text{ with } \tilde{c}_2 \in \{\underline{c}_2, \bar{c}_2\},$$

where $\tilde{c}_2$ is the monopolist's report to the government about its type c_2.

For incentive compatibility, the following incentive constraints must be satisfied: for the bad type

$$\bar{t} + \alpha_1 \bar{p}_1 \bar{q}_1 + \alpha_2 \bar{\mu} \bar{p}_2 \bar{q}_2 - (\alpha_1 c_1 \bar{q}_1 + \alpha_2 \bar{\mu} \bar{c}_2 \bar{q}_2) - C(\bar{\mu})$$
$$\geq \underline{t} + \alpha_1 \underline{p}_1 \underline{q}_1 + \alpha_2 \mu \underline{p}_2 \underline{q}_2 - (\alpha_1 c_1 \underline{q}_1 + \alpha_2 \underline{\mu} \bar{c}_2 \underline{q}_2) - C(\underline{\mu}),$$
(6.6)

and for the good type

$$\underline{t} + \alpha_1 \underline{p}_1 \underline{q}_1 + \alpha_2 \underline{\mu} \underline{p}_2 \underline{q}_2 - (\alpha_1 c_1 \underline{q}_1 + \alpha_2 \underline{\mu} \underline{c}_2 \underline{q}_2) - C(\underline{\mu})$$
$$\geq \bar{t} + \alpha_1 \bar{p}_1 \bar{q}_1 + \alpha_2 \bar{\mu} \bar{p}_2 \bar{q}_2 - (\alpha_1 c_1 \bar{q}_1 + \alpha_2 \underline{c}_2 \bar{\mu} \bar{q}_2) - C(\bar{\mu}).$$
(6.7)

The government's program is therefore:

$$\max_{\{\underline{q}_1, \underline{q}_2, \underline{\mu}, \underline{U}, \bar{q}_1, \bar{q}_2, \bar{\mu}, \bar{U}\}} \nu\{\alpha_1(S(\underline{q}_1) + \lambda \underline{p}_1 \underline{q}_1) + \alpha_2 \underline{\mu}(S(\underline{q}_2) + \lambda \underline{p}_2 \underline{q}_2)$$
$$- (1 + \lambda)(\alpha_1 c_1 \underline{q}_1 + \alpha_2 \underline{\mu} \underline{c}_2 \underline{q}_2$$
$$+ C(\underline{\mu})) - \lambda \underline{U})\} + (1 - \nu)\{\alpha_1(S(\bar{q}_1)$$
$$+ \lambda \bar{p}_1 \bar{q}_1) + \alpha_2 \bar{\mu}(S(\bar{q}_2) + \lambda \bar{p}_2 \bar{q}_2)$$
$$- (1 + \lambda)(\alpha_1 c_1 \bar{q}_1 + \alpha_2 \bar{\mu} \bar{c}_2 \bar{q}_2 + C(\bar{\mu})) - \lambda \bar{U}\}$$

s.t. (6.4), (6.5), (6.6), and (6.7).

Then, we have the following result:

Proposition 6.2: *If $|S''|$ is large enough, under asymmetric information, the optimal regulatory policy entails:*

(1) If $c_2 = \underline{c}_2$, the optimal price and the optimal size of network for the rural area are the same as under complete information;

(2) If $c_2 = \bar{c}_2$, asymmetric information leads to a higher price and a smaller network for the rural area than those under complete information.

More specifically,

$$\underline{p}_1^{SB} = \bar{p}_1^{SB} = p_1^*, \underline{p}_2^{SB} = \underline{p}_2^*; \underline{\mu}^{SB} = \underline{\mu}^*,$$

$$\frac{\bar{p}_2^{SB} - \bar{c}_2}{\bar{p}_2^{SB}} = \frac{\lambda}{1+\lambda}\frac{1}{\eta} + \frac{\lambda}{1+\lambda}\frac{\nu}{1-\nu}\frac{\Delta c_2}{\bar{p}_2^{SB}},$$

$$(1+\lambda)C'(\bar{\mu}^{SB}) = \alpha_2\left[S(\bar{q}_2^{SB}) + \lambda\bar{p}_2^{SB}\bar{q}_2^{SB} - (1+\lambda)\bar{c}_2\bar{q}_2^{SB}\right.$$

$$\left. - \lambda\frac{\nu}{1-\nu}\Delta c_2\bar{q}_2^{SB}\right].$$

Proof: See the appendix.   ∎

Under asymmetric information the regulator has to give up an information rent $\Pi = \alpha_2\bar{\mu}\Delta c_2\bar{q}_2$ to the efficient firm to satisfy incentive compatibility. Both the optimal price and the optimal size of the network for the rural area (when $c_2 = \bar{c}_2$) are distorted at the optimum to mitigate this rent. Indeed, the optimal price in the rural area $\bar{p}_2$ is increased (respectively, consumption $\bar{q}_2$ decreased) and the optimal size of network $\bar{\mu}_2$ decreased in comparison with the first-best allocations.

Proposition 6.2 says that, when price discrimination is permitted, under asymmetric information consumers in the rural area face a higher price due to the informational cost and therefore consume a lower level of services. Furthermore, people without connection are less likely to be connected because the investment cost is also increased by the information rent. So in this sense both the connected and disconnected consumers of the rural area are affected adversely by asymmetric information.

6.4 Optimal regulation under uniform pricing

In this section, we derive the optimal regulatory policy when uniform pricing is imposed. As before, we first consider the benchmark case in which there is complete information about the cost of providing services in the rural area, c_2. For expositional simplicity, more notation is introduced: $\bar{p} = p(\bar{c}_2)$, $\bar{q} = q(\bar{p})$, $\underline{p} = p(\underline{c}_2)$, and $\underline{q} = q(\underline{p})$. Other notational conventions are defined as in section 6.3.

Under complete information the following participation constraints must be satisfied: for the bad type

$$\bar{t} + (\alpha_1 + \alpha_2 \bar{\mu})\bar{p}\bar{q} - (\alpha_1 c_1 + \alpha_2 \bar{c}_2 \bar{\mu})\bar{q} - C(\bar{\mu}) \geq 0, \qquad (6.8)$$

and for the good type

$$\underline{t} + (\alpha_1 + \alpha_2 \underline{\mu})\underline{p}\underline{q} - (\alpha_1 c_1 + \alpha_2 \underline{c}_2 \underline{\mu})\underline{q} - C(\underline{\mu}) \geq 0. \qquad (6.9)$$

The government's problem is then to optimize the following objective function:

$$\max_{\{\underline{p},\underline{\mu},\bar{p},\bar{\mu}\}} W = v\{(\alpha_1 + \alpha_2 \underline{\mu})(S(\underline{q}) + \lambda \underline{p}\underline{q}) - (1 + \lambda)[(\alpha_1 c_1$$
$$+ \alpha_2 \underline{\mu}\underline{c}_2)\underline{q} + C(\underline{\mu})] - \lambda \underline{U}\} + (1 - v)\{(\alpha_1$$
$$+ \alpha_2 \bar{\mu})(S(\bar{q}) + \lambda \bar{p}\bar{q}) - (1 + \lambda)[(\alpha_1 c_1 + \alpha_2 \bar{\mu}\bar{c}_2)\bar{q}$$
$$+ C(\bar{\mu})] - \lambda \bar{U}\}$$

s.t. (6.8) and (6.9).

Then, optimal regulation entails:

Proposition 6.3: *Suppose the government has complete information about c_2. Assume that $|S''|$, $C''(\cdot)$, and α_2 are large enough. Then uniform pricing decreases both the price* *and the size of the network for the rural area in comparison with those under price discrimination.* More specifically,

$$\frac{\underline{p}^{**} - \frac{\alpha_1 c_1 + \alpha_2 \underline{c}_2 \mu^{**}}{\alpha_1 + \alpha_2 \mu^{**}}}{\underline{p}^{**}} = \frac{\bar{p}^{**} - \frac{\alpha_1 c_1 + \alpha_2 \bar{c}_2 \bar{\mu}^{**}}{\alpha_1 + \alpha_2 \bar{\mu}^{**}}}{\bar{p}^{**}} = \frac{\lambda}{1 + \lambda} \frac{1}{\eta}$$

$$(1 + \lambda)C'(\underline{\mu}^{**}) = \alpha_2 [S(\underline{q}^{**}) + \lambda \underline{p}^{**} \underline{q}^{**} - (1 + \lambda)\underline{q}^{**} \underline{c}_2]$$

$$(1 + \lambda)C'(\bar{\mu}^{**}) = \alpha_2 [S(\bar{q}^{**}) + \lambda \bar{p}\bar{q}^{**} - (1 + \lambda)\bar{q}^{**} \bar{c}_2].$$

Proof: See the appendix. ∎

Under complete information the optimal allocation with uniform pricing can be implemented without giving up an information rent. Again, the prices are determined by the Ramsey rule. However, the relevant cost is the average marginal cost

$$\frac{\alpha_1 c_1 + \alpha_2 \underline{c}_2 \underline{\mu}}{\alpha_1 + \alpha_2 \underline{\mu}} \text{(respectively,} \frac{\alpha_1 c_1 + \alpha_2 \bar{c}_2 \bar{\mu}}{\alpha_1 + \alpha_2 \bar{\mu}})$$

when the marginal cost in the rural area is $\underline{c}_2$ (respectively, $\bar{c}_2$), and that average marginal cost is lower than the marginal cost $\underline{c}_2$ (respectively, $\bar{c}_2$). The average marginal cost in the rural area is higher than in the urban area. Thus, uniform pricing indeed leads to the redistributive outcome of a lower price for the rural area and a higher price for the urban area regardless of the size of the network – i.e. $p_1^* < \underline{p}^{**} < \underline{p}_2^*$ and $p_1^* < \bar{p}^{**} < \bar{p}_2^*$. But as we will see soon, pricing favoritism towards the rural area is achieved with a distortion towards a smaller size of the network.

When the monopolistic firm is endowed with a high-cost technology – i.e. $c_2 = \bar{c}_2 - C'(\bar{\mu})$ is the marginal cost of network expansion in the rural area. As before, two benefits of network expansion need to be taken into account: One is the net surplus effect from consumption, $S(\bar{q}) - (1 + \lambda)\bar{q}\bar{c}_2$; the other is the revenue effect resulting from the social cost of public funds. But unlike under price discrimination, the net effect entails that $S(\bar{q}) + \lambda \bar{p}\bar{q} - (1 + \lambda)\bar{q}\bar{c}_2$ is a decreasing function of $\bar{q}$ at $\bar{q}^{**}$ rather than a constant function. The reason is that uniform pricing creates a distortion towards a lower price in the rural area, which in turn causes a distortion to the size of the network. Thus, $\underline{\mu}^{**} < \underline{\mu}^*$ and $\bar{\mu}^{**} < \bar{\mu}^*$.

A few remarks about uniform pricing are in order. In practice, one often observes that USOs are implemented by uniform pricing (for example, for postal or telephone services). While such a regulatory policy may have some political advantages in implementation, one may wonder whether it is the right approach to favor the rural area. For instance, the government might design its redistributive policy alternatively by changing the weights of consumers for different areas in the objective function. To illustrate this point, assume the government puts a weight $\omega > 1$ on the net consumer surplus in the rural area, which implies that it values more the surplus of these consumers. By simple manipulation the government's objective function can be written as:

$$W = \alpha_1(S(q_1) - p_1 q_1) + \alpha_2 \mu \omega(S(q_2) - p_2 q_2) - (1+\lambda)t + U$$
$$= \alpha_1(S(q_1) + \lambda p_1 q_1) + \alpha_2 \mu \omega[S(q_2) + (\frac{1+\lambda}{\omega} - 1)p_2 q_2]$$
$$- (1+\lambda)(\alpha_1 c_1 q_1 + \alpha_2 c_2 \mu q_2 + C(\mu)).$$

We thus obtain:

$$\frac{p_2^{\omega} - c_2}{p_2^{\omega}} = (1 - \frac{\omega}{1+\lambda})\frac{1}{\eta}$$
$$(1+\lambda)C'(\mu^{\omega}) = \alpha_2[\omega(S(q_2^{\omega}) + (\frac{1+\lambda}{\omega} - 1)p_2^{\omega} q_2^{\omega})$$
$$- (1+\lambda)c_2 q_2^{\omega}].$$

To compare these results with those under uniform pricing, we substitute $p_2^{\omega} = \bar{p}^{**}$ into the above pricing function to get $\omega = (1+\lambda)[1 - \frac{\bar{p}^{**} - \bar{c}_2}{\bar{p}^{**}}\eta]$. One can show that $\omega(S(\bar{q}^{**}) + (\frac{1+\lambda}{\omega} - 1)\bar{p}^{**}\bar{q}^{**} - (1+\lambda)\bar{c}_2\bar{q}^{**} > S(\bar{q}^{**}) + \lambda\bar{p}^{**}\bar{q}^{**} - (1+\lambda)\bar{c}_2\bar{q}^{**}$.[3] In

---

[3] Since $\frac{\bar{p}^{**} - \bar{c}_2}{\bar{p}^{**}} - \frac{\lambda}{1+\lambda}\frac{1}{\eta} < 0$, by collecting terms one has $(\frac{\lambda}{1+\lambda}\frac{1}{\eta} - \frac{\bar{p}^{**} - \bar{c}_2}{\bar{p}^{**}})[S(\bar{q}^{**}) - \bar{p}^{**}\bar{q}^{**}] > 0$.

words, uniform pricing induces a smaller network with the same price for the rural area and achieves a lower level of social welfare for a weight ω which induces the same price in the rural area. We can therefore conclude that favoring the rural area with a proper price discrimination is a better way of implementing redistribution than by uniform pricing, if it is politically feasible.

Assume now that the social planner has asymmetric information about c_2. The regulatory policy under uniform pricing can be defined as the following direct revelation mechanism:

$\{p(\tilde{c}_2), \tilde{\mu}(\tilde{c}_2), t(\tilde{c}_2)\}$ with $\tilde{c}_2$ in $\{\underline{c}_2, \bar{c}_2\}$.

Then, the following incentive constraints need to be satisfied: for the bad type

$$\bar{t} + (\alpha_1 + \alpha_2\bar{\mu})\bar{p}\bar{q} - (\alpha_1 c_1 + \alpha_2\bar{c}_2\bar{\mu})\bar{q} - C(\bar{\mu})$$
$$\geq \underline{t} + (\alpha_1 + \alpha_2\underline{\mu})\underline{p}\underline{q} - (\alpha_1 c_1 + \alpha_2\underline{\mu}\bar{c}_2)\underline{q} - C(\underline{\mu}), \qquad (6.10)$$

and for the good type

$$\underline{t} + (\alpha_1 + \alpha_2\underline{\mu})\underline{p}\underline{q} - (\alpha_1 c_1 + \alpha_2\underline{c}_2\underline{\mu})\underline{q} - C(\underline{\mu})$$
$$\geq \bar{t} + (\alpha_1 + \alpha_2\bar{\mu})\bar{p}\bar{q} - (\alpha_1 c_1 + \alpha_2\bar{\mu}\underline{c}_2)\bar{q} - C(\bar{\mu}). \qquad (6.11)$$

The government needs to solve the following program for the optimal regulatory policy:

$$\max_{\{\underline{q},\underline{\mu},\underline{U},\bar{q},\bar{\mu},\bar{U}\}} \nu\{(\alpha_1 + \alpha_2\underline{\mu})(S(\underline{q}) + \lambda\underline{p}\underline{q}) - (1 + \lambda)((\alpha_1 c_1$$
$$+ \alpha_2\underline{c}_2\underline{\mu})\underline{q} + C(\underline{\mu})) - \lambda\underline{U}\} + (1 - \nu)\{(\alpha_1 + \alpha_2\bar{\mu})(S(\bar{q})$$
$$+ \lambda\bar{p}\bar{q}) - (1 + \lambda)[(\alpha_1 c_1 + \alpha_2\bar{c}_2\bar{\mu})\bar{q} + C(\bar{\mu})] - \lambda\bar{U}\}$$

s.t. (6.8), (6.9), (6.10), and (6.11).

We can now state the next result:

Proposition 6.4: *Suppose the government has asymmetric information about c_2. Assume that $|S''|$, C'', and α_2 are large enough. Then,*

(1) When the size of information asymmetry Δc_2 is large enough:

    (i) If $c_2 = \underline{c}_2$, the optimal regulatory rule is the same as under complete information with uniform pricing;

    (ii) If $c_2 = \bar{c}_2$, the price is higher and the size of the network is smaller in the rural area relative to that under complete information with uniform pricing. Moreover, the price is lower and the size of network is smaller than that under discriminatory pricing.

More specifically, the optimal regulatory policy entails:

$$\underline{p}^{USB} = \underline{p}^{**}, \mu^{USB} = \mu^{**}$$

$$\frac{\bar{p}^{USB} - \frac{\alpha_1 c_1 + \alpha_2 \bar{c}_2 \bar{\mu}^{USB}}{\alpha_1 + \alpha_2 \bar{\mu}^{USB}}}{\bar{p}^{USB}} = \frac{\lambda}{1+\lambda}\frac{1}{\eta} + \frac{\lambda}{1+\lambda}\frac{\nu}{1-\nu}$$

$$\times \frac{\alpha_2 \Delta c_2 \bar{\mu}^{USB}}{\alpha_1 + \alpha_2 \bar{\mu}^{USB}}\frac{1}{\bar{p}^{USB}}$$

$$(1+\lambda)C'(\bar{\mu}^{USB}) = \alpha_2[S(\bar{q}^{USB}) + \lambda \bar{p}^{USB}\bar{q}^{USB}$$

$$-(1+\lambda)\bar{q}^{USB}\bar{c}_2 - \lambda\frac{\nu}{1-\nu}\Delta c_2 \bar{q}^{USB}].$$

(2) When the size of information asymmetry Δc_2 is small enough, bunching occurs and optimal regulation entails:

$$\frac{p^{USB} - \frac{\alpha_1 c_1 + \alpha_2[\nu\underline{c}_2 + (1-\nu)\bar{c}_2]\mu^{USB}}{\alpha_1 + \alpha_2 \mu^{USB}}}{p^{USB}} = \frac{\lambda}{1+\lambda}\frac{1}{\eta}$$

$$+ \frac{\lambda}{1+\lambda}\frac{\nu\alpha_2 \Delta c_2 \mu^{USB}}{\alpha_1 + \alpha_2 \mu^{USB}}\frac{1}{p^{USB}}$$

$$C'(\mu^{USB}) = \alpha_2[\frac{S(q^{USB}) + \lambda p^{USB}q^{USB}}{1+\lambda}$$

$$- (\nu\underline{c}_2 + (1-\nu)\bar{c}_2)q^{USB} - \frac{\lambda}{1+\lambda}\nu\Delta c_2 q^{USB}].$$

Proof: See the appendix.   ■

The complete information optimal regulatory rule under uniform pricing is obtained when $c_2 = \underline{c}_2$ – i.e. there is no distortion at the top. However – since the government has to give up an information rent $\alpha_2 \bar{\mu} \Delta c_2 \bar{q}$ to the firm to induce truthful revelation of its information, both the price and the size of network are distorted as a result of the efficiency–rent-extraction trade-off when the firm has a high-cost technology.

Uniform pricing has two effects on the pricing decision: One is the direct effect of asymmetric information which leads to a higher price; the other is the average marginal cost effect caused by uniform pricing, which can induce either an increase or a decrease of the price, depending on the change in the size of the network. But if the size of information asymmetry Δc_2 is large enough, with uniform pricing the price for the rural area will be higher than that under complete information.

To determine the optimal network investment, one needs now to take into account three effects: In addition to the surplus effect and the revenue effect, there is a direct effect of asymmetric information which calls for a decrease in the size of the network. The net effect is to induce a smaller network if Δc_2 is large enough.

Next we compare these results with those under discriminatory pricing. Again, there are two effects that need to be considered. The average marginal cost effect which leads to a decrease of price has now a counter effect. But one can show that the price for the rural area under uniform pricing is always lower than under discriminatory pricing. Indeed, denoting

$$\bar{\bar{p}} \equiv \frac{\alpha_1 p_1 + \alpha_2 \bar{\mu}\, \bar{p}_2}{\alpha_1 + \alpha_2 \bar{\mu}}$$

the average price under price discrimination, one can show that the price under uniform pricing is equal to the average price under discrimination (i.e. $\bar{\bar{p}} = \bar{p}^{USB}$ for a given size of the network). Moreover, one can show that the size of the network under uniform pricing is smaller than that with discriminatory pricing. We thus conclude that under asymmetric information, while uniform pricing favors the people in the rural area, it does so at the expense of network expansion in the rural area.

An interesting result under uniform pricing is that bunching occurs if Δc_2 is small enough. In this case, optimization of the social welfare calls for the consumption and the network investment to be decreasing functions of c_2. Indeed, we have seen that in the optimal allocation under complete information monotonicity is satisfied if α_1 is large enough. But in the presence of asymmetric information, if Δc_2 is small enough, the second-order condition of truthtelling is violated. Then screening is not possible with uniform pricing.[4]

6.5 Universal service policy under collusion

Let us now introduce the possibility of collusion. We want to illustrate in a very simple setting the impact of collusion on the optimal regulatory policy. For this purpose, we add to the basic principal–agent relationship between the government and the monopolist firm a hierarchical level representing the regulator of the firm. A special feature in this chapter is that in addition to the threat of collusion between the regulator and the firm, collusion may also arise between the regulator and other interest groups such as consumers in the rural area and taxpayers.

Following Tirole (1986), we assume that the regulator's role is to bridge the government's informational gap on c_2. Suppose the regulator has the utility function:

$$R(s) = s \text{ and } s \geq 0, \tag{6.12}$$

---

[4] For an exposition of this nonresponsiveness result in a model with a single action, see Laffont and Martimort (2002, p. 53).

where s is the regulator's reward. The regulator is risk neutral but is protected by limited liability. Therefore, to obtain the regulator's participation he should get at least his reservation utility level, which is normalized to be zero. Assume that the regulator is endowed with an information technology with which he learns a private signal ($\sigma = c_2$) about the monopolist's cost in the rural area with probability ξ and learns nothing ($\sigma = \phi$) with probability $1 - \xi$. For simplicity, we assume that the regulator's information is known to the monopolistic firm and other possible interest groups. In other words, side contracting is assumed to take place under complete information. To make use of the regulator's information σ, the government asks him to report the signal he has received, i.e. $r \in \{\underline{c}_2, \bar{c}_2, \phi\}$. The critical assumption is that the signal the regulator reports is hard information – i.e. when a signal is reported to the government, it is hard evidence. However, the regulator can hide his information and report that the signal is ϕ. If the regulator learns nothing, he must report $\sigma = \phi$. Thus, the regulator has discretion only when he receives a signal which reveals the firm's private information. The regulator's information technology can be summarized by table 6.1, describing the probability of each state of nature.

The timing of the regulatory game in the presence of a collusion threat between the regulator and the monopolist and other interest groups is as follows: A grand contract is offered by the government after the firm, the regulator, and other interest groups learn their respective information. Then the regulator makes a take-it-or-leave-it offer to the firm and

Table 6.1. *Information structure*

	type $\bar{c}_2$	type $\underline{c}_2$
$\sigma = \bar{c}_2$	$\nu\xi$	0
$\sigma = \phi$	$\nu(1 - \xi)$	$(1 - \nu)(1 - \xi)$
$\sigma = \underline{c}_2$	0	$(1 - \nu)\xi$

other interest groups and they decide whether to accept this side contract. The government then asks for a report from the regulator about the monopolist's cost. When evidence is reported by the regulator, the regulatory contract is chosen under complete information; but when the regulator reports that he has learned nothing, the revelation game under asymmetric information is played as in section 6.4. Finally the firm decides whether to accept the grand contract, and both the grand contract and the side contract will be executed if they are accepted.[5]

Collusion under discriminatory pricing

Before we proceed, the following notations are introduced: $\bar{q}_2^c = q(c_2 = \bar{c}_2, \sigma = \bar{c}_2), \underline{q}_2^c = q(c_2 = \underline{c}_2, \sigma = \underline{c}_2)$, $\bar{q}_2^{c\phi} = q(c_2 = \bar{c}_2, \sigma = \phi)$, and $\underline{q}_2^{c\phi} = q(c_2 = \underline{c}_2, \sigma = \phi)$. Other notations such as $\underline{\mu}^c$, $\underline{\mu}^{c\phi}$, $\bar{\mu}^c$, and $\bar{\mu}^{c\phi}$ are similarly defined.

To analyze when collusion matters, assume that the second-best contract under discriminatory pricing is still offered under the threat of collusion. Let us look first at what happens if the state of nature is $c_2 = \underline{c}_2$ and $\sigma = \underline{c}_2$. In this case the firm gets an information rent of $\alpha_2 \bar{\mu}^{SB} \Delta c_2 \bar{q}_2^{SB}$ if the regulator hides the information that the firm has an efficient type. So there is a stake of collusion for the good-type firm to bribe the regulator for his silence. Therefore, the government has to satisfy the following collusion-proofness constraint to induce truthtelling of the regulator:

$$\underline{s}^f \geqslant k_1 \alpha_2 \Delta c_2 \bar{\mu}^{c\phi} \bar{q}_2^{c\phi}, \tag{6.13}$$

where $\underline{s}^f$ is the reward of the regulator if he reveals that the firm is type $\underline{c}_2$ and where $k_1 = \frac{1}{1+\lambda_1}$ and λ_1 represents the transaction cost between the regulator and the firm. To focus

---

[5] Note that under our assumption about the manager's information technology, the posterior beliefs after an inconclusive signal (∅) are identical to the prior beliefs:

$$\hat{v} = \frac{v(1-\xi)}{v(1-\xi) + (1-v)(1-\xi)} = v.$$

on the interesting case we assume $\lambda_1 > \lambda$.[6] Extending proposition 6.2 to take into account the cost of collusion-proofness we know that for $c_2 = \underline{c}_2$ the price and the size of the network are not distorted, regardless of the regulator's report. So consumers in the rural area are not affected by the presence of collusion and they do not have any stake of collusion in this state of nature. Similarly, consumers in the urban area do not want to collude with the regulator because of complete information about c_1. Another potential interest group is the taxpayers, who are obliged to fund any deficit due to the lack of a budget constraint for the firm. Nevertheless, since neither the size of network nor the prices are distorted by the presence of asymmetric information, they will pay the same amount of taxes under asymmetric information as under complete information. So the taxpayers do not want to collude with the regulator either. Therefore, $\underline{s}^f > 0$ is the only incentive payment to the regulator needed to induce his truthful report.

Suppose the state of nature is $c_2 = \bar{c}_2$ and $\sigma = \bar{c}_2$. In this case, the firm does not obtain any information rent even if the regulator hides the evidence. So the monopolistic firm does not want to collude with the regulator. Similarly, consumers in the urban area do not benefit from collusion. Moreover, we know from proposition 6.2 that consumers in the rural area will get a surplus of $\alpha_2 \bar{\mu}^{SB}(S(\bar{q}_2^{SB}) - \bar{p}_2^{SB}\bar{q}_2^{SB})$ if the signal is concealed by the regulator, and $\alpha_2 \bar{\mu}^*(S(\bar{q}_2^*) - \bar{p}_2^*\bar{q}_2^*)$ if the signal is truthfully revealed. Since asymmetric information leads to an increase of the price and a decrease of the size of network for the rural area under price discrimination and $S(q) - pq$ is an increasing function of q in the relevant region, the rural consumers would obtain less surplus from collusion and therefore they do not have any incentive to collude with the regulator.

---

[6] Otherwise, side contracting incurs a lower transaction cost than the social cost of public funds and it is optimal to let collusion take place. So avoiding collusion is not an issue.

For the taxpayers, however, if $\sigma = \bar{c}_2$ is reported to the government, they will pay:

$$T^c = \alpha_1 \bar{q}_1^*(c_1 - \bar{p}_1^*) + \alpha_2 \bar{\mu}^* \bar{q}_2^*(\bar{c}_2 - \bar{p}_2^*) + C(\bar{\mu}^*)$$

and

$$T^{c\phi} = \alpha_1 \bar{q}_1^{SB}(c_1 - \bar{p}_1^{SB}) + \alpha_2 \bar{\mu}^{SB} \bar{q}_2^{SB}(\bar{c}_2 - \bar{p}_2^{SB}) + C(\bar{\mu}^{SB})$$

if σ is hidden. Since asymmetric information induces a higher price and a smaller network in the rural area, one can check that $T^{c\phi} < T^c$. In other words, the taxpayers will pay less to fund the deficit if the regulator hides the information that $\sigma = \bar{c}_2$. Thus, the interest group of taxpayers would like to collude with the regulator if they can overcome the transaction costs involved and ask the regulator to hide the signal $\sigma = \bar{c}_2$ in order to save a tax payment of $T^c - T^\phi$. In this case the government has to satisfy the following collusion-proofness constraint:

$$\bar{s}^t \geqslant k_2[\alpha_2 \bar{\mu}^c \bar{q}_2^c(\bar{c}_2 - \bar{p}_2^c) - \alpha_2 \bar{\mu}^{c\phi} \bar{q}_2^{c\phi}(\bar{c}_2 - \bar{p}_2^{c\phi})$$
$$+ (C(\bar{\mu}^c) - C(\bar{\mu}^{c\phi}))], \tag{6.14}$$

where $k_2 = \frac{1}{1+\lambda_2}$ and λ_2 is the transaction cost of side contracting between the regulator and the interested group of taxpayers. Again, we assume $\lambda_2 > \lambda$ to focus on the interesting case in which collusion is indeed an issue, and we assume that the government's program remains convex.

By the collusion-proofness principle, we can without loss of generality focus on the following program to solve for the optimal regulatory policy under the threat of collusion:

$$\max_{\{\underline{q}_1^c, \underline{q}_2^c, \underline{q}_2^{c\phi}, \underline{\mu}^c, \underline{\mu}^{c\phi}, \bar{q}_1^c, \bar{q}_2^c, \bar{q}_2^{c\phi}, \bar{\mu}^c, \bar{\mu}^{c\phi}\}} \nu\xi\{\alpha_1(S(\underline{q}_1^c) + \lambda \underline{p}_1 \underline{q}_1^c)$$

$$+ \alpha_2 \underline{\mu}^c(S(\underline{q}_2^c) + \lambda \underline{p}_2^c \underline{q}_2^c) - (1 + \lambda)((\alpha_1 c_1 \underline{q}_1^c + \alpha_2 \underline{c}_2 \underline{q}_2^c \underline{\mu}^c$$

$$+ C(\underline{\mu}^c)) - \lambda \underline{s}^f\} + \nu(1 - \xi)\{\alpha_1(S(\underline{q}_1^{c\phi}) + \lambda \underline{p}_1^{c\phi} \underline{q}_1^{c\phi})$$

$$+ \alpha_2 \underline{\mu}^{c\phi}(S(\underline{q}_2^{c\phi}) + \lambda \underline{p}_2^{c\phi} \underline{q}_2^{c\phi}) - (1 + \lambda)((\alpha_1 c_1 \underline{q}_1^{c\phi}$$

$$+ \alpha_2 \underline{c}_2 \underline{q}_2^{c\phi} \underline{\mu}^{c\phi} + C(\underline{\mu}^{c\phi})) - \lambda \underline{U}\} + (1 - \nu)\xi\{\alpha_1(S(\bar{q}_1^c)$$

$$+ \lambda \, \bar{p}_1^c \bar{q}_1^c) + \alpha_2 \bar{\mu}^c (S(\bar{q}_2^c) + \lambda \, \bar{p}_2^c \bar{q}_2^c) - (1 + \lambda)(\alpha_1 c_1 \bar{q}_1^c$$
$$+ \alpha_2 \bar{c}_2 \bar{q}_2^c \bar{\mu}^c + C(\bar{\mu}^c)) - \lambda \bar{s}^t\} + (1 - \nu)(1 - \xi)\{\alpha_1 (S(\bar{q}_1^{c\phi})$$
$$+ \lambda \, \bar{p}_1^{c\phi} \bar{q}_1^{c\phi}) + \alpha_2 \bar{\mu}^{c\phi} (S(\bar{q}_2^{c\phi}) + \lambda \, \bar{p}_2^{c\phi} \bar{q}_2^{c\phi}) - (1 + \lambda)(\alpha_1 c_1 \bar{q}_1^{c\phi}$$
$$+ \alpha_2 \bar{c}_2 \bar{q}_2^{c\phi} \bar{\mu}^{c\phi} + C(\bar{\mu}^{c\phi}))\}.$$

Note that when the state of nature is $c_2 = \underline{c}_2$ and $\sigma = \underline{c}_2$, the government does not need to give up an information rent but has to give an incentive payment $k_1 \alpha_2 \Delta c_2 \bar{\mu}^{c\phi} \bar{q}_2^{c\phi}$ to the regulator to induce truthful revelation of information. Then, regulation is made under complete information. When the state of nature is $c_2 = \underline{c}_2$ and $\sigma = \phi$, however, regulatory policies are made under asymmetric information. In this case, the government not only needs to pay the regulator's reservation utility level but has to give up an information rent $\alpha_2 \Delta c_2 \bar{\mu}^{c\phi} \bar{q}_2^{c\phi}$ to the low-cost firm.

When the state of nature is $c_2 = \bar{c}_2$ and $\sigma = \bar{c}_2$, the monopolistic firm does not get an information rent. But the regulator is paid an incentive payment of $\bar{s}^t = k_2 [\alpha_2 \bar{\mu}^c \bar{q}_2^c (\bar{c}_2 - \bar{p}_2^c) - \alpha_2 \bar{\mu}^{c\phi} \bar{q}_2^{c\phi} (\bar{c}_2 - \bar{p}_2^{c\phi}) + C(\bar{\mu}^c) - C(\bar{\mu}^{c\phi})]$ to reveal his information.

We thus obtain the following result:

Proposition 6.5: *Under the same assumptions as proposition 6.2[7] and under price discrimination, the optimal regulatory response to the threat of collusion calls for:*

(i) When the state of nature is $c_2 = \bar{c}_2$ and the regulator reports $\sigma = \phi$, the optimal size of the network is smaller than without the threat of collusion. Moreover the optimal price for the rural area is higher than that in the absence of collusion if and only if $k_1 > \frac{\lambda}{1+\lambda}(1 - \frac{1}{\eta})k_2 / [1 - \frac{\lambda}{1+\lambda}\frac{1}{\eta}]$. But the optimal rural price is lower if k_1 is small;

---

[7] For simplicity we also assume that the second-order condition for truthtelling is satisfied. Otherwise, bunching occurs and collusion leads to less screening.

(ii) When the state of nature is $c_2 = \bar{c}_2$ and the regulator reports $\sigma = \bar{c}_2$, the optimal price for the rural area is higher and the optimal size of the network for the rural area is smaller than those in the absence of collusion.

More specifically, the optimal regulatory policy entails:

$$\underline{p}_1^c = \underline{p}_1^{c\phi} = \underline{p}_1^*, \underline{p}_2^c = \underline{p}_2^{c\phi} = \underline{p}_2^*, \underline{\mu}^c = \underline{\mu}^{c\phi} = \underline{\mu}^*$$

$$\frac{\bar{p}_2^{c\phi} - \bar{c}_2}{\bar{p}_2^{c\phi}}[1 + \frac{\lambda}{1+\lambda}\frac{\xi}{1-\xi}k_2] = \frac{\lambda}{1+\lambda}\frac{1}{1-\xi}\frac{1}{\eta}[\xi k_2 + (1-\xi)]$$

$$+ \frac{\lambda}{1+\lambda}\frac{\nu}{1-\nu}\frac{1}{1-\xi}\frac{\Delta c_2}{\bar{p}_2^{c\phi}}[k_1 \xi$$

$$+ (1-\xi)]\frac{\bar{p}_2^c - \bar{c}_2}{\bar{p}_2^c}(1 + \frac{\lambda}{1+\lambda}k_2) = \frac{\lambda}{1+\lambda}\frac{1}{\eta}(1 + k_2)$$

$$C'(\bar{\mu}^{c\phi})[(1+\lambda) - \lambda\frac{\xi}{1-\xi}k_2] = \alpha_2[S(\bar{q}_2^{c\phi}) + \lambda\bar{p}_2^{c\phi}\bar{q}_2^{c\phi}$$

$$- (1+\lambda)\bar{c}_2\bar{q}_2^{c\phi} - \lambda\frac{\nu}{1-\nu}\frac{\bar{q}_2^{c\phi}\Delta c_2}{1-\xi}(k_1\xi + (1-\xi))$$

$$- \lambda\frac{\xi}{1-\xi}k_2\bar{q}_2^{c\phi}(\bar{p}_2^{c\phi} - \bar{c}_2)]$$

$$C'(\bar{\mu}^c)((1+\lambda) + \lambda k_2) = \alpha_2[S(\bar{q}_2^c) + \lambda\bar{p}_2^c\bar{q}_2^c - (1+\lambda)\bar{c}_2\bar{q}_2^c$$

$$+ \lambda k_2\bar{q}_2(\bar{p}_2^c - \bar{c}_2)].$$

Under our assumption the participation constraint of the high cost, the incentive constraint of the low cost, and the collusion-proof constraints (6.13) and (6.14) are the only binding constraints. When the state of nature is $c_2 = \underline{c}_2$ and $\sigma = \underline{c}_2$, since the good-type firm obtains an information rent of $\alpha_2\Delta c_2\bar{\mu}^{c\phi}\bar{q}_2^{c\phi}$ if the regulator reports $r = \phi$, the optimal regulatory response to the threat of collusion between the firm and the regulator is to increase the price $\bar{p}_2^{c\phi}$ and decrease the size of network $\bar{\mu}^{c\phi}$. In other words, incentives are weakened to reduce the stake of collusion.

But when the state of nature is $c_2 = \bar{c}_2$ and $\sigma = \bar{c}_2$, the taxpayers have a tax saving of $\alpha_2\bar{\mu}^c\bar{q}_2^c(\bar{c}_2 - \bar{p}_2^c) - \alpha_2\bar{\mu}^{c\phi}\bar{q}_2^{c\phi}$

$(\bar{c}_2 - \bar{p}_2^{c\phi}) + (C(\bar{\mu}^c) - C(\bar{\mu}^{c\phi}))$ if the regulator conceals his information. In this case, prevention of collusion calls for a decrease of the price $\bar{p}_2^{c\phi}$ and an increase of the size of the network $\bar{\mu}^{c\phi}$. Observe that both incentive payments to the regulator $\underline{s}^f$ and $\bar{s}^t$ depend on the output $\bar{q}_2^{c\phi}$. So we face an interesting case in which, from the point of view of the government, the monopolistic firm and taxpayers have opposite interests to collude with the regulator. As a result, the existence of one collusion-proofness constraint hardens the other one, even though the collusion-proofness constraints are associated with different states of nature. However, it turns out that the need to reduce the stake of collusion between the regulator and the firm dominates that between the regulator and the interest group of taxpayers if k_1 is large enough. Consequently, the rural price will be higher than that without collusion. Conversely, the presence of collusion will induce a lower price for the rural area if k_1 is small.

It is interesting to note that this result is different from Laffont and Tirole (LT, p. 490) where the existence of an interest group (the environmentalists) increases the rent of the firm.

Collusion under uniform pricing

Now let us consider the collusion issue under uniform pricing. For expositional simplicity we introduce the following notations: $\bar{q}^{uc} = q(c_2 = \bar{c}_2, \sigma = \bar{c}_2)$, $\underline{q}^{uc} = q(c_2 = \underline{c}_2, \sigma = \underline{c}_2)$, $\bar{q}^{uc\phi} = q(c_2 = \bar{c}_2, \sigma = \phi)$, and $\underline{q}^{uc\phi} = q(c_2 = \underline{c}_2, \sigma = \phi)$. Other notations such as μ^{uc}, $\underline{\mu}^{uc\phi}$, $\bar{\mu}^{uc}$, and $\bar{\mu}^{uc\phi}$ are similarly defined.

Before considering when collusion matters, remember that with the information structure of our model, the regulator has discretion only when he receives a conclusive signal. Assume now that the second-best result under uniform pricing is offered in the presence of collusion. If $c_2 = \underline{c}_2$ and

$\sigma = \underline{c}_2$, the good-type firm will get an information rent of $\alpha_2 \Delta c_2 \bar{\mu}^{c\phi} \bar{q}^{c\phi}$ if the regulator hides the information. Thus, the government has to satisfy the following collusion-proofness constraint to induce truthtelling of the regulator:

$$\underline{s}^{uf} \geqslant k_1 \alpha_2 \Delta c_2 \bar{\mu}^{uc\phi} \bar{q}^{uc\phi}, \tag{6.15}$$

where $k_1 = \frac{1}{1+\lambda_1}$ and $\lambda_1 > \lambda$ is the transaction cost between the regulator and the firm.

As with discriminatory pricing, consumers in the rural area do not have any stake of collusion because neither the price nor the size of the network is distorted if $c_2 = \underline{c}_2$. The consumers in the urban area do not have an incentive to collude with the regulator either even though they are adversely affected by uniform pricing. It is also the case for taxpayers, who will pay the same amount of taxes regardless of the regulator's report.

Suppose the state of nature is $c_2 = \bar{c}_2$ and $\sigma = \bar{c}_2$. The firm no longer has any stake of collusion because it does not get an information rent when $c_2 = \bar{c}_2$. We know from proposition 6.4 that when the size of asymmetric information is large enough, the price for the rural area is higher and the size of the network smaller if the regulator hides his information. Thus, $\alpha_2 \bar{\mu}^{uc}(S(\bar{q}^{uc}) - \bar{p}^{uc}\bar{q}^{uc}) > \alpha_2 \bar{\mu}^{uc\phi}(S(\bar{q}^{uc\phi}) - \bar{p}^{uc\phi}\bar{q}^{uc\phi})$, i.e. the consumers in the rural area obtain less surplus if the regulator does not report truthfully and therefore they have no incentive to collude. Similarly, the urban consumers do not want to collude with the regulator in this state of nature.

Note that the taxpayers will pay $T^{uc} = (\alpha_1 c_1 + \alpha_2 \bar{c}_2 \bar{\mu}^{uc})\bar{q}^{uc} - (\alpha_1 + \alpha_2 \bar{\mu}^{uc})\bar{p}^{uc}\bar{q}^{uc} + C(\bar{\mu}^{uc})$ if the signal is revealed and $T^{uc\phi} = (\alpha_1 c_1 + \alpha_2 \bar{c}_2 \bar{\mu}^{c\phi})\bar{q}^{uc\phi} - (\alpha_1 + \alpha_2 \bar{\mu}^{uc\phi})\bar{p}^{uc\phi}\bar{q}^{uc\phi} + C(\bar{\mu}^{uc\phi})$ if not. Since $(\alpha_1 c_1 + \alpha_2 \bar{c}_2 \mu)q - (\alpha_1 + \alpha_2 \mu)pq + C(\mu) > 0$ if $C'(\cdot)$ is large enough, the taxpayers will save a tax payment of $T^{uc} - T^{uc\phi} > 0$ if the regulator reports $r = \phi$. So they have incentives to collude with the regulator. Thus, the government needs to satisfy the following collusion-proofness constraint:

$$\bar{s}^{ut} \geqslant k_2[(\alpha_1 c_1 + \alpha_2 \bar{c}_2 \bar{\mu}^{uc})\bar{q}^{uc} - (\alpha_1 + \alpha_2 \bar{\mu}^{uc})\bar{p}^{uc}\bar{q}^{uc} + C(\bar{\mu}^{uc})$$
$$- (\alpha_1 c_1 + \alpha_2 \bar{c}_2 \bar{\mu}^{uc\phi})\bar{q}^{uc\phi} + (\alpha_1 + \alpha_2 \bar{\mu}^{uc\phi})\bar{p}^{uc\phi}\bar{q}^{uc\phi}$$
$$- C(\bar{\mu}^{uc\phi})], \tag{6.16}$$

where $k_2 = \frac{1}{1+\lambda_2}$ and λ_2 denotes the transaction cost of side contracting between the regulator and the interest group of taxpayers.

By the collusion-proofness principle, the optimal regulatory policy is obtained by solving the following program:

$$\max_{\{\underline{q}^{uc}, \underline{q}^{uc\phi}, \underline{\mu}^{uc}, \underline{\mu}^{uc\phi}, \bar{q}^{uc}, \bar{q}^{uc\phi}, \bar{\mu}^{uc}, \bar{\mu}^{uc\phi}\}} v\xi\{(\alpha_1 + \alpha_2\underline{\mu}^{uc})(S(\underline{q}^{uc})$$

$$+ \lambda \underline{p}^{uc}\underline{q}^{uc}) - (1 + \lambda) \times [(\alpha_1 c_1 + \alpha_2\underline{c}_2\underline{\mu}^{uc})\underline{q}^{uc}$$

$$+ C(\underline{\mu}^{uc})] - \lambda\underline{s}^{uf} - \lambda\underline{U}^{uc}\}$$

$$+ v(1 - \xi)\{(\alpha_1 + \alpha_2\underline{\mu}^{uc\phi})(S(\underline{q}^{uc\phi}) + \lambda\underline{p}^{uc\phi}\underline{q}^{uc\phi})$$

$$- (1 + \lambda)[(\alpha_1 c_1 + \alpha_2 c_2\underline{\mu}^{uc\phi})\underline{q}^{uc\phi} + C(\underline{\mu}^{uc\phi})] - \lambda\underline{U}^{uc\phi}\}$$

$$+ (1 - v)\xi\{(\alpha_1 + \alpha_2\bar{\mu}^{uc})(S(\bar{q}^{uc}) + \lambda\bar{p}^{uc}\bar{q}^{uc})$$

$$- (1 + \lambda)[(\alpha_1 c_1 + \alpha_2\bar{c}_2\bar{\mu}^{uc})\bar{q}^{uc} + C(\bar{\mu}^{uc})] - \lambda\bar{s}^{ut} - \lambda\bar{U}^{uc}\}$$

$$+ (1 - v)(1 - \xi)\{(\alpha_1 + \alpha_2\bar{\mu}^{uc\phi})(S(\bar{q}^{uc\phi}) + \lambda\bar{p}^{uc\phi}\bar{q}^{uc\phi})$$

$$- (1 + \lambda)[(\alpha_1 c_1 + \alpha_2\bar{c}_2\bar{\mu}^{uc\phi})\bar{q}^{uc\phi} + C(\bar{\mu}^{uc\phi})] - \lambda\bar{U}^{uc\phi}\}$$

s.t. (6.7), (6.8), (6.9), (6.10), (6.15), and (6.16).
Thus, optimal regulation entails:

Proposition 6.6: *Under the same assumptions as proposition 6.4, suppose uniform pricing is required and there is a threat of collusion. Then,*

(1) When the state of nature is $c_2 = \bar{c}_2$ and $\sigma = \phi$:

    (i) The price for the rural area is lower and the size of network is smaller than with discriminatory pricing,

    (ii) The price for the rural area will be higher and the size of network smaller than in the absence of collusion if k_1 is large enough;

(2) When $c_2 = \bar{c}_2$ and $\sigma = \bar{c}_2$, both the price and the size of the network for the rural area are distorted in comparison with those under complete information with uniform pricing.

More specifically,

$$\underline{p}^{uc} = \underline{p}^{uc\phi} = \underline{p}^{**}, \underline{\mu}^{uc} = \underline{\mu}^{uc\phi} = \underline{\mu}^{**}$$

$$\frac{\bar{p}^{c\phi} - \frac{\alpha_1 c_1 + \alpha_2 \bar{c}_2 \bar{\mu} c^\phi}{\alpha_1 + \alpha_2 \bar{\mu}^{c\phi}} (1 - \frac{\lambda}{1+\lambda} \frac{\xi}{1-\xi} k_2)}{\bar{p}^{c\phi}}$$

$$= \frac{\lambda}{1+\lambda} \frac{1}{\eta} + \frac{\lambda}{1+\lambda} \frac{\xi}{1-\xi} k_2 (1 - \frac{1}{\eta})$$

$$+ \frac{\lambda}{1+\lambda} \frac{\nu}{1-\nu} \frac{1}{1-\xi} \frac{\alpha_2 \Delta c_2 \bar{\mu}^{uc\phi}}{\alpha_1 + \alpha_2 \bar{\mu}^{uc\phi}} \frac{1}{\bar{p}^{c\phi}} [k_1 \xi + (1-\xi)]$$

$$\frac{\bar{p}^{uc} - \frac{\alpha_1 c_1 + \alpha_2 \bar{c}_2 \bar{\mu}^{uc}}{\alpha_1 + \alpha_2 \bar{\mu}^{uc}} (1 + \frac{\lambda}{1+\lambda} k_2)}{\bar{p}^{uc}} = \frac{\lambda}{1+\lambda} \frac{1}{\eta} - \frac{\lambda}{1+\lambda} k_2 (1 - \frac{1}{\eta})$$

$$C'(\bar{\mu}^{uc\phi})(1 - \frac{\lambda}{1+\lambda} \frac{\xi}{1-\xi} k_2)$$

$$= \alpha_2 [\frac{S(\bar{q}^{uc\phi}) + \lambda \bar{p}^{uc\phi} \bar{q}^{uc\phi}}{1+\lambda} - \bar{c}_2 \bar{q}^{uc\phi}$$

$$- \frac{\lambda}{1+\lambda} \frac{\nu}{1-\nu} \frac{1}{1-\xi} \bar{q}^{uc\phi} \Delta c_2 (k_1 \xi + (1-\xi))$$

$$- \frac{\lambda}{1+\lambda} \frac{\xi}{1-\xi} k_2 (\bar{p}^{uc\phi} - \bar{c}_2) \bar{q}^{uc\phi}]$$

$$C'(\bar{\mu}^{uc})(1 + \frac{\lambda}{1+\lambda} \frac{\xi}{1-\xi} k_2) = \alpha_2 [\frac{S(\bar{q}^{uc}) + \lambda \bar{p}^{uc} \bar{q}^{uc}}{1+\lambda} - \bar{c}_2 \bar{q}^{uc}$$

$$- \frac{\lambda}{1+\lambda} k_2 (\bar{c}_2 - \bar{p}^{uc}) \bar{q}^{uc})].$$

As for the case of discriminatory pricing, incentives of the monopolistic firm are weakened by the existence of the interest group of taxpayers. Moreover, the allocations are distorted when $c_2 = \bar{c}_2$ and the regulator learns this information and reports it to the government. However, in both the states of nature $c_2 = \bar{c}_2$ and $\sigma = \phi$ and $c_2 = \bar{c}_2$ and $\sigma = \bar{c}_2$, the price for the rural area is lower and the size of the network is smaller than those under discriminatory pricing.

6.6 Conclusion

In this chapter, we have analyzed with a formal model the optimal regulatory policy associated with USOs. In particular, we have examined how the optimal universal service policy is affected by asymmetric information and the threat of collusion under both discriminatory pricing and uniform pricing. Our findings show that under both discriminatory pricing and uniform pricing, asymmetric information leads to a higher price and a smaller network in the rural area and the collusion threat weakens the incentives given to the firm. In addition, we find that while uniform pricing may indeed achieve the redistributive goal of a lower price for the rural area, it is achieved at the cost of a smaller network.

One of the main policy implications from our results is that when uniform pricing is used to favor consumers in the rural area, the consumers which are not connected may be adversely affected because less investment is devoted to the expansion of the network. Thus, uniform pricing may not achieve the goal claimed by policy makers of promoting expansion of access to infrastructure network, which is most urgent in developing countries. On the contrary, the expansion of network may be delayed even though connected consumers in the rural area are favored. Therefore, one general lesson we can draw from this chapter is that one cannot isolate the network investment problem from pricing policy.

Since LDCs have not yet developed a sufficient infrastructure network to provide services to the whole society, network expansion constitutes an extremely important development strategy for these countries. Indeed, in many LDCs the poor are willing to pay a high price for access to the basic services. But since the network is not there, they are deprived of the services. So in this sense the governments in LDCs should devote more attention to giving incentives for network investments rather than distorting prices.

Another insight coming from this model is that there are multiple interest groups which have stakes in a specific universal service policy. This result provides a better description of the losers and winners in the universal service policy game. In addition, since the existence of multiple interest groups calls for different regulatory responses, our results show that there are many collusion-proofness constraints and that the universal service policy is easier to be manipulated.

Appendix

Proof of proposition 6.1: The first-order conditions with respect to $\bar{q}_1$, $\bar{q}_2$, $\bar{\mu}$ (and similarly those with respect to $\underline{q}_1$, $\underline{q}_2$, $\underline{\mu}$) are:

$$\alpha_1(S'(\bar{q}_1) + \lambda \bar{p}_1'\bar{q}_1 + \lambda \bar{p}_1) - (1 + \lambda)\alpha_1 c_1 = 0 \qquad (A.1)$$

$$\alpha_2 \bar{\mu}(S'(\bar{q}_2) + \lambda \bar{p}_2'\bar{q}_2 + \lambda \bar{p}_2) - (1 + \lambda)\alpha_2 \bar{\mu}\bar{c}_2 = 0 \qquad (A.2)$$

$$\alpha_2(S(\bar{q}_2) + \lambda \bar{p}_2\bar{q}_2) - (1 + \lambda)(\alpha_2\bar{c}_2\bar{q}_2 + C'(\bar{\mu})) = 0. \qquad (A.3)$$

Since $C'' > 0$, a sufficient condition for the concavity of the objective function is $|S''|$ large enough.

The determination of $\bar{p}_2$ and $\bar{\mu}$ is illustrated in figure 6A.1.

Equation (A.2) determines $\bar{q}_2$ according to the Ramsey rule.[8] For this level of $\bar{q}_2$, (A.3) determines $\bar{\mu}$.

Proof of proposition 6.2: Since only $\bar{q}_2$ and $\bar{\mu}$ are affected by asymmetric information, we consider only the first-order conditions with respect to $\bar{q}_2$ and $\bar{\mu}$:

$$- \nu\lambda\alpha_2\Delta c_2\bar{\mu} + (1 - \nu)[\alpha_2(S'(\bar{q}_2) + \lambda \bar{p}_2'\bar{q}_2 + \lambda \bar{p}_2) - (1 + \lambda)\alpha_2\bar{c}_2]\bar{\mu} = 0 \qquad (A.4)$$

---

[8] There is of course a one-to-one relationship between $\bar{p}_2$ and $\bar{q}_2$.

$\overline{p}_2$

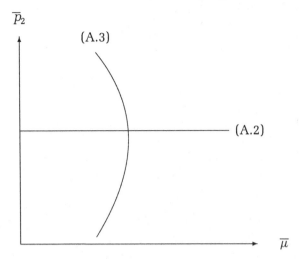

Figure 6A.1   Optimal contract with complete information

$$- \nu \lambda \alpha_2 \Delta c_2 \bar{q}_2 + (1 - \nu)[\alpha_2 (S(\bar{q}_2) + \lambda \bar{p}_2 \bar{q}_2)$$
$$- (1 + \lambda)(\alpha_2 \bar{c}_2 \bar{q}_2 + C'(\bar{\mu}))] = 0 \qquad (A.5)$$

$|S''|$ large enough ensures concavity.
Denote

$$U(c_2, \tilde{c}_2) \equiv t(\tilde{c}_2) + \alpha_1 p_1(\tilde{c}_2) q(p_1(\tilde{c}_2)) + \alpha_2 \mu(\tilde{c}_2) p_2(\tilde{c}_2) q(p_2(\tilde{c}_2))$$
$$- (\alpha_1 c_1 q(p_1(\tilde{c}_2)) + \alpha_2 c_2 \mu(\tilde{c}_2) q(p_2(\tilde{c}_2))) - C(\mu(\tilde{c}_2))$$

the utility the firm obtains when its report about c_2 is $\tilde{c}_2$.
Proceeding as if c_2 were a continuous variable the first-order
condition for truthtelling is:

$$\dot{t} + \alpha_1(\dot{p}_1 q_1' p_1 + \dot{p}_1 q_1) + \alpha_2 \dot{\mu} p_2 q_2 + \alpha_2 \mu(q_2 \dot{p}_2 + p_2 \dot{p}_2 q_2')$$
$$- (\alpha_1 c_1 q_1' \dot{p}_1 + \alpha_2 c_2(\dot{\mu} q_2 + \mu q_2' \dot{p}_2)) - C'(\mu)\dot{\mu} = 0.$$

The second-order condition for truthtelling is:

$$-\alpha_2(\dot{\mu} q_2 + \mu q_2' \dot{p}_2) \geq 0.$$

Since $q_2' < 0$, a sufficient second-order condition is $\dot{\mu} < 0$
and $\dot{p}_2 > 0$. So, the strategy is to solve the problem in the

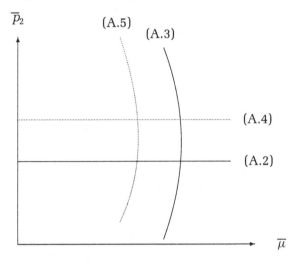

Figure 6A.2 Optimal contract under incomplete information

absence of the second-order condition and check *ex post*
that the sufficient condition $\ddot{\mu} < 0$ and $\dot{p}_2 > 0$ is satisfied (see
Guesnerie and Laffont, 1984).
We can easily represent the impact of asymmetric information on figure 6A.1 by looking at (A.4) and (A.5). We obtain
figure 6A.2.
Therefore $\bar{p}_2^{SB} > \bar{p}_2^* > \underline{p}_2^* = \underline{p}_2^{SB}$ and $\bar{\mu}^{SB} < \bar{\mu}^* < \underline{\mu}^* = \underline{\mu}^{SB}$.
So the second-order condition of incentive compatibility is
satisfied.   ∎

Proof of proposition 6.3: The first-order conditions with
respect to $\bar{q}$ and $\bar{\mu}$ are:

$$(\alpha_1 + \alpha_2\bar{\mu})(S'(\bar{q}) + \lambda\,\bar{p}'\bar{q} + \lambda\,\bar{p}) - (1 + \lambda)(\alpha_1 c_1 + \alpha_2\bar{c}_2\bar{\mu}) = 0$$
$$(A.6)$$
$$\alpha_2(S(\bar{q}) + \lambda\,\bar{p}\bar{q}) - (1 + \lambda)(\alpha_2\bar{c}_2\bar{q} + C'(\bar{\mu})) = 0. \qquad (A.7)$$

From second-order conditions, the objective function is concave if the following conditions are satisfied:

$$(\alpha_1 + \alpha_2\bar{\mu})(S''(\bar{q}) + \lambda\,\bar{p}''\bar{q} + 2\lambda\,\bar{p}') < 0 - C''(\bar{\mu})(\alpha_1$$

$$+\alpha_2\bar{\mu})(S''(\bar{q}) + \lambda\,\bar{p}''\bar{q} + 2\lambda\,\bar{p}) > (1+\lambda)[\frac{\alpha_1\alpha_2(c_1 - c_2)}{\alpha_1 + \alpha_2\bar{\mu}}]^2.$$

So a sufficient condition for the concavity of the objective function is $|S''|$ large enough.

Since $\frac{\alpha_1 c_1 + \alpha_2 c_2\mu}{\alpha_1 + \alpha_2\mu} < c_2$, we have $\bar{p}^{**} < \bar{p}_2^*$ and $\underline{p}^{**} < \underline{p}_2^*$. Moreover, since $\bar{p}_2^*$ maximizes $\frac{S(\bar{q}_2)+\lambda\,\bar{p}_2\bar{q}_2}{1+\lambda} - \bar{c}_2\bar{q}_2$ and $\frac{S'(\bar{q}^{**})+\lambda\,\bar{p}^{**\prime}\bar{q}^{**}+\lambda\,\bar{p}^{**}}{1+\lambda} - \bar{c}_2 < 0$ by substituting the first-order conditions, one obtains $\bar{\mu}^{**} < \bar{\mu}^*$. Similarly, $\mu^{**} < \mu^*$. Finally, we can show that $\frac{d\bar{p}}{d\bar{\mu}} = \frac{c_1}{1-\frac{\lambda}{1+\lambda}\frac{1}{\eta}}\frac{\alpha_1\alpha_2(\bar{c}_2-c_1)}{(\alpha_1+\alpha_2\bar{\mu})^2} > 0$ and $C''(\bar{\mu})\frac{d\bar{\mu}}{d\bar{q}} = \alpha_2(\frac{S'(\bar{q})+\lambda\,\bar{p}\bar{q}+\lambda\,\bar{p}}{1+\lambda} - \bar{c}_2) < 0$. Therefore, both the pricing curve and the network coverage curve are increasing functions of $\bar{p}$.

Differentiating the following equations with respect to c_2:

$$\frac{p - \frac{\alpha_1 c_1 + \alpha_2 c_2\mu}{\alpha_1 + \alpha_2\mu}}{p} = \frac{\lambda}{1+\lambda}\frac{1}{\eta}$$

$$C'(\mu) = \alpha_2[\frac{S(q)+\lambda pq}{1+\lambda} - c_2 q],$$

we have:

$$C''\frac{d\mu}{dc_2} = \alpha_2[\frac{dq}{dc_2}\frac{S'+\lambda p'q + \lambda p - (1+\lambda)c_2}{1+\lambda} - q]$$

$$\frac{dq}{dc_2} = \frac{q'}{1-\frac{\lambda}{1+\lambda}\frac{1}{\eta}}\frac{(\alpha_1+\alpha_2\mu)\alpha_2\mu + \alpha_1\alpha_2(c_2 - c_1)\frac{d\mu}{dc_2}}{(\alpha_1+\alpha_2\mu)^2}.$$

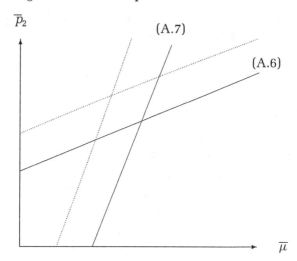

Figure 6A.3   Optimal contract under incomplete information and uniform pricing

Then, one can solve for $\frac{dq}{dc_2}$ and $\frac{d\mu}{dc_2}$:

$$\frac{dq}{dc_2} = \frac{1}{\Delta}\left[-\frac{q'\mu C''}{(1 - \frac{\lambda}{1+\lambda}\frac{1}{\eta})(\alpha_1 + \alpha_2\mu)} + \frac{\alpha_1\alpha_2(c_2 - c_1)qq'}{(1 - \frac{\lambda}{1+\lambda}\frac{1}{\eta})(\alpha_1 + \alpha_2\mu)^2}\right]$$

$$\frac{d\mu}{dc_2} = \frac{1}{\Delta}\left[q - \frac{\alpha_2 q'\mu(S'(q) + \lambda p'q + \lambda p - (1+\lambda)c_2)}{(1 - \frac{\lambda}{1+\lambda}\frac{1}{\eta})(\alpha_1 + \alpha_2\mu)(1+\lambda)}\right],$$

where $\Delta = -\frac{C''}{\alpha_2} + \frac{\alpha_1\alpha_2 q'(c_2-c_1)(S'(q)+\lambda p'q+\lambda p-(1+\lambda)c_2)}{(1-\frac{\lambda}{1+\lambda}\frac{1}{\eta})(\alpha_1+\alpha_2\mu)^2(1+\lambda)}$. A sufficient condition for $\frac{dq}{dc_2} \leqslant 0$ and $\frac{d\mu}{dc_2} \leqslant 0$ is both C'' and α_2 are large enough.

We obtain figure 6A.3.

For $\bar{c}_2$ not too large with respect to c_1, the curves associated with (A.6) and (A.7) cut as shown in figure 6A.3. An increase of $\bar{c}_2$ as shown in the figure has ambiguous effects unless C'' and α_2 are large enough. Then the second-order conditions are satisfied and the solution is as described in proposition 6.3.   ∎

Proof of proposition 6.4: The first-order conditions are:

$$-\nu\lambda\alpha_1\Delta c_2\bar{\mu} + (1-\nu)[(\alpha_1 + \alpha_2\bar{\mu})(S'(\bar{q}) + \lambda\bar{p}\bar{q} + \lambda\bar{p})$$

$$-(1+\lambda)(\alpha_1 c_1 + \alpha_2\bar{c}_2\bar{\mu})] = 0$$

$$-\nu\lambda\alpha_1\Delta c_2\bar{q} + (1-\nu)[\alpha_2(S(\bar{q}) + \lambda\bar{p}\bar{q})$$

$$-(1+\lambda)(\alpha_2\bar{c}_2\bar{q} + C'(\bar{\mu}))] = 0.$$

One can show that a sufficient condition for the concavity of the objective function is $|S''|$ large enough.

Denote $U(c_2, \tilde{c}_2) \equiv t(\tilde{c}_2) + (\alpha_1 + \alpha_2\mu(\tilde{c}_2))p(q(\tilde{c}_2))q(\tilde{c}_2) - (\alpha_1 c_1 + \alpha_2 c_2\mu(\tilde{c}_2))q(\tilde{c}_2) - C(\mu(\tilde{c}_2))$ as the firm's utility when $\tilde{c}_2$ is its report about c_2. The first-order condition for truthtelling is (for a continuous variable c_2):

$$\dot{t} + \alpha_2\dot{\mu}\,p(q)q + (\alpha_1 + \alpha_2\mu)(\dot{p}\dot{q}q + p\dot{q}) - \alpha_2 c_2\dot{\mu}q$$

$$-(\alpha_1 c_1 + \alpha_2 c_2\mu)\dot{q} - C'(\mu)\dot{\mu} = 0.$$

The second-order condition is:

$$-\alpha_2\dot{\mu}q - \alpha_2\mu\dot{q} \geq 0.$$

One can see that a sufficient condition for the second-order condition to be satisfied is $\bar{p}^{USB} > \underline{p}^{USB}$ and $\bar{\mu}^{USB} < \underline{\mu}^{USB}$ which implies:

$$\frac{\alpha_1 c_1 + \alpha_2\bar{c}_2\bar{\mu}^{USB}}{\alpha_1 + \alpha_2\bar{\mu}^{USB}} + \frac{\lambda}{1+\lambda}\frac{\nu}{1-\nu}\frac{\alpha_2\Delta c_2\bar{\mu}^{USB}}{\alpha_1 + \alpha_2\bar{\mu}^{USB}}$$

$$> \frac{\alpha_1 c_1 + \alpha_2\underline{c}_2\underline{\mu}^{**}}{\alpha_1 + \alpha_2\underline{\mu}^{**}}$$

$$\frac{S(\bar{q}^{USB}) + \lambda\bar{p}^{USB}\bar{q}^{USB}}{1+\lambda} - \bar{q}^{USB}\bar{c}_2 - \frac{\lambda}{1+\lambda}\frac{\nu}{1-\nu}\Delta c_2\bar{q}^{USB}$$

$$< \frac{S(\underline{q}^{**}) + \lambda\underline{p}^{**}\underline{q}^{**}}{1+\lambda} - \underline{q}^{**}\underline{c}_2.$$

Thus, a sufficient condition for the second-order condition of truthtelling to be satisfied is Δc_2 large enough. However, if Δc_2 small enough, we have $\bar{p}^{USB} < \underline{p}^{USB}$ and $\bar{\mu}^{USB} > \underline{\mu}^{USB}$. Then, bunching occurs so that $\bar{p}^{USB} = \underline{p}^{USB} = p^{USB}$ and $\bar{\mu}^{USB} = \underline{\mu}^{USB} = \mu^{USB}$.

Let us now compute the condition that ensures $\bar{p}^{USB} > \bar{p}^{**}$ and $\bar{\mu}^{USB} < \bar{\mu}^{**}$. From the first-order conditions we have:

$$\frac{\alpha_1 c_1 + \alpha_2 \bar{c}_2 \bar{\mu}^{USB}}{\alpha_1 + \alpha_2 \bar{\mu}^{USB}} + \frac{\lambda}{1+\lambda} \frac{\nu}{1-\nu} \frac{\alpha_2 \Delta c_2 \bar{\mu}^{USB}}{\alpha_1 + \alpha_2 \bar{\mu}^{USB}}$$
$$> \frac{\alpha_1 c_1 + \alpha_2 \bar{c}_2 \bar{\mu}^{**}}{\alpha_1 + \alpha_2 \bar{\mu}^{**}}$$

or $\bar{p}^{USB} > \bar{p}^{**}$ if Δc_2 is large enough. Similarly, $\bar{\mu}^{USB} < \bar{\mu}^{**}$ if Δc_2 is large enough. Finally, since $\frac{\alpha_1 c_1 + \alpha_2 \bar{c}_2 \bar{\mu}^{USB}}{\alpha_1 + \alpha_2 \bar{\mu}^{USB}} + \frac{\lambda}{1+\lambda} \frac{\nu}{1-\nu} \frac{\alpha_2 \Delta c_2 \bar{\mu}^{USB}}{\alpha_1 + \alpha_2 \bar{\mu}^{USB}}$ is always smaller than $\bar{c}_2 + \frac{\lambda}{1+\lambda} \frac{\nu}{1-\nu} \Delta c_2$, we have $\bar{p}^{USB} < \bar{p}_2^{SB}$. Moreover, since $\bar{p}_2^{SB}$ optimizes $\frac{S(\bar{q}_2) + \lambda \bar{p}_2 \bar{q}_2}{1+\lambda} - \bar{q}_2 \bar{c}_2 - \frac{\lambda}{1+\lambda} \frac{\nu}{1-\nu} \Delta c_2 \bar{q}_2$, we have $\bar{\mu}^{USB} < \bar{\mu}^{SB}$. ∎

7

Design of regulatory institutions in developing countries

7.1 Introduction

The question of multiregulation in developing countries has many dimensions. First, one can think of geographical decentralization as one aspect of the problem. Should we have federal regulation in federal states or should we decentralize regulation in each state? For example, should we recommend federal regulation of telecommunications in Brazil or a two-tier system of state and federal regulation as in the United States or the European Union (EU)? Or, for water distribution, should we recommend regulation at the level of provinces rather than national regulations? These questions show that we must have a clear understanding of the pros and cons of decentralization to deal with our topic. Second, what is the desirable industrial scope of a regulator, or how many industries a regulator should supervise, is another question to answer when designing regulation. Should we have one regulator per industry, or one regulator for all industries, as in Panama and Jamaica, or should we recommend one for each industry, as in Mexico and Canada? Should the optimal design evolve over time, as the integration of gas and electricity regulations in the United Kingdom might suggest? Third, regulation has several functional dimensions, including regulation of prices, quality, environmental effects, entry and can be *ex ante*, as traditional regulation, or rather *ex post*, as competition policy. Should we have a single national body to deal with regulation and antitrust, as in Australia? Should we have separated regulators for price regulation, quality regulation, and environmental regulation, as in the regulation of water in the United Kingdom? What should be the responsibility of ministries versus those of independent regulators? These are the questions we would like to answer when designing regulation in a developing country. These questions are at the heart of current political disputes, as this quote of Boris Berezovsky opposing Vladimir Putin shows:

> On the whole, the horizontal and vertical division of power is a guarantee against arbitrary rule and the usurping of power...In other words, a bad elected leader is better than a good leader appointed from above because the system of appointing leaders is defective in principle. The point of a federal organization of Government lies in the rational balancing of real, objective contradictions between central and local interests.
>
> (*Moscow Times, June 1, 2000*)

These questions are also as old as economics, as this citation of Adam Smith testifies:

> Public works of a local nature should be maintained by local revenue because the abuses which sometimes creep into the local and provincial administration of a local or provincial revenue, how enormous so ever they may appear, are in reality, however almost always very trifling, in comparison with those which commonly take place in the administration and expenditure of a great empire.
>
> (*The Wealth of Nations, 1776*)

Three viewpoints must be integrated when trying to make some recommendations: lessons from the long experience of developed countries, the recent, often incomplete experiences of some developing countries, and the recommendations of economic theory. Given technologies and available resources, including human resources, the normative approach of economic theory looks for the design of regulatory structures which maximize social welfare. A complementary viewpoint is to worry about the political implementation of new institutions such as regulatory rules, which immediately leads to the historical viewpoint and the path dependence of institutional evolution.

In section 7.2 we review the major historical experiences of regulation in industrialized countries. Section 7.3 includes a synthesis of what we can derive from economic theory. Section 7.4 presents the most exciting recent experiments in industrialized countries. Section 7.5 discusses some selected examples of Latin American countries. Section 7.6 concludes.

7.2 Lessons from history in industrialized countries

Historically, regulatory agencies seem to have sprung up in the late nineteenth century and in the twentieth century in industrialized countries according to each country's needs without reference to a theoretical framework for optimal regulatory design. The degree of centralization of regulatory institutions, as well as the degree of specialization of agencies, has been decided without much reference to any theory of institutions. Looking back at the evolution of regulatory institutions in industrialized countries, a historical path dependence emerges, agencies being created one after another when firms or public pressure demanded them.

The evolution of regulation until the Second World War

Regulation has typically emerged locally at the level of municipalities, before evolving towards state and federal regulation, when needed. Since regulation entails a power of giving up rents, control by political entities was necessary to ensure some accountability. The allocation of regulatory authority has therefore closely followed the political structure of the states. Regions in France and *Länder* in Germany took up regulatory responsibilities when technical or coordination issues justified it. Intervention by the upper level of government was more or less extensive, depending on the degree of political and administrative centralization in the country. In the case of local services such as buses or waste collection, regulation has often remained local since there were no possible economies of scale in centralized regulation, and therefore no justification for depriving municipalities of their regulatory power. Some degree of centralized regulation of water comes from the necessity to coordinate extraction and distribution and from environmental concerns. Municipalities or regions have often kept control of the design and allocation of concessions.

Nationalization as a response

The British post office and telegraph services
In Britain, the first thirty years of telephony were characterized by formal competition. The Postmaster General began issuing licenses in 1880 to private and municipal suppliers. Yet network effects rapidly gave rise to *de facto* regional unregulated monopolies. Public pressure ended in the nationalization of the service in 1912, when statutory monopoly was granted to the Post Office. Telecommunications were in this respect different from other utilities, which remained fragmented in the United Kingdom until the Second World War. This came from a rapid perception in this industry of the difficulties involved in coordinating private networks.

Although Parliament had a large degree of discretion and made frequent changes in the legislation, the Post Office, despite its public status, retained a large degree of autonomy, especially concerning technical decisions. Regulation consisted merely of rate-of-return mechanisms, with interventions on tariffs by the government for macroeconomic control. Regulation opposed the will of the Treasury to use the industry as a revenue resource. This partly explains the lack of investment in the network and of technological upgrading until the 1960s. The industry was then characterized by poor service and long waiting lists.

Britain's telegraph company was nationalized in 1869, at the same time as the Post Office. The Post Office kept monopoly over long-distance telephony lines, in order to protect telegraph investments from a too intense telephony competition. Since the Post Office was a government department, all its expenses had to be approved by the Treasury and revenues turned over to the Treasury.

While daily expenses were under complete control of the Treasury, parliament could not distinguish between expenses incurred for telephony, telegraph, or postal services. Political control seems to have been only formal, actual control belonging to the bureaucracy after 1911 (Hills, 1986). The election in 1979 of the Thatcher government issued in the 1981 Telecommunications Act, which created British Telecom and opened telephony services to competition. British Telecom was privatized and Oftel, the office for the regulation of telecommunications, was established in 1984.

Railways in France
State intervention began in 1823 but was the continuation of previous intervention in other transportation modes, such as canals. As stressed by Dobbin (1994), in his interesting comparison of railroads in the United States, Britain, and France in the nineteenth century, the primary concern of French politicians and officials was to develop a coherent and rational rail system. This translated into developing it under government planning.

The government attracted private capital by guaranteeing a return on capital and restricting entry in the industry by establishing six regional monopolies. The Ponts et Chaussées administrative body designed the routes that appeared most necessary, and exclusive concessions of ninety-nine years were auctioned off. Concessions were granted under administrative oversight by civil servants who had no legislative mandate (see Dobbin, 1994, p. 107).

Regional and local governments were almost excluded from the design of railways planning, which was considered to be of national interest: railways were seen as a way to achieve order and regional integration. Adolphe Thiers, Minister of Commerce and Public Works, supported public planning on efficiency and political grounds. This strongly contrasts with the building of railways in the United States, where local governments were very active, and where concessions were granted according to expected financial viability. In France, on the other hand, the main criterion was an optimal use of the nation's resources, given the existing roads and canals.

A debate on whether railways should be public or private arose in 1837, and continued in parliamentary commissions. The need for private funds had to be traded with the ability for the central government to preserve the public interest. A compromise was reached, in which construction was mixed (half of the capital was provided by the government, the other half by private investors) and operation was private, under a system of concessions and franchises. Ongoing corruption led to several scandals, to which the central government responded by increased state controls in 1880. This response corresponded to the prevailing feeling that the central government was acting in the public interest. This again contrasts with the response chosen by the United States in the same situation and nearly the same period, which consisted in limiting state intervention to remove discretionary power from the hands of local politicians.

The debate about the public or private management of railways arose again when the first concessions came to an end.

Nationalization was decided in 1937, with the creation of the Société Nationale des Chemins de Fer, still in operation.

The United States' complex regulatory system

The United States is a very large federal country, in which states are highly autonomous, particularly regarding businesses that remain within their borders. This particular feature partly explains the regulatory system that emerged in the twentieth century. A will to rely on market mechanisms for attaining efficiency and a distrust of state intervention are other characteristics that have conditioned the evolution of regulation over time.

Two competition agencies

The Sherman Act voted at the end of the nineteenth century provided a sound framework for dealing with firms' abuse of power. Yet at the time it was seen as insufficient and was not well enforced to control utilities. Specific regulatory agencies were created to answer the demands of firms; it is indeed a striking feature that some degree of regulation was asked for by firms, to protect them either from local political extortion or from abuse of power by clients or suppliers.

Competition was viewed as potentially very harmful for high fixed or sunk costs industries, in particular railroads and utilities. Indeed fierce competition with little or no interconnection in the late nineteenth and early twentieth centuries resulted in waste and frequent bankruptcies in railroads and telecommunications. In 1912, the courts decided to react to this trend by imposing interconnection; the judgement in *United States* v. *Terminal Railroad Association of St. Louis* (224 U.S. 383) obliged railroads that were controlling terminal facilities to offer access to rivals on reasonable terms. The court appealed to the Interstate Commerce Commission (ICC) to set fair access prices. This decision led to the "essential facilities doctrine." It also reinforced the legitimacy of utility regulators by calling for access regulation in addition to more standard types of regulation. Yet it was seen at the time as proving that the terms of the Sherman Act were too vague and too much subject to interpretation.

In 1914 Congress passed two laws reducing the power of judges: The Clayton Act and the Federal Trade Commission Act. The Clayton Act reduced the discretion of courts by specifying special *per se* forbidden practices, such as exclusive dealing, interlocking directorates, and mergers resulting from purchasing stock (see Kovacic and Shapiro, 2000, for an interesting survey of antitrust policy in the United States since 1890). The Federal Trade Commission Act created the FTC, an independent administrative agency in charge of promoting competition. The mandate of the FTC was *de facto* very close to that of the Department of Justice in the part concerning enforcement of the Sherman Act. The creation of overlapping agencies was publicly motivated by the fact that the Department of Justice was overloaded with work. Yet it seems reasonable to think that the creation of the FTC had been motivated by some other reason, since in theory creating a specialized bureau within the Department of Justice would have been sufficient: specialization need not imply separation. Moreover, the fact, underlined by Kovacic and Shapiro (2000), that the FTC Act "ended the executive's branch monopoly on public enforcement of antitrust laws" seems to indicate some political motives.

Kovacic and Shapiro (2000) argue that this separation came, at least in part, from the desire to better control antitrust enforcement, after the much-debated *Standard Oil* v. *United States* (221 U.S. 1 (1911)), and, to a lesser extent, the 1912 *Terminal Railway* decisions. If one accepts this argument, then separation of regulators can be seen as a way of relying on competition between regulators to limit their discretion.

Federal sector agencies and state multi-sector commissions
The first state Public Utility Commissions (PUCs) were set up to answer a need expressed by local firms for more regulation. The general tendency was to look for regulation by the "closest" political body: first municipalities, that owned their regulatory power from their ability to sell and auction concessions for water, electricity, mining, etc. Then when municipalities appeared corrupt, extortive, or unable to deal with firms located in several areas, state regulation began, with the creation of PUCs.

The strong autonomy of US states gave them the constitutional power to have their own agencies in order to regulate intra-state issues. Due to a size effect, the PUCs have remained multisectoral agencies. Conversely, the large size of the country made it more realistic to set up sector-specific or even industry-specific federal regulatory agencies. The 1946 Administrative Procedures Act gave to regulatory commissions the authority to make industry-wide rules. Most state commissions use quasi-judiciary proceedings; they follow the example of the Interstate Commerce Commission, which set up a model of regulation in the 1880s. This way of regulating permits the maintenance of a strong accountability of regulators, even though they benefit from a large amount of discretion.

The complexity of telecommunications regulation
The end of the nineteenth and the beginning of the twentieth century saw strong competition between local exchange operators, with usually at least two operators in each city (among which was a Bell). Since most companies did not interconnect, Bell used network effects to gain a competitive advantage over independent competitors, and a larger consumer base. This advantage was further strengthened by AT&T denying interconnection with its inter-city network to independent companies for long-distance calls. This behavior was challenged by the Department of Justice. The Head of AT&T,

A. Kingsbury, settled the dispute in 1913 by signing a commitment (the "Kingsbury commitment") to follow some rules, including offering interconnection to all. In 1921, a large part of this commitment became irrelevant after forceful lobbying of Congress ended in the adoption of the Willis–Graham Act, which exempted AT&T from antitrust laws when acquiring additional companies. An aggressive policy of consolidation followed, leading to the creation in 1934 under the Communications Act of the Federal Communications Commission (FCC). This Act remained valid for more than sixty years, until the Telecommunications Act of 1996.

The 1934 Communications Act established the FCC, giving it the power to approve new services, compel interconnection, suspend rates, and allocate frequencies. The Act required that rates be "just and reasonable," but no precise definition of these terms was given. It also put "common carriers" under an obligation to provide service to the public. Indeed at the time, AT&T provided 90 percent of the telecommunications network but covered less than 50 percent of the country in terms of land area.

The independence of the federal regulator   The 1934 Act ensured independence of the federal regulatory agency by several provisions. First, the FCC is responsible to (and its budget is decided by) Congress and not the executive branch. Second, the five Commissioners governing the FCC are nominated by the President and confirmed by the Senate. There cannot be more than three of them from the same political party, which constitutes a balance-of-power mechanism and should ensure some insulation from political pressures. Third, to prevent capture by the industry, the Commissioners can not have any financial interest in an industry related to the work of the FCC.

Regulatory problems   One of the main difficulties encountered by regulators was the complexity of the relationship

linking AT&T, the Bell operating companies, Bell Laborato-
ries, and Western Electric. Regulation consisted in a relatively
simple rate-of-return regulation. As early as 1938, a report of
the FCC stressed that the vertical monopoly of the company
allowed it to actually escape regulation; AT&T charged very
high rates to local operating companies, that then incorporated these prices in their costs, and therefore in the rate-base
used by the regulator. This ended after long and hot debates
in the divestiture of AT&T in 1980. Other difficulties linked
to the regulatory framework came from the lack of clear allocation of authority between the different regulators. The 1996
Act strongly increased the authority of the FCC by investing
it with the power and duty to adopt very detailed rules and
standards. This provision should not give rise to much concern about excessive discretion of the Commission since the
Department of Justice and the state Commissions can challenge its authority.

*Unclear allocation of tasks between state and Federal Com-
missions* The case of telecommunications illustrates the
complexity quite well. As stated in section 1 of the 1934
Act, the FCC was responsible for regulating prices, mergers,
and acquisitions, but for inter-state services only. Intra-state
services remained under the control of state Commissions,
which frequently decided to grant monopoly licenses to operators (most of them Regional Bell Operating Companies). The
1996 Act modified this feature by allowing the FCC to intervene in the local exchange market. But the provision lacked
clarity regarding the precise allocation of authority between
the FCC and the state Commissions, thereby giving rise to
judicial uncertainty and potential disputes.

   An unclear allocation of authority can be used in an opportunistic manner by firms so as to delay the implementation
of regulatory rules. Consider, for instance, the suit brought
by incumbent local exchange carriers and state regulators
against the FCC in 1996. The FCC issued a First Report and

Order in which it prescribed the use of pricing based on Total Element Long-Run Incremental Cost. This was challenged on the ground that local competition provisions should be designed and implemented by the states and not by the FCC. A decision was taken in October 1996 by the Court of Appeals for the Eighth Circuit, asserting that the FCC lacked jurisdiction to issue pricing rules. The decision was finally overturned by the Supreme Court in January 1999. This dispute was very costly and induced much delay in the implementation of the 1996 Act.

Allocation of power between the FCC and the Department of Justice   Under the 1996 Act, the FCC has to consult the Department of Justice before deciding whether to let the Regional Bell Operating Companies enter the long-distance market. The FCC and the Department of Justice share responsibility in the area of mergers and acquisitions. Both can review mergers in an independent way and with a different statutory authority. This system has costs and benefits. The benefits come from the possibility that the two agencies use different approaches, the Department of Justice focusing more on the competition issue. The costs lie in the duplication of costs, in the delays incurred before reaching a definitive decision, and in the regulatory uncertainty. The overlapping of responsibilities means in particular that inconsistencies can occur, especially since the review process is different according to the agency. For instance, in 1997, the Department of Justice approved the Bell Atlantic–NYNEX merger without conditions, contrary to the FCC, that required that measures to open markets be taken before accepting the merger.

Main findings

Historical evidence shows that two main factors have affected the design of regulatory institutions, namely the technical characteristics of the industry and the political organization of the state.

The impact of technical characteristics
Regulation seems to have generally started at a local level, municipalities first beginning to use their power of allocating licenses and concessions and of issuing price and safety regulations. Whether regulation has been taken over by higher levels of government has depended on the structure of the industry itself. When there were no economies of scale in regulation, municipalities have retained power. Economies of scale arose when there were externalities in the operation of firms between neighboring areas and needs for regional coordination (as in the design of railways or in the interconnection of telecommunications and electricity networks), or when regulation required specific skills and expertise.

Regulation of local transportation, waste collection, and treatment did not demand much technical expertise. Moreover no externalities between municipalities existed. Therefore, local government kept control over regulation in these industries. Water regulation generally remained at a local level, except regarding environmental concerns. Karhl (1982) also relates how financial constraints have affected the behavior of municipalities in US water management. Private investment achieved major projects in the nineteenth century, but only projects that could use locally available water, without movements of water from one hydrologic basin to another. When the need to move water across basins appeared, financial issues arose since firms were not willing to invest due to the regulatory risk derived from having two local regulatory authorities.

Railroads, telecommunications, or electricity, on the other hand, are industries that operate on a much larger geographical scale. High expertise is required to understand the functioning of the industry. Duplicating specific skills at the lower levels of government would clearly be wasteful, and the economies of scale in having a centralized regulation could easily be perceived by public opinion. National regulation therefore emerged in Europe. In the United States, the large size of the states explains why states retained sizeable regulatory powers, federal regulators being in charge of regulation only when inter-state issues arose.

The impact of governmental and political structures
A second factor that seems to have played a crucial role in the design of regulation in industrialized countries is the general structure of government. Effective regulation needs both administrative bodies to execute it and political entities to ensure its legitimacy. Regulatory structures have therefore been closely linked to the organization of the state. When regulatory needs arose in Europe and in the United States, it was natural first to use the existing structure to deal with problems quickly. Regulation was in general first undertaken by the local political entities that had the legislative legitimacy required, i.e. municipalities or regions. The case of railroads in France is an exception since an administrative body first undertook to regulate the industry without any legislative mandate, but this reflects the informal authority of technocrats in the French state at that time.

Once an entity began regulating an industry, the regulatory structure was very slow to change. This is because regulation entails a strong power of creating and distributing rents and political and administrative bodies are reluctant to relinquish it. Removing authority from an existing structure has thus proved difficult. Nevertheless, it was easier to do so when public opinion was aware of problems in the existing structures. Scandals linked to corruption, for instance, have usually been followed by a change in the regulatory structure, either towards more centralized regulation (as in France), or towards less public intervention (as in the United States). A poor quality of service leading to widespread discontent has also stimulated reforms in the regulatory structure.

The impact of the political structure of government over the regulatory system can be seen by comparing the approaches of France, the United Kingdom, and the United States. France, with a very centralized political system, quickly adopted national centralized regulation, except for water or local transportation, for which municipalities still retained a large degree of control. The United Kingdom adopted centralized regulation but with the participation of regional entities and monopolies with substantial power. This reflected the political autonomy of the regions and their determination to have sufficient regulatory power. In the United States, states retained large regulatory powers due to the autonomy of the states and their large size.

The example of railway design and management in France illustrates two observations. The first is the importance of the *cultural environment* in choosing regulatory structures. France, having a culture of state intervention and state benevolence, reacted to regulatory issues by further increasing the role of government in economic life, contrary to the United States, for instance, where beliefs in market mechanisms led to very different outcomes. Second, *expanding or reforming existing institutions* is more common than creating new ones. This may be due to the savings from avoiding investment in a new structure, or to the efforts of existing institutions to obtain more power by obtaining broader mandates. In most countries, when new institutions have been created, they have usually been designed by copying existing agencies: In Britain, parliament used the outline of the early factory inspectorates to design the railways regulatory agency. Similarly, the United States followed the model given by state banking commissions when designing their regulatory agencies. The main structure of the ICC (1887) was later reproduced in the Federal Reserve Board in 1913, the FTC in 1914, the Federal Power Commission in 1930, or the FCC in 1934, with little adjustments.

Lastly, it should be noticed that the notion of independent regulators dates back to the beginning of the twentieth century in the United States and to the 1980s in Europe and elsewhere. This is because the answer to regulatory problems in the United States was independent regulation, while the answer in other countries was nationalization of the infrastructure services.

7.3 Organization theory

This section reviews the various trade-offs shown by organization theory, which affect the choice between a single regulator versus multi-regulators. To do so, we proceed in four steps. In the first, we maintain the myth of the benevolent informed government but assume bounded rationality in its decision making. In the second step, we assume decentralization of information and the strategic behavior of agents. Still maintaining the benevolence of the government, we assume in the third step that the lack of complete contracts limits the mechanisms that the government can implement. Finally, the fourth step eliminates the benevolence assumption and takes into account the fact that governments are under the influence of interest groups. Along the way, we analyze how conclusions are affected by the specific characteristics of developing countries.

Bounded rationality and centralization

Sah (1991) pointed out that the role of human fallibility or bounded rationality has not been studied in the debates about diversification versus concentration of political authority. Even if we stick to a view of government as a benevolent informed principal, assuming government's bounded rationality leads to some insights into the structuring of power. For example, the multiplication of agencies, which have authority to contest mergers in the United States (Department of Justice, FTC, State Attorneys-General, private parties), might be an example of multiregulation motivated by bounded rationality arguments, as Sah and Stiglitz (1986) pointed out. Sah and Stiglitz (1986) provided a model of bounded rationality which sheds some light on the centralization–decentralization issue. A decision maker can make two types of errors in a decision problem such as the choice of a project, the choice of a manager, or the choice of a rule. Type-I error is accepting a bad project or a bad manager and Type-II error is rejecting a good project or manager. Let p_1 and p_2 be the probability of making Type-I error and Type-II error, respectively.

Suppose we have two available decision makers. A first question would be: Should we organize decision making as a hierarchy, where an acceptance decision has to be made by both, or as a polyarchy in which a single decision maker can make the decision and a project which is rejected by one can be examined by the other decision maker?

In a hierarchy, the probability of accepting a good project is $(1 - p_2)^2$ and the probability of accepting a bad project is p_1^2. In a polyarchy these probabilities are, respectively, $(1 - p_2)(1 + p_2)$ and $p_1(2 - p_1)$. Let W and $-V$ be the value of a good and bad decision, respectively, and suppose that v is the probability of a good project. In a hierarchy expected social welfare is $v(1 - p_2)^2 W - (1 - v)p_1^2 V$, instead of $v(1 - p_1^2)W - (1 - v)(2 - p_1)p_1 V$ in a polyarchy. A hierarchy is better if $(1 - v)(2 - p_1)p_1 V > (1 - p_2)p_2 W$.

A hierarchical decision process corresponds to centralization while a polyarchical one corresponds to decentralization. The above reasoning gives the following insights. When mistakes are very costly and bad projects quite common, centralization is better, while decentralization is favored if good projects with high value are common. Although the robustness of this conclusion should be checked in other bounded rationality models, the following recommendations derive from it. Centralization is favored for questions which can threaten society, such as public health or security issues, while decentralization is favored for projects which have great potential value and weak downside effects. Suppose now that the decision makers differ in their abilities to make decisions, and let us associate decentralization with a larger number of decision makers. Then, if decision makers are chosen randomly a less centralized society has the advantage of a greater diversification of its performance. Welfare will have the same mean but a higher volatility under greater centralization. The effect of human fallibility is that more centralized societies will have more volatile performances. However, decision makers are not chosen randomly, and to the extent that the single decision maker of a centralized system can be well chosen (in a good merit-based selection of decision makers), centralization is favored. This is particularly true for decision problems, which are well identified *ex ante* and for which appropriate selection mechanisms can be designed, but it is not necessarily true in a changing world where the diversity of decision makers of a decentralized system might induce a greater ability to react to unanticipated events. So far, we have neglected the possibility of gains from coordination and economies of scale, which favor centralization. However, centralization requires communication and as communication is also fallible, limiting communication, and therefore centralization, also has value.

What lessons can we derive for developing economies? The greater imperfection of decision making and the higher costs of communication (of the Sah–Stiglitz, 1986 type) militate in favor of decentralization. Decentralization is also favored because the merit-based selection system for the central authorities will be less efficient in those countries relative to developed countries. However, the extreme lack of human resources in the regulatory area, and the large opportunity cost of those resources, militates in favor of centralization to the extent that economies of scale exist. These are the

Table 7.1. *Bounded rationality and decentralization*

Relevant aspects	Developing relative to developed countries
Cost of communication	Decentralization
Cost of regulators	Centralization
Imperfection of decision making process	Decentralization
Quality of selection	Decentralization

reasons for envisaging regional regulation encompassing several countries, as well as multi-sector regulators and even an integrated regulation and competition policy. The prospect of improving quickly the expertise of a limited number of regulators with international support appears great. If new information technologies can be developed in these countries, better communication costs also militate in favor of centralization as well, but not relative to developed countries. Those regulatory questions, as important as they are, do not threaten the survival of those countries. So the added value of hierarchical systems (which multiply decision makers in a centralized way) seems limited. We obtain conflicting results, as summarized in table 7.1.

Benevolent uninformed government

The next analysis considers the case of a benevolent government in a world where the regulated agents have private information. If all concerned parties are rational agents and the judicial system allows signing complete contracts, the revelation principle gives a useful benchmark: Any form of regulation by government can be replicated by a centralized mechanism in which all agents transmit their private information to the government in an incentive compatible way, which then issues orders for verifiable variables and recommendations for moral hazard variables. Therefore, according to the revelation principle, centralization remains optimal despite the superior information of the periphery.[1] The government may behave more proactively with respect to its asymmetric information; it can use intermediaries who will mitigate the extent of asymmetric information. Regulatory agencies can be viewed as such intermediaries and we can raise the question of the optimal structuring of these agencies. A few studies are relevant for this discussion.

In Dewatripont and Tirole (1999), the separation between two bodies is based on the notion of *advocate*. Two types of information can be searched for. Favorable type-1 information favors decision A, favorable type-2 information favors decision B, while no information or two pieces of favorable information lead to no decision. Assume further that rewards for information can be provided only if a decision is taken. The two costly activities of search for information create negative externalities one on the other. Indeed, after finding type-1 information for which he can be rewarded by a payment conditional on decision A, the regulator has no incentive to search for type-2 information. This is because this could lead only to no decision and therefore to no reward. By having two regulators, each in charge of searching for one type of information only, and to the extent that these two regulators do not collude, better incentives can be provided. Indeed, when searching for one type of information, one regulator does not internalize the fact that, if he succeeds, he creates a negative externality on the other regulator. The two moral hazard variables are the search for information and transmission of this information when the search is successful.

It is often thought that, when two activities (say, gas and electricity) interact, a single regulator (as in England today, and soon in France) is preferred. However, having two

---

[1] Some authors argue in favor of decentralization because information is decentralized. However, this argument is not valid under the assumptions of the Revelation Principle. The desirability of decentralization of decisions demands further imperfections, such as costly communication or some other form of bounded rationality.

regulators may provide better incentives to regulators. Similarly, one may want to separate the Ministry of Finance, in charge of looking for reasons for not spending on a project, from spending ministries such as the Ministry of Industries, Transportation, or Agriculture. To what extent this argument compensates for the loss of coordination that separation creates is of course an empirical question.

Laffont and Martimort (1999) have modeled the idea of separating regulators as follows. In their supervision function, regulators have in general some degree of discretion. Rather than transmitting the acquired information to the government who can then decrease the information rents of the agents, the regulators can be captured by the agents for not revealing this information and share the information rents with the agents (Laffont and Tirole, 1991a). Laffont and Martimort (1999) show that separating the supervision functions between several regulators often makes side-contracting more difficult, and therefore less distortive of the regulatory response of the government to collusion. Note the importance in the reasoning of taking into account the regulatory response of the government which makes use of the lack of coordination of the regulators. Not taking into account this institutional response may lead to the misleading idea that centralized regulation is better to address corruption because decentralized corruption leads (with a free-riding argument) to excessive corruption (Shleifer and Vishny, 1994).

The major weakness of all the above arguments is that they rely on the implicit assumption that the separated regulators will not collude.[2] Indeed, most of the literature on mechanism design that uses the competition of agents to create incentives has made this naïve assumption. Perfect collusion

---

[2] It is very important to take into account collusive behavior in these discussions about structural regulation. Faure-Grimaud, Laffont, and Martimort (2000) show, in a principal–supervision–one agent adverse selection problem, that the optimal collusion-proof contract is equivalent to decentralization to the supervisor of the choice of the agent's contract. In other words, if the principal cannot prevent collusion, he is as well off giving up control of the agent completely.

Table 7.2. *Benevolence of governments and decentralization*

Relevant aspects	Developing relative to developed countries
Cost of public funds	Several regulators
Transaction cost of collusion	Several regulators
Size of agency problem	Several regulators
Cost of regulators	One regulator
Enforcement of separation	One regulator

would bring us back to the single-regulator framework. However, to the extent that government controls the information technologies made available to agents, it can create asymmetries of information among them. As emphasized in Laffont and Martimort (1997, 2000), asymmetric information between colluding agents creates transaction costs, which are beneficial to the principal. Collusion is then imperfect and separation of powers can be designed to be collusion-proof between regulators. Of course, such considerations weaken the value of this institutional design.

Finally, let us note the dangers of reciprocal supervision, which favors reciprocal collusive activities at low transaction costs (Laffont and Meleu, 1997).

What particular insight can we derive for developing countries? Chapter 8 shows that most characteristics of developing countries (cost of public funds, transaction costs of collusion, size of asymmetric information) favor more separation in a framework of the Laffont and Martimort (1999) type. Unfortunately, those same parameters also make it more costly to implement a collusion-proof separation of powers. We summarize the arguments in table 7.2.

Benevolent government with contractual constraints

We review here the various types of contractual constraints which affect the optimal structuring of regulation.

Incomplete contracts
Laffont and Zantman (2002) argue that local politicians are better informed about local conditions than the central government. The justification given is that local politics creates the incentives for acquisition of information by these politicians. However, the constitution does not permit a complete contract which would enable the center to remunerate those politicians for information transmission. Consequently, it may be better to decentralize some collective decisions rather than using a centralized process with no prior information. The same foundation underlies the trade-off studied by Gilbert and Picard (1996) where local decision makers are better informed but their objectives are biased and unknown to the central government. The better information of local authorities is balanced with the greater information rents (capture) that those local authorities leave to regulated firms (Caillaud, Jullien, and Picard 1996).

Aghion and Tirole (1997) pointed out that information structures are endogenous. The choice to decentralize decisions also creates more incentives to acquire information locally. However, the value of this is limited by the fact that local preferences differ from the preferences of the center.

Tiebout's (1956) model of decentralization can also be interpreted as a response to incomplete contracts. There, the difficulty is the elicitation of willingness to pay for local public goods to achieve the right partition of the population into communities and the right levels of local public goods within those communities. This could be achieved by a grand mechanism which uses nonlinear and personalized transfers to elicit the relevant information with the best rent extraction–efficiency trade-off. Alternatively, if payments are constrained to be uniform within each community, decentralization of the level of public goods to communities within which agents self-select themselves by voting with their feet is a second-best mechanism of information revelation.[3]

One can expect contracts between the center and the periphery to be even more incomplete in developing than in developed countries, and there is no particular reason why local preferences should be more biased, or coordination problems worse. This creates a bias in favor of decentralization when local information is good. This explains the trend towards local decision making for managing water resources, forests, etc. On the other hand, for issues like health and some environmental matters, local information may be weaker than central government information that has better access to international data, and the benefits of decentralization are blurred.

Lack of commitment

The lack of commitment is also a particular form of contract incompleteness. The delegation of authority for decision making to agents who have particular objective functions may be a way to solve the commitment deficiency. For example, if the government can not commit to resist a merger, then delegating the right to decide to a competition agency may be optimal. However, delegation may tie the government to inefficient decisions. Thus delegation in the context of a benevolent government requires setting up incentives for the members of the agency which will lead them to favor competition.

Contract theory (Baron and Besanko, 1994, for example) shows that under the assumption of repeated relationships, adverse selection, and perfectly temporally correlated types, it is *ex ante* optimal to commit to use each period the optimal static contract in the rent-extraction–efficiency trade-off. However, after the first period, this contract is not *ex post* optimal, and the partners in the contract would like to

---

[3] Bardhan and Mookherjee (1999) suggest that the role of this type of mobility is less likely to be relevant in developing countries.

renegotiate. Although efficiency demands that the government has the credibility to commit not to renegotiate, governments often do not have the ability to commit not to renegotiate with the regulated agents.[4] Note that the optimal mechanism is renegotiation-proof, since then the principal can anticipate the outcome of renegotiation and mimic it. The optimal renegotiation-proof mechanism leads to semi-separating equilibria in which agents only partially reveal their types in the first period in order to maintain an information rent in the second period. By inducing a first-period equilibrium in which the principal remains uninformed, the principal commits to not extract completely the information rent of tomorrow, since the optimal *ex post* renegotiated contract entails an information rent for the agent. In this way, the principal commits to some *ex post* inefficiency. A strong result can be achieved when the government has two lines of activities and commits to have a regulator for each. The noncooperative behavior of the regulators in the second period may lead to a lower rent being awarded to the agent, i.e. it indirectly yields a commitment to a greater inefficiency (see Martimort, 1999).

Problems of credibility are likely to be even worse in developing countries than in developed ones and this would tend to favor decentralization and delegation. However, several features of developing countries weaken the strength of that conclusion. First, delegating decision making to overcome the lack of commitment is more difficult in developing countries. Second, the capacity of increasing efficiency through competition among agencies depends on the agency's ability to resist capture, and such ability seems lower in developing countries due to lower transaction costs. Third, increasing commitment by establishing several agencies relies on the

---

[4] Dewatripont (1989) first modeled this contractual opportunism emphasized by Williamson (1985), but the full characterization of optimal mechanisms when the government cannot commit not to renegotiate was achieved in Laffont and Tirole (1990).

assumption that those agencies will not collude; however, collusion seems easier in developing countries.

Nonbenevolent government

The previous sections assumed that the government was benevolent and was maximizing social welfare. In this section, this assumption is dropped. Therefore, accountability of governments plays a crucial role in the choice of centralized versus decentralized mechanisms. For Seabright (1996), the difference between centralized and decentralized government is a matter over which groups of electors are collectively given the power. He argues that local politicians have a greater accountability, because they will be controlled (through election mechanisms) by voters who have a greater probability of influencing their reelection than politicians in the central government. This gain may counter-balance any loss coming from the lack of coordination that decentralization entails.

Bardhan and Mookherjee (1999) use the Bernheim and Whinston (1986) political economy model of capture to compare centralization and decentralization, and argue that, perhaps contrary to a widely shared belief, decentralization is not necessarily worse from the point of view of capture.

Crémer and Palfrey (1996) study how voting procedures affect the choice of centralization or decentralization at the constitutional level. The main assumptions are the following. First, collective decisions are made by the majority rule,[5] with the further constraint that centralization requires uniform rules,[6] which favors policy moderation. Second, agents are risk averse. Third, each voter must arbitrate between her forecasts about the identity of the median voter in her region

---

[5] Majority rules yield decisions that generically do not maximize social welfare.

[6] See also Besley and Coate (1998).

or in the whole country. They show that a two-stage procedure in which representatives elected by voters decide on the choice of centralization versus decentralization with a majority vote is more favorable to centralization than direct voting by agents. Similarly, Bolton and Roland (1997) study preferences of regions on alternative mechanisms for assigning public goods. The preference of regions for separate mechanisms (i.e. a mechanism in which decisions on public goods are taken within the region) is more likely when the median incomes in regions are different from the aggregate median income (political effect), when positive externalities between regions are low (efficiency effect), and when production levels differ between regions (tax effect).

Laffont and Pouyet (2002) show that competition between national regulators leads to too high-powered incentive schemes as each regulator tries to reimburse less of the cost than the other regulator to induce a strategic allocation of costs. Combining this distortion with a political system, they show that centralization (which internalizes externalities between regulators but suffers from an excessive fluctuation of policies due to the majority game) can be dominated by decentralization (which induces too high-powered incentive schemes from the regulators but destroys the discretion of politicians). A high cost of public funds associated with developing countries favors centralization because of the costly high-powered incentive schemes of decentralization.

The lack of confidence in governments leads to a limitation of their mandates. Consequently, governments can commit for only a short period. In an adverse selection principal–agent context, this leads to the ratchet effect. This means that the agent hides, does not reveal his true type (he uses a mixed strategy) to maintain a rent in the future, since he knows that future regulators will leave him no rent if they are fully informed about his type (Laffont and Tirole, 1988). Olsen and Torsvick (1995) show that committing to have several regulators (who will leave more rents in the future to the agent through their noncooperative behavior if the regulated activities are complements) helps mitigate the ratchet effect. Less pooling in the first period is needed to indirectly commit to the same information rent in the second period. Although nonbenevolence at all levels may be an even greater problem in developing than in developed countries because of the lack of appropriate institutions and counterpowers, it is not clear in which direction this tilts the choice between centralization and decentralization. As pointed out by Bardhan and Mookherjee (1999): "Simple generalizations about relative capture are therefore hazardous on the basis of theory alone."

7.4   Experiences in industrialized countries

Independent and industry-specific regulators in Great Britain

General system structure
The United Kingdom has a two-party political system with majority control of both the executive and legislative branches of government. The government has a large amount of discretion to modify regulatory rules whenever it deems it necessary. This would be a factor of regulatory risk *a priori.* Yet, as underlined by Spiller and Vogelsang (1996), informal norms constitute a strong check on the discretionary power of the government. These norms include the permanency of bureaucracy, most officials remaining in office after majority changes, the fact that the government publishes its intended reforms in white papers (allowing concerned parties to react), and an important degree of informal delegation of power from the minister to regulators. Since the United Kingdom has a tradition of strong enforcement of contracts, a way to reassure investors has been to rely on regulation by contracts: Detailed licenses are used to impose obligations on utilities. Licenses

for telecommunications were issued as early as 1880, for instance. The UK regulatory system is one of the clearest examples of independent and industry-specific regulators. The regulatory system works as follows: A single Director-General per sector is appointed by the Minister.[7] Directors-Generals can be appointed for more than one term and their independence is strengthened by the fact that they cannot be removed from office unless there is proven incompetence or misconduct. They are ultimately accountable to parliament and their budget is voted by the Treasury. This design reflects the strong will of the government to ensure the independence of regulators. Oversight of regulators is ensured by the Competition Commission, the courts, and parliamentary committees (see Green and Rodriguez-Pardina, 1999). Firms can appeal to the Competition Commission (formerly the Monopolies and Mergers Commission, MMC).

Although Great Britain relies on industry-specific regulators, it has recognized the need for closer cooperation in sectors that are strong substitutes, by completing the merger in 1999 of Ofgas (the agency regulating gas) and Offer (the agency regulating electricity) into a new regulatory body, Ofgem (the Office of Gas and Electricity Markets).

The debate about water regulation
The United Kingdom has chosen to have functional regulation within the water industry. Several distinct agencies have received specific (nonoverlapping) mandates over the industry, according to the function of regulation to be carried out – economic regulation, quality oversight, or promotion of competition. The Office of Water Regulation (Ofwat) has the responsibility for controlling prices and ensuring the viability of suppliers, whereas the Drinking Water Inspectorate oversees the quality of tap water, and the Environment

---

[7] Commissions have now replaced single directors (electricity, gas).

Agency is responsible for maintaining the quality of water in rivers and canals. The industry is also, like the other utilities, subject to the 1992 Competition and Services (Utilities) Act and the 1998 Competition Act.

This separation of regulatory functions in different entities contrasts with the structure chosen for other sectors. The Office of the Rail Regulator, for instance, is in charge of consumer protection, enforcing domestic competition laws when railroads are concerned, safety and health issues, and the environmental effects of railroads. It may of course be argued that environmental concerns are less important in the rail industry than for water, and therefore do not require specific supervision. Yet the experience of the water sector helps highlight the pros and cons of functional regulation. Since the definition of mandates has been quite clear, the issue is not so much overlapping (as for the United States, for instance) as the externalities at the firms' level of specialized regulations. This experiment of having multiple functional regulators has been criticized and cited as the cause of several problems in the water industry. For instance, Ofwat has been particularly criticized for not taking social and public costs and benefits sufficiently into account when considering investment programs in the water sector. It has also been pointed out that investment incentives given by Ofwat and by the environmental regulator are often conflicting and unclear.

The experience of New Zealand

New Zealand regulation is an exception to the general rule of separation of regulation and competition policy. Its novel approach, used to regulate first telecommunications and then power, relies only on general competition laws, enforced by courts and by an industry-wide competition authority.

The notion of self-regulation has been introduced, with councils composed of industry participants to set the main rules and access conditions. This form of regulation is consistent with the idea that these industries will become competitive enough for regulation to gradually disappear. However, relying on negotiated agreements between firms on interconnection pricing and other such issues has proved rather unsatisfactory, and New Zealand is again shifting to specific regulatory tools.

Telecom, the incumbent in charge of telecommunications, which is privately owned, has control over the local loop and competes with other providers for most other services linked to telecommunications. As early as 1988, measures to facilitate competition were taken including cost-based charges for interconnection, the obligation to consult the industry to set up those charges, and the operation of Telecom's subsidiaries as separate profit centers. These obligations and others, linked in particular to universal service, are known as the "Kiwi share obligations."

Three features characterized the New Zealand approach:

- First, regulation relied only on the Kiwi share obligations and on general competition rules, as written in the Commerce Act of 1986, without sector-specific regulation or legislation. The Commerce Commission was in charge of overseeing not only mergers, but also pricing schedules and access terms related to the telecommunications sector.
- Second, Telecom was subject to information disclosure requirements.
- Third, the industry had to negotiate access and other measures without governmental intervention.

A concern that this form of light control of the industry was not sufficient to restrain abuse of power by Telecom led to the establishment of a Ministerial Inquiry in February 2000. The final version of the Inquiry's report was released on September 29, 2000. The number of cases brought to courts since this type of light regulation was put in place has shown that specific characteristics of the telecommunications industry make it quite difficult to convict a firm of abuse of dominant position, as required by the Commerce Act.

The government has decided to modify competition rules to have them better applied to the telecommunications and electricity industries. Thus the concept of taking advantage of a substantial degree of market power will replace the concept of abuse of dominant position in section 36 of the Commerce Act. Similarly, section 47 will prohibit acquisitions that would have the effect of substantially lessening market competition in a market – rather than, as now, those that lead to acquisition or strengthening of dominance.

The example of New Zealand shows that a very innovative approach of using only well-developed competition authorities to oversee a self-regulating industry may not be doomed to immediate failure. Yet after some years, the government has recognized the necessity still to have regulatory control in industries which are not competitive enough for the moment. It seems that the transition from protected monopoly to competition is not sufficiently advanced as yet for formal regulation to be suppressed. Relying on competition laws only is inefficient in a transition period, even when these laws are developed and well enforced.

Australia: an original combination
Australia is a federation of states in which states have large degrees of autonomy and can follow very different policies. The current regulatory system of Australia has been designed in such a way as to correct the problems perceived in New Zealand's regulation. Regulation is organized around a federal multisectoral and multi-functional competition authority, the Australian Competition and Consumer Commission (ACCC), specialized agencies, and state regulation. The system is relatively complex, since some issues are resolved at the national level, while others are left to regional governments. It is also very innovative due to the important role given to the ACCC.

The example of telecommunications

Until 1975, post services and the post-master operated domestic telecommunications, whereas international services were operated by the Overseas Telecommunications Commission. Both were public enterprises. Telecommunications and postal services were separated in 1975. Despite a move towards a mode of functioning more similar to that of private firms, a 1988 review showed that competition was virtually nonexistent. In 1989, the Telecommunications Act liberalized markets and created AUSTEL, a sector-specific regulatory agency, in order to separate regulatory and operational functions.

Until 1995, the telecommunications industry was under a traditional oversight structure, regulation being in the charge of AUSTEL and the allocation of frequencies in the charge of the Spectrum Management Agency (SMA).

In 1993, the Himler Report recommended an economy-wide regulation of all matters related to competition and access. AUSTEL and the SMA were abolished and all the former functions of AUSTEL linked to competition (in particular, interconnection) were taken over by the ACCC. A new agency, the Australian Communications Authority (ACA) was given authority over the technical issues dealt with by AUSTEL, as well as spectrum management. This choice corresponds to the insight that specialized expertise is needed for very technical issues.

The multi-sector agency has a mandate over the most sensitive issues faced in the industry. The oversight undertaken by this agency entails lighter regulation than would have been effected by a specialized regulatory agency. However, regulations still allow for more standard intervention (on prices, for instance) in case this turns out to be needed. The institutional framework is therefore more flexible than in New Zealand. The law also includes consultation processes to facilitate coordination between the ACCC and the ACA.

Several industry associations have also been set up to encourage participation in the regulatory process by all members of the industry: The Telecommunications Access Forum deals with access issues, the Australian Communications Industry Forum develops technical and operational standards, and the Telecommunications Industry Ombudsman settles unresolved complaints made by small users such as residential or small business consumers (Kerf and Geradin, 1999).

The telecommunications sector, like other sectors in Australia, is also under the supervision of regional regulatory agencies for all intra-regional matters. Regional regulators have a fair degree of independence in intra-regional problems.

A multifunction and multisector agency: the ACCC
The ACCC was created by merging the Trade Practices Commission and the Price Surveillance Authority. It took over a nonnegligible part of specialized regulators' duties by endorsing responsibility for promotion of competition in a general sense. For instance, the regulatory body in charge of telecommunications was suppressed after the creation of the ACCC.

The ACCC is in charge of competition promotion, safety, intellectual rights, access issues, and organizing coordination and exchange of information between the different regulators. It is an original integrated structure, composed of sectoral and functional bureaus with coordination entities. It deals with product safety, consumer protection, mergers and restrictive trade practices, and access, in sectors as diverse as telecommunications, electricity, gas, transports, and airports.

The ACCC comprises numerous specialized Commissions and Offices, according to sectors and to geographical areas (e.g. the South Australian Independent Pricing and Access Regulation, the Office of Water Regulation). Offices are located in all the capital cities of the country, plus Townsville and Tamworth. Local offices seem to be needed in this large country, despite the advances in communication and transport technologies. The Utility Regulators Forum ensures coordination of the regulatory activities within the ACCC. Created in 1997, this division was established in recognition of the need for cooperation between state-based regulators in a federal system according to the Mission Statement on the ACCC web site (http://www.accc.gov.au, 2000).

Justifications for a multisector and multifunction agency
The creation in Australia of a comprehensive competition authority has given rise to a debate about the range of problems that it should tackle. The need for a broad agency has been particularly felt with respect to the introduction of competition in regulated utilities. Designing access regimes for electricity or tradable water rights is an example of issues in which regulation and competition are closely related.

Fels (1996) argues that traditional narrow competition policy relies on independent nonpolitical agencies and courts. When moving to a comprehensive view of competition policy (including safety norms, trade policies, regulation of public utilities, and so on), it is no longer possible to isolate the agency from political processes. In Australia the ACCC is independent and nonpolitical but major policy changes remain determined by legislators and governments. All the state governments agreed in 1996, and for the following five years, to review all the regulations likely to affect competition. The National Competition Council was appointed to review this process and administer the access regime (Fels, 1996; OECD, 1999).

The Himler committee based its decision to favor a national authority rather than state agencies on three main arguments. The first was that markets were now more national than regional, particularly as advances in transport and communications permit many firms to develop national trade networks (Fels, 1996). Second, many goods and services in sectors governed by state or territory laws were protected from exposure to competition by other national firms, due to constitutional and ownership limitations. And finally, a national competition policy would ensure consistency of pro-competitive reforms and "avoid the costs linked to industry-specific and sub-national regulatory arrangements" (Fels, 1946). The second argument seems to show defiance from state regulators who may favor regional firms at the expense of other competitors. The third argument underlines the difficulty of coordinating the actions of state agencies and the costs of separation across sectors and states.

7.5   Experiences in Latin America

Multisectoral agencies in small countries

Several countries, such as Bolivia, Costa Rica, Jamaica, and Panama, have chosen to have a multisector regulatory agency rather than specialized bodies. This choice seems particularly rational in small countries in which the duplication costs associated with setting up several sector-specific agencies would outweigh the benefits of focused regulation, and in which there is a lack of available human capital and expertise.

Bolivia: a compromise between coordination and specialization

Bolivia has set up a regulatory system that constitutes a balanced compromise between a multisectoral agency and specialized regulators. It is composed of sector-specific branches that are under the supervision of a coordination entity. The structure can therefore be seen as very close to a multisectoral agency with specialized bureaus, yet it leaves more independence to the branches, which makes it more acceptable to officials who would be reluctant to forgo their regulatory power over an industry.

Regulation is primarily under the Ministerio de Desarrollo Económico (Ministry of Economic Development), composed of four branches: Transports, Communications and Civil Aeronautics; Energy; Minerals and Steel; and Domestic Trade and Industry. A Vice-Ministry of Sectorial Coordination supervises all these four divisions, directly under the Minister of Economic Development.

This innovative structure reflects a compromise between sectoral regulation, demanded by former sectoral regulators, and multisectoral coordination, as desired by the government at the time this ministry was designed in 1996.

A drawback of such an organization is that if it helps reduce the threat of capture of regulators by the industry, it may not insulate the agency sufficiently from political interference. This may be costly since it increases the risk perceived by investors, and therefore the return on capital they will demand before agreeing to invest in the country.

Jamaica

Jamaica chose very early to set up a multisectoral agency to regulate utilities: This agency was created in 1966 by the Public Utilities Commission Act and has remained nearly unchanged since then. Given the size of the country, creating specialized agencies would have been extremely costly in terms of duplication of administrative and material costs, as well as of human expertise. Coordination of policies appears here a less relevant reason for a multisectoral agency than pure cost–benefit analysis and resource constraints.

Telecommunications are operated by a protected monopoly, the Jamaica Telephone Company. It has a monopoly not only on basic telephony but also on all the associated services, including equipment supply. The firm is also guaranteed a high rate of return, which has been strongly criticized. Yet according to Spiller and Sampson (1996), given political constraints, permitting such a rate-of-return contract with a monopoly may have been the best available regulation system.

Jamaica is characterized by a strong judiciary with independent and reliable judges. Yet its parliamentary system gives the government in office enough power to change legislation whenever needed. The judiciary cannot therefore guarantee enforcement of current regulatory rules since these may be subject to important changes. Although a strong judiciary system may seem at first sight to imply regulatory certainty for regulated firms, this is not the case whenever laws and jurisdictions can be easily modified by the executive, as in Jamaica. Moreover the political system is composed of two parties that are alternately in power for short periods of time. Reversals of political majorities tend to be extremely frequent, making the political environment very unstable for companies. To add to the fear of regulatory expropriation, telecommunications are a very sensitive area, since they are a service used mainly by the middle-class and rich voters who constitute the "swing voters" in Jamaica. Each party therefore has strong incentives to maintain low prices in local telephony in order to strengthen its chance at the next elections.

In such a context, the main problem when designing regulatory institutions may be to find commitment devices to reduce uncertainty and the possibility of expropriation by the government. This was made possible in Jamaica by using contracts: Contracts between the government and the regulated firm cannot be modified unilaterally by the government and are credible instruments since they can be enforced by the judiciary. As underlined by Spiller and Sampson, licenses are long-term contracts that constitute a commitment not to expropriate investors. In addition, granting a monopoly for all services allows cross-subsidization, used in order to maintain low prices for local calls. It is moreover a way to attract investors by committing to high rents. The costs of this arrangement are that it requires leaving high rents to the firm and forgoing the benefits of competition for the long period during which the exclusive concession contract is valid.

Both the use of a multisectoral agency and the choice of licenses ensuring rather large rates of return appear as optimal choices given the institutional and economic characteristics of the country.

Competition authorities and specific industrial regulators: Argentina[8]

Argentina has three independent agencies for electricity, gas, and telecommunications. All agencies are financed by taxes on firms or end-consumers in their industry, yet their actual level of autonomy varies, the structure of appeal being one of the important factors in regulators' credibility and actual independence. The study of Argentineàn agencies shows that financial autonomy and nomination procedures are similar among the sector agencies. The Competition Agency has appropriate legal independence.

Argentina has chosen to have two separate agencies created by law for regulating gas and electricity, ENARGAS and ENRE, respectively. They have been given more chances at first than other agencies since they have independent and sufficient funding, a skilled staff, and are autonomous. They are accountable to both the executive and legislative branches. Yet the first appeal is to the ministry, and not the courts, which means that the government may be able to reverse regulatory decisions.

The regulation of electricity is divided quite rationally between a federal regulation of transmission, and a state regulation of distribution, even though this creates some problems of coordination for large consumers who can sign contracts with generators outside the state. But the regulation of gas (transmission and distribution) is a federal responsibility. This seems to be due to the fact that the gas industry was a public firm federally run at the time of privatization and

---

[8] This corresponds to the institutional arrangements prevailing prior to the January 2002 crisis, which has led to a redistribution of regulatory powers in Argentina, with the outcome at present unclear.

liberalization, and the federal government kept the full regulatory powers. So not only does a single regulator not regulate electricity and gas but they are also regulated at different levels.

The privatization of telecommunications, the first undertaken by the government to show its commitment to reform, has a poor record, even if some of the initial difficulties have been solved. The regulation of telecommunications is divided between the Comisión Nacional de Telecomunicaciónes (CNT) and the Secretariat of Telecommunications. The CNT was created by decree in 1990 and following no legislative debate, making the agency accountable to the executive only, which implies a much lower level of independence. The CNT has changed ministries twice (due to a merging of the Ministry of Public Works into the Ministry of the Economy) and lacks autonomy and expertise. The first committee was staffed with former members of the Secretariat of Telecommunications that had not supported privatization. The first years of regulation proved quite unsatisfactory, and the staff of the CNT was changed rapidly. Yet once the credibility of the agency was lost, it was difficult to regain it. The agency has remained very slow in dealing with problems and its accountability is limited. The separation of regulation between the CNT and the Secretariat has also proven costly: coordination of end-user rates and of access rates, for instance, has been difficult to implement. Controversies have arisen between the two regulators. This cost of separation must weighed against the benefits, in terms of reduced capture and increased enforcement.

The new law of 1999 establishes the transfer of decision capacity from the public administration to the Competition Tribunal by the creation of a new antitrust body as an autonomous agency empowered to impose sanctions that can be appealed in the corresponding federal court. Formerly, the National Competition Commission was entitled only to issue non-binding reports, whereas the Secretary for Competition

Defense pronounced the final resolution. Under the new law, a great institutional leap forward is evidenced by the fact that Tribunal sentences end the official channel, with no need for a decision from the political authority. Furthermore, the law enacts[9] the abolition of every attribution of authority on competition issues granted to other government agencies or entities.

According to Law 25.156 of 1999, the National Tribunal for the Defense of Competition is organized as a self-financing and independent agency. However, in 2001, the tribunal was not yet working.

Decentralization of regulatory responsibilities

Decentralization of specific tasks in a centralized country: Mexico

Mexico is a clear example of decentralization of selected tasks in a centralized country. Saleth and Dinar (1999) underline that, although Mexico has a strongly centralized government, a trend towards decentralizing water supply functions to state and municipal governments has emerged. Water resource management is under the responsibility of the central government but actual management of many tasks is carried out at a local level. Saleth and Dinar (1999) nonetheless note that a main challenge faced by Mexico with regard to water is better use of local information. They suggest using the information available in the National Registry of Water Users to allocate water more efficiently between competing users. Adequate institutions for allocating water across regions and sectors are still lacking; this suggests that some mechanism to obtain transmission of the information available at the local level is necessary.

---

[9] Section 59 of the Competition Law establishes that any jurisdictional powers concerning the subject matter and purpose of this law conferred on other governmental agencies are revoked.

The regulation of the seaport industry is also an area in which the government has chosen to introduce more decentralization. Trujillo and Nombela (1999) stress as a factor of success the trend towards decentralization that can be observed for the seaport industry in Latin America. In the general law of 1992, the Mexican government chose to relinquish control over port administration, terminal operation, and provision of other services associated with ports. Authority was decentralized to Port Authorities that manage the port they are in charge of, according to the specification of their concession contract.

Regulation of water services: conflicts between local and central authorities

The regulation of water distribution suffers from a conflict between local and central authorities. In most Latin American countries, with a few exceptions such as Chile, responsibility for water supply relies on municipalities. In some cases such responsibility is established by a high-ranking law and even by the constitution. General regulations for setting tariffs according to similar criteria across the country are therefore politically and socially rejected, and political reluctance to accept central regulatory institutions is common.

Several models can be found regarding the regulation of water distribution in Latin American countries. A first is characterized by the lack of regulation either at the local or central level and by public enterprises providing and regulating the service. Brazil is an example of this model. Moreover, in Brazil, efforts to establish water regulations and increasing private participation give rise to conflicts between the federal, the state, and the municipal governments. As the conflicts prevent large private sector participation, the need for independent regulatory bodies to attract investment is now a relevant issue.

Water regulations in Argentina rely in some cases on central government, and in others on the provinces and even municipalities. However, conflicts of regulations did not prevent private participation, and ad hoc solutions to regulatory questions were established. In the case of Buenos Aires, the solution was an independent entity, Ente Tripartito de Obras y Servicios Sanitarios (ETOSS), that has to protect the interests of the national government that owns water assets, of the municipality of Buenos Aires, and of the provinces. Since these three layers of government can be controlled by different political parties, strong tensions may arise. The provinces have followed different paths as to the structure of regulation. Some states (Córdoba, Salta) have created multi-industry regulators (for distribution of electricity, water, and transport) while others have industry-specific regulators (Buenos Aires, Tucumán).

The models of Colombia and Peru are quite similar. Conflicts do not arise, but the regulatory agencies do not enforce the law. A central regulatory agency is in charge of supervising and regulating the distribution of water supply. Such entities were created by a law that removed some responsibilities from municipalities. However, as municipal companies keep supplying and distributing the potable water, the capacity of the regulatory agency to enforce the law is limited. For example, the law established that tariffs should be set so that services are financially viable, yet most companies experience losses year after year and the corresponding agencies are not able to enforce appropriate tariffs.

Trading off between investors' security and excess profits

Two types of regulator must be feared: A regulator with no power and under the direct control of the government that uses pricing and investment requirements, for instance, to extract too much of the firms' profit. On the other hand, a very independent agency may be more easily captured by the industry. The government, having relinquished control over the regulator, will not be able to reduce the rents left to the firms. The first case will induce very little investment by regulated firms. The changes in investment levels in Chile's telecommunications across time may be explained by a move from the first type of regulation (leading to expropriation), to a system more favorable to investors. The second situation may lead to political difficulties and consumers and voters being discontented by high prices and large entrepreneurial profits, as in the case of Mexico.

The regulation of telecommunications in Chile
Chile was among the very first countries to promote competition in utilities and to introduce it in power generation and long-distance telephony, as in the United States and the United Kingdom. Competition was introduced in data and cable TV services and private networks following the privatization of the main telecommunications companies in the late 1980s. Galal (1996) distinguishes three phases in the regulation of telecommunications in Chile. The first went from the 1930s to 1971 and corresponded to regulation and private ownership. The second, from 1971 to 1982, was one in which the long-distance operators (CTC, created in 1930, and ENTEL, created in 1964) were nationalized. The nationalization was initiated by socialist president Salvador Allende after his election in 1971, and was not challenged by dictator Augusto Pinochet after his military coup in 1973. The third phase began in 1982, when privatization and deregulation of telecommunications was undertaken.[10] Chile's telecommunications went through the two contrasted types of regulatory uncertainty in a very brief period. Indeed, the companies first suffered from expropriation of investments in the early 1970s: At that time, the socialist government of Salvador Allende used an adjustment of prices lower than the inflation rate to increase consumers' surplus, despite the concession contract

---

[10] Galal (1996) notes that the number of lines doubled in four years after the privatization of CTC and ENTEL.

that guaranteed a rate of return of 10 percent to the firms. When Augusto Pinochet came into power in 1973, a reversal of policy occurred. In particular, a state holding company, CORFO, that had become the joint owner of CTC and ENTEL, obtained in practice more influence than the regulatory authorities.

Competition policy is one of the tools used to regulate firms. Supervision of competition law is quite decentralized, with a fairly clear allocation of tasks among the different levels. Compliance with competition laws is ensured by Regional Preventative Commissions (one in each capital of the country) for purely regional cases, by a Central Preventative Commission, that intervenes whenever cases involve more than one region, and by a Resolutary Commission with large investigation powers. A representative of the Ministry of Economy chairs the Preventative Commissions and each includes a representative of the Ministry of Finance, whereas a Member of the Supreme Court chairs the Resolutary Commission. This organization takes into account the stakes of the ministries concerned, while defining allocation of authority and preeminence rules. The fact that different ministries have interests in the Commissions appears a credible way of ensuring judiciary security; the allocation of tasks is relatively clear and there seems to be a good monitoring of regional agencies.

The same will to design clear rules and decision-making processes can be found in the organization of sectoral regulatory agencies. A particular feature of the Chilean system is that regulators have little discretion since the rules they apply are very precise. For instance, regulators set prices on the basis of the estimated cost of a model operator. This increases the need for the regulator to explain and justify its decisions. Moreover, the rules are usually set in sectoral laws so that the legislative process reinforces their legitimacy. Chile has chosen to have great certainty in its regulatory environment, at the cost of a lack of flexibility.

Chile's (1993) Law also leaves very little discretion to regulators as to the way in which they should implement redistributive policies. Aid is carefully targeted at low-income users through a comprehensive subsidy scheme. A special fund was created in 1994 to facilitate access to public telephones in rural areas and in low-income urban areas.[11] Such subsidy schemes and investment programs are more costly to set up than downward pressures on tariffs, but they avoid creating distortions in prices. They have moreover the important advantage of reassuring investors since they constitute a (partial) commitment to cost-covering tariffs: With targeted aid, social motives cannot be used as a pretense for expropriating their investment from the firms. The firms operating in the country perceive the regulatory risk as being much lower than in neighboring countries, and therefore are more willing to invest even when rates of return are lower. Yet the current system has drawbacks. The boundaries between the segments that should be competitive and where entry should remain restricted are not clear, which is an explanation for the large number of suits that have been filed against the incumbents CTC and ENTEL, mainly on grounds of anticompetitive behavior in providing interconnection. This lack of precision in regulation is quite costly in terms of judiciary disputes, but it may be rationalized by the necessity to keep some flexibility in an industry that is rapidly changing. A blurred definition of segments can be seen as an indirect way of regaining flexibility while giving discretionary powers to the courts rather than to the regulators (recall that Chile has a tradition of a strong and independent judiciary).

The new regulation of telecommunications in Mexico
A frequent difficulty arising a few years after the privatization of a public monopoly, in developed as in developing

---

[11] In 1997, 10 percent of the population lived in towns in which there was no public phone (see Wellenius, 1997).

countries, is the discontent of the population and even political unrest. Indeed attracting private capital requires committing to high rents, sometimes by granting a monopoly position, or by setting a generous price cap or rate of return for the first years of operation of the privatized firm. But excessively high profits are usually seen as a failure of regulation, or as a sign that the regulator is captured. The regulation of telecommunications in Mexico examplifies these problems.

Mexican telecommunications services were operated until 1990 by a state-owned enterprise, Telmex. After its privatization in 1990, Telmex was been left virtually unregulated. Following the 1995 Telecommunications Law, telephony markets were opened to competition in 1997. Yet this opening to competition was rather theoretical since in 1998 Telmex still enjoyed a dominant position in five markets, according to the CFC, Mexico's competition commission. In an OECD report on regulatory reform, the 1995 Telecommunications Law was assessed as a good tool but it was underlined that "the regulator has inadequate powers to regulate, particularly in regard to regulation of the incumbent in markets where it has substantial market power." The local population has shown growing discontent due to the high cost of service and its poor quality. In particular, although a regulation allowing Telmex to charge high access rates was justified by the necessity to leave its profits high enough to encourage network expansion, no new line was added in 1996 or in 1997. Faced with harsh criticisms, Cofetel, the telephony regulator, tried to introduce more stringent obligations for Telmex. Yet the government appeared to fear a negative impact on the stock market in case of too severe regulation. In October 1997, for instance, Minister Carlos Ruiz Sacristan replied to pressures for diminishing Telmex's market power by asserting that one had "to be careful not to negatively impact the stock market." Here again, the need not to discourage investment appears as a strong constraint on regulation. This argument can of course be used to hide private agenda reasons for helping the firm make large profits. Attracting investors by reducing too greatly the effectiveness of and scope for intervention of the regulator may be politically very costly and makes it hard to end the "golden period" that immediately follows privatization when introducing competition or adjusting regulated prices becomes necessary.

7.6 Conclusions

Centralization versus decentralization

The main arguments in favor of centralization and decentralization fall into one of the categories in table 7.3.

Differentiation versus coordination

According to Smith (2000), decentralization permits regulatory objectives and approaches to be shaped by local conditions, priorities, and preferences. Yet *a priori* nothing prevents, from an economic point of view, a centralized regulator differentiating rules according to regional specificities. Two major arguments may nevertheless comfort Warrick Smith's viewpoint: Bounded rationality and capture. If transmitting and processing information is costly, then the centralized regulator will be obliged to use uniform rules. Such costs depend on communication technologies and location of expertise. As for capture, uniform rules across the board are often a necessary regulatory response when dangers of capture are too

Table 7.3. *Decentralization versus centralization*

Pro-decentralization	Pro-centralization
Differentiation	Coordination
Local information	National expertise
Creative competition	No destructive competition
Enforcement	Control over regions

high. So knowledge of both the precise nature of the information required and of the national and local political conditions is needed to conclude whether centralized or decentralized institutions will be better adapted to design regulations suited to local conditions.

Smith (2000) also discusses the negative effects of a lack of coordination between decentralized regulators. The four major issues concerning decentralized regulation are: (a) Potential misalignment between jurisdictional and industry boundaries, (b) Controlling spillover effects, (c) Interjurisdictional trade, (d) Concerns over destructive competition. These arguments describe various spillover effects when excessive competition between uncoordinated regulators takes place.

Local information versus national expertise
Smith (2000) points out that centralization enables us to address information asymmetries between firms and consumers. Indeed, when asymmetric information rests with firms, high technical expertise to evaluate available information is needed, and in most developing countries only national regulators have this type of expertise. This is less true for information concerning consumers, even if reliable statistical information might not be available locally. On the other hand, local accountability of politicians is certainly greater when decisions are based on information available locally. This is because local electors will be able to better judge the quality of regulation, if they share the information on which regulatory choices are based.

National expertise is better mobilized through centralized mechanisms. This argument militates strongly in favor of centralization – at least, in a first step of development. It is an evolving criterion, which must be assessed in each specific case and in which the international community can play a great role by transferring technical expertise in those countries.

Creative versus destructive competition
An argument frequently put in favor of decentralization is that it promotes creative competition among regulators. This competition may reduce the discretion of politicians and improve accountability. The efficiency of regulators can then be assessed using yardstick competition. Yet this competition may be excessive and lead to a waste of resources. A problem that may arise is that of "forum shopping," i.e. of firms deciding to settle in the localities that have the most favorable legislation and regulations. While this induces competition between regulators in order to attract firms, a consequence may well be too lax regulation enabling firms to earn extremely large profits. The ability of the central government to retain enough control to prevent this type of behavior by decentralized regulators is a criterion to be taken into account when considering decentralization.

Better enforcement versus better control by the central government
Decentralization permits better enforcement by local authorities, at the cost of some loss of control. Large countries such as the United States, Brazil, or Russia have had to give sufficient responsibilities to their states and regions to induce more participation in enforcement activities at the local level. This implies a loss of control by the federal state in a world of incomplete contracts and asymmetric information, which may be less costly than setting up independent federal enforcement mechanisms.

Ambiguous results on corruption and capture
Smith (2000) cites as a drawback of a decentralized system the potentially greater risk of political and industry capture. Even though it is true that greater proximity may decrease the transaction costs of capture, we have argued that both empirically and theoretically, this is a debatable point. A good knowledge of local politics is essential before one can assess the greater or smaller risk of capture involved in decentralization.

Centralization versus decentralization: a summary
of arguments

To strike a balance between these arguments is quite complex, and general rules cannot be provided. As Smith (2000) points out, the jurisdictional size, the industry characteristics, the nature of the regulatory issue, and the regulatory capacity (including human resources in expertise and vulnerability to capture) are the relevant variables. Benefits and costs of decentralization have to be assessed for each country, keeping in mind that the institutional structure is important in defining the degree of control that the central government will effectively have. Several Latin American countries have begun decentralizing responsibilities, yet the general consensus is that this decentralization is largely formal and has little actual impact on the functioning of the state. A good knowledge of the country's specificities is indispensable to evaluate the actual consequences of reforms.

Nevertheless, normative conclusions are clear in a few cases. For example, telecommunications, which is a network industry spanning the whole country and requiring high technical expertise, is a leading candidate for national, and even federal, regulation. Similar considerations apply to the regulation of transmission grids in electricity, gas transportation, or long-distance railways, which exhibit the same characteristics. At the other extreme, price regulation of the local distribution of water, electricity, and gas should be decentralized to benefit from local information and better accountability. This is not incompatible with national or federal oversight concerning corruption issues or some dimensions of regulation requiring a lot of expertise, such as quality regulation, certification of operators, etc.

At the implementation level, also, one must take into account the initial allocation of responsibilities those political bodies may have. Even if one may desire a reallocation of powers, the priority may often be to improve the regulations themselves, to favor horizontal or vertical cooperation

Table 7.4. *Arguments for and against industry-specific regulations*

Pro-specialization	Pro-multi-sector
Differentiation	Blurring industry boundaries
Specific expertise	Sharing resources
Diversification of risks	Better coordination
Creative competition	No destructive competition

of existing authorities to prepare the ground for politically acceptable reforms of institutions.

Industry-specific agency versus multisectoral agency

In a similar way, the main arguments in favor of, and against, industry-specific regulation can be summarized in table 7.4.

Differentiation versus blurring industry boundaries
Differentiation arguments similar to those in favor of decentralization demand a specific sector agency, while multisector agencies are more able, when there is imperfect communication and cooperation of regulators, to deal with changing industries whose boundaries are loosely defined and rapidly moving. For instance, for telecommunications, the Report on the Ministerial Inquiry into Telecommunications (2000) in New Zealand stresses this aspect of the industry and has preferred to use the term "electronic communications," in order to avoid restricting its analysis only to a part of the economy.

Industry-specific expertise and focus versus sharing resources
Only the bounded rationality of regulators may justify the advantage of industry-specific expertise, since nothing prevents an integrated regulatory agency from having specific

departments permitting specialized expertise and differentiated treatments. But again the issue of availability of regulatory resources for developing countries appears crucial. There seem to be sizeable economies of scope in regulatory activities and this argument is particularly important in developing countries. Moreover, having a multisectoral agency may foster expertise in cross-cutting issues, as was argued for Australia after the Himler Report was published and when the creation of the ACCC was being considered. This argument is linked to the idea that communication between regulators is not perfect. Notice that fierce competition between regulators may result in limited communication; the communication issue may thus be worsened by separation of regulators across industries.

Diversifying the risk of institutional failure
versus coordination
Having industry-specific regulation may be argued to permit more experimentation in regulatory design. Yet this argument, as in the case of decentralization, is not valid in a world of benevolent unconstrained and rational regulators. Here again bounded rationality *à la* Sah–Stiglitz (1986) is a possible explanation for why a multisectoral agency may not be able to avoid the risk of unadapted regulation. Yet multisector agencies may be favored, as indicated by Smith (2000), to reduce the risks of economic distortions. Reducing economy-wide risks is one of the benefits of better coordination.

Creative competition versus avoiding
destructive competition
The arguments are similar to those described in assessing the benefits of decentralization. Yet the specificity of industries limits the scope of such competition and of yardstick mechanisms.

Industry-specific agency versus multisectoral agency:
a summary of arguments
In an attempt to summarize the arguments we can say the following: Bounded rationality and the creation of incentives for regulators favor specific regulation, while coordination and scarce expertise favor integrated regulation. Capture and accountability are ambiguous. No single approach is always superior. The best solution depends on the size of the economy, the scope of regulatory responsibilities, the nature of the industries, and the regulatory capacity. In spite of lack of general rules, the situation of the poorest developing countries militates in favor of integrated regulation.

An important historical point is relevant here. In most countries the reform of utilities proceeds industry by industry. It is institutionally much simpler to establish a new regulator for each industry. Then, one must encourage cooperation between regulators and eventually some mergers such as those we observe currently in gas and electricity, due to the greater interaction of these industries through the massive production of electricity with gas turbines.

8

Separation of regulatory powers and development

8.1 Introduction

It is well recognized now that the design of proper institutions is crucial to development. Among the characteristics of governmental institutions, separation of powers stands as a cornerstone of democracy. Article 16 of the French Declaration of Human Rights of 1789 goes as far as saying "A society in which the guarantee of rights is not assured, nor the separation of powers provided for, has no constitution." Indeed, since Montesquieu (1748), separation of powers has been explicitly recognized as vital:

> Tout serait perdu si le même homme, ou le même corps des principaux et des nobles, ou du peuple, exerçaient les trois pouvoirs: celui de faire des lois, celui d'exécuter des résolutions publiques, et celui de juger les crimes ou les différents des particuliers.
>
> *(Montesquieu, 1748, p. 589)*[1]

Hamilton and Madison in *The Federalist Papers* (Madison, Hamilton, and Jay, 1788) referred to Montesquieu as "the oracle who is always consulted and cited on this subject." They put these principles into practice for the American Constitution within a broader view of checks and balances. It is only

---

[1] "Everything would be lost if the same man, or the same body of the principals or the nobility, or of the people, were to control the three powers: to draft laws, to implement public decisions, and to judge the crimes and disputes."

recently that economists have started modeling the value of separation of powers.[2]

A first reason for duplicating regulation agencies is *yardstick competition*. Using the correlation of the signals obtained by these agencies enables the principal to extract in a costless way their information rents. This idea was modeled by Shleifer (1985) in the case of perfect correlation and Crémer and McLean (1988) in the case of an arbitrary degree of nonzero correlation.[3]

A second reason for separation of powers is to act as a device against *regulatory capture*. This general idea has been known for a while by political scientists (Wilson, 1980; Moe, 1986; Mueller, 1997). The Public Choice school has emphasized the fact that institutional rules may be designed to discourage rent seeking behavior. Rose-Ackerman (1978) and Congleton (1984) have argued that increasing the number of individuals who must be bribed before getting a permit may be optimal. Laffont and Martimort (1999) have provided a modeling of this idea, which must be distinguished from yardstick competition, which is a pure informational competition. Recent studies of relative capture of local and central governments include Seabright (1996), Bardhan and Mookherjee (1999), and Laffont and Pouyet (2002).

A third reason, reported in Moe (1986), is that separation of powers may be beneficial when *intertemporal commitment* is limited. It may act as an indirect way to commit. Agency models have been developed to capture this idea (Olsen and Torsvick, 1993; Tirole, 1994; Martimort, 1999).

A fourth reason, modeled by Sah and Stiglitz (see 1986, 1991, for example) is that it may be an efficient way of dealing with the risk of *errors*.

---

[2] We refer mainly to the modeling literature in terms of adverse selection because we will use this framework. There exists a parallel literature for models with moral hazard, especially for the first motivation given below.

[3] Auriol and Laffont (1992) consider a stochastic structure with a common part and idiosyncratic shocks. Then, yardstick competition decreases but does not eliminate rents. Dana and Spier (1994) obtain a similar outcome with limited liability of regulators.

A fifth reason (based on a model of multi-tasks with some incomplete contracting; see Dewatripont, Jewitt, and Tirole, 1999) is that separation of missions makes it easier to provide powerful *reputational incentives.* Even though decentralization and separation of powers are often discussed in development economics, we are not aware of any research which inquires if the characteristics of LDCs affect the trade-offs involved in these institutional choices. This chapter is a first attempt at this task in a model where separation of powers in a regulatory framework is a tool of yardstick competition against regulatory capture. Section 8.2 lays out the model. The power of a regulator is his ability to enter collusive agreements with the regulated firm. Section 8.3 describes optimal benevolent regulation with one or two signals. Sections 8.4 and 8.5 characterize the optimal collusion-proof regulation with one regulator and two regulators, respectively. We identify some parameters of the model which take higher values in developing countries. The comparative statics on these parameters provides in section 8.6 the answer to our question of how the value of separation of powers varies with the level of development. It shows that most indicators suggest that separation of powers is even more valuable in developing countries than in more developed ones. As a mitigating factor, section 8.7 reveals that the cost of implementing the separation of powers increases with underdevelopment. Section 8.8 sketches a political economy model to discuss the endogeneity of the particular institution that is the separation of powers. Section 8.9 concludes.

8.2 The model

We consider a slight variation of the model in chapter 2. A public good is provided by a regulated monopolist, which has private information about its cost function. Producing q units of public good has a cost θq. The marginal cost θ can take one of two values $\{\underline{\theta}, \bar{\theta}\}$ with respective probabilities v and $1 - v$. Let $\Delta\theta = \bar{\theta} - \underline{\theta} > 0$. Denoting t the transfer from the government to the firm, to obtain participation of the firm, a participation constraint must be satisfied for all values of the information parameter θ, namely

$$U = t - \theta q \geq 0.$$

Consumers derive a utility $S(q)$, with $S' > 0$, $S'' < 0$, from public good consumption. Funding of public good production requires indirect taxation with a cost of public funds $\lambda > 1$, hence consumers' welfare is

$$S(q) - (1 + \lambda)t.$$

As usual, social welfare is defined as

$$S(q) - (1 + \lambda)\theta q - \lambda U.$$

Under asymmetric information about θ, the benevolent social maximizer is obliged to give up a costly information rent to the firm.[4] To mitigate this cost, the social maximizer delegates to regulators the task of supervising the firm. A regulator observes a hard signal correlated with θ which enables the social maximizer to decrease the information rent of the firm. More specifically, consider the case of two supervision technologies.

Technology i provides a signal σ_i in $\{\phi, \underline{\theta}\}$, $i = 1, 2$. The signal σ_i either is noninformative ($\sigma_i = \phi$), or identifies in a verifiable way the value of θ when $\theta = \underline{\theta}$.

The stochastic structure of the signals is given by:

$$p_{11} = \Pr(\sigma_1 = \underline{\theta} \quad \text{and} \quad \sigma_2 = \underline{\theta}/\theta = \underline{\theta})$$
$$p_{12} = \Pr(\sigma_1 = \underline{\theta} \quad \text{and} \quad \sigma_2 = \phi/\theta = \underline{\theta}) ;$$
$$p_{21} = \Pr(\sigma_1 = \phi \quad \text{and} \quad \sigma_2 = \underline{\theta}/\theta = \underline{\theta})$$
$$p_{22} = \Pr(\sigma_1 = \phi \quad \text{and} \quad \sigma_2 = \phi/\theta = \underline{\theta}).$$

---

[4] The model is similar to the one in chapter 2 when cost is not observed. It is a Baron and Myerson (1982) model rather than a Laffont and Tirole (1986) model. The results of this chapter can be easily extended to the model of chapter 2.

The regulator i receives from the social maximizer an income s_i. He has no private wealth and his utility function is

$$R(s_i) = s_i \geq 0.$$

The regulator i is risk neutral but faces a limited liability constraint. We will distinguish two cases. First, the case of a single regulator who has access to both information technologies. Second, the case where a different regulator is associated with each information technology.

8.3 Duplication of informative signals and benevolent regulation

Suppose first that the regulator is benevolent and observes only the signal σ_1.

With probability $p_{11} + p_{12}$ he is informed that $\theta = \underline{\theta}$ when it is indeed the case. He truthfully reports his signal. Then, the government is fully informed and implements the optimal complete information regulation, i.e.

$$S'(\underline{q}^*) = (1 + \lambda)\underline{\theta} \quad ; \quad \underline{t}^* = \underline{\theta}\underline{q}^* \tag{8.1}$$

which equates the marginal utility of production to the marginal social cost and leaves no rent to the firm.

When the signal is "uninformative," the government updates its belief that $\theta = \underline{\theta}$ as

$$\hat{v} = \Pr(\theta = \underline{\theta}/\sigma_1 = \phi) = \frac{v(p_{22} + p_{21})}{v(p_{22} + p_{21}) + (1 - v)} < v \tag{8.2}$$

and chooses the regulation which maximizes expected social welfare under incentive and participation constraints,[5] i.e.

---

[5] From the revelation principle, there is no loss of generality in restricting the analysis to pairs of contracts $\{(\underline{t}, \underline{q}); (\bar{t}, \bar{q})\}$ which specify a transfer and a production level for each type. Then we denote $\underline{U} = \underline{t} - \underline{\theta}\underline{q}$; $\bar{U} = \bar{t} - \bar{\theta}\bar{q}$.

solves:

$$\max_{\{q,\underline{U},\bar{q},\hat{v}\}} \hat{v}\left[S(\underline{q}) - (1+\lambda)\underline{\theta}\underline{q} - \lambda\underline{U}\right] + (1-\hat{v})$$

$$\times \left[S(\bar{q}) - (1+\lambda)\bar{\theta}\bar{q} - \lambda\bar{U}\right] \qquad (8.3)$$

s.t.

$$\underline{U} \geq \bar{U} + \Delta\theta\bar{q}$$

$$\bar{U} \geq \underline{U} - \Delta\theta\underline{q}$$

$$\underline{U} \geq 0$$

$$\bar{U} \geq 0.$$

From standard reasoning,[6] we know that $\bar{U} = 0$ and $\underline{U} = \Delta\theta\bar{q}$, hence the optimal regulation is characterized by:

$$S'(\underline{q}^\phi) = (1+\lambda)\underline{\theta} \; ; \; \underline{t}^\phi = \underline{\theta}\underline{q}^\phi + \Delta\theta\bar{q}^\phi \qquad (8.4)$$

$$S'(\bar{q}^\phi) = (1+\lambda)\bar{\theta} + \lambda\frac{v(p_{22} + p_{21})}{1-v}\Delta\theta \qquad (8.5)$$

and $\bar{t}^\phi = \bar{\theta}\bar{q}^\phi$.

No rent is given up to the inefficient type $\bar{\theta}$ and a downward distortion of production for the inefficient type is made to decrease the information rent, $\Delta\theta\bar{q}^\phi$, of the efficient type.

We can model informational competition with an additional benevolent regulator who observes the signal σ_2. Now, the government is informed that $\theta = \underline{\theta}$ with probability $p_{11} + p_{12} + p_{21}$ when $\theta = \underline{\theta}$ and, then, it implements the optimal complete information regulation. When $\sigma_1 = \sigma_2 = \phi$, the posterior probability that $\theta = \underline{\theta}$ is

$$\frac{vp_{22}}{vp_{22} + 1 - v},$$

leading to an optimal regulation characterized by

$$S'(\bar{q}^{\phi\phi}) = (1+\lambda)\bar{\theta} + \lambda\frac{vp_{22}}{1-v}\Delta\theta. \qquad (8.6)$$

---

[6] See chapter 2.

The duplication of regulators has a pure informational value when their signals are not perfectly correlated and it enables the government to enhance efficiency. Indeed, in the optimal trade-off between rent extraction and efficiency, the expected cost of the rent is now lower since, following an uninformative signal, the probability of facing an efficient firm is now lower. However, with benevolent regulators, the separation of regulators has no incentive value and the same result would obtain if a single regulator was observing both signals.

Remark: For simplicity we have considered a version of the Baron–Myerson (1982) regulation model with adverse selection, in which higher incentives mean higher production levels. We could have used the Laffont–Tirole (1993) procurement model with both adverse selection and moral hazard with cost observability. In this latter model, higher incentives mean higher effort levels. All our results hold with such an interpretation.   ∎

In the next section we consider the possibility of collusion between regulators and the regulated firm.

8.4   Optimal regulation with a single regulator

When the regulator is not benevolent, he can collude with the firm and hide his informative signals in exchange for a bribe. However, optimal regulation entails no collusion.[7] The collusion-proof constraint is written:

$$s \geq k\Delta\theta\bar{q}^{\phi}. \tag{8.7}$$

Indeed, the firm is willing to offer to the regulator as much as its rent $\Delta\theta\bar{q}^{\phi}$ when the signals are hidden, since it

---

[7] For this collusion-proof principle, see LT, which shows that if the regulator entails no cost it is always better to use it when internal side contracts have transaction costs at least as large as λ.

has no rent when they are revealed. The parameter k represents the inverse of the transaction costs of collusion.[8] If $k = 0$, the regulator behaves as if he was benevolent. If $k = 1$, collusion entails no transaction costs. A low value of k in $(0, 1)$ may reflect several institutional features. It may correspond to a higher "morality" of regulators, a better control of corruption, or greater difficulties of a *quid pro quo* in side contracting – for example, difficulties in using money. To avoid collusion, a payment s satisfying (8.7) must be made to the regulator when he reports the verifiable signal $\sigma = \underline{\theta}$.

When the regulator is not benevolent, the following additional expected social cost is incurred to ensure collusion-proofness:

$$\lambda v(p_{11} + p_{12} + p_{21})k\Delta\theta\bar{q},$$

since it must be paid to the regulator each time the firm is efficient (with probability v) and identified as such by the regulator (with probability $(p_{11} + p_{12} + p_{21})$).[9]

Reoptimizing expected social welfare with this additional cost yields immediately (8.1) when the firm is efficient and the signals are informative, and the following new distortions when the signals are uninformative:

$$S'(\underline{q}_I^{\phi}) = (1 + \lambda)\underline{\theta} \quad ; \quad \underline{t}^{\phi} = \underline{\theta}\underline{q}_I^{\phi} + \Delta\theta\bar{q}_I^{\phi} \qquad (8.8)$$

$$S'(\bar{q}_I^{\phi}) = (1 + \lambda)\bar{\theta} + \frac{\lambda v}{1 - v}\Delta\theta(p_{22} + k(p_{11} + p_{12} + p_{21})). \qquad (8.9)$$

Summarizing we have:

---

[8] $k = \frac{1}{1+\mu}$ where μ is the transaction cost of collusion. See LT and Faure-Grimaud, Laffont, and Martimort (2000) for a discussion of these exogenous transaction costs. We also assume without loss of generality that all the bargaining power belongs to the regulator and that the firm is informed of the regulator's message. This eliminates possibilities of extortion by threatening to report $\underline{\theta}$ when ϕ has occurred.

[9] It is weighted by λ because we include the regulator's welfare in the utilitarian social welfare function. Otherwise it would be $(1 + \lambda)$.

Proposition 8.1: *The optimal regulatory response against capture leads to lower incentives for production of the inefficient type*

$$\bar{q}_I^\phi < \bar{q}^{\phi\phi},$$

and to a lower information rent for the efficient type

$$\Delta\theta\bar{q}_I^\phi < \Delta\theta\bar{q}^{\phi\phi}.$$

Asymmetric information is now more costly since it requires incentive payments (for regulators) proportional to the information rents, even when the signals are informative. The information rents are more costly and, to mitigate them, a greater production inefficiency for the inefficient type is accepted. Note that both consumers and the firm lose from the need to fight potential capture. In addition to the technical cost of the regulator's information technology, there is an additional incentive cost of delegation.

In this simple model, four parameters are candidates to characterize less developed countries. First, it is well known that developing countries have a high cost of public funds (λ high). One can expect that governments in these countries suffer from more asymmetric information and less efficient technologies ($\Delta\theta$ higher with $\bar{\theta}$ higher), that collusion is less easily detected (k higher), and that the supervision technology is less efficient (for example, p_{22} higher).

Note from (8.9) that all these features militate in favor of lower $\bar{q}_I^\phi$. Hence

Proposition 8.2: *Optimal incentive mechanisms should be lower-powered in LDCs.*[10]

---

[10] This conclusion is valid as long as the incentive scheme does not rely on accounting data difficult to obtain. In the Laffont–Tirole (1986) model, incentive schemes require cost information. Proposition 8.2 is then valid only if cost data are available. Otherwise, the regulator is obliged to use a high-powered scheme (see chapter 2).

Proposition 8.2 shows a kind of vicious circle since less development calls for less efficiency of high-cost types.[11]

Let us now separate powers – i.e. associate one regulator with each supervision technology.

8.5 Optimal regulation with two regulators

When regulators are not benevolent, it is straightforward to show that optimal regulation here entails, too, collusion-proofness. It remains to write the collusion-proof constraints with two regulators.

Let r_1 and r_2 in $\{\phi, \underline{\theta}\}$ be the reports made by the regulators and $t_1(r_1, r_2)$, $t_2(r_1, r_2)$ the transfers made by the government to the regulators as a function of their reports. The social maximizer wishes to induce truthtelling of regulators as a Nash equilibrium.

Consider regulator 1 who has observed $\sigma_1 = \underline{\theta}$. He does not know what regulator 2 has observed, but he anticipates that regulator 2 truthfully reveals his signal.

Regulator 1's expected utility if $r_1 = \underline{\theta}$ is:

$$\Pr(\sigma_2 = \underline{\theta}/\sigma_1 = \underline{\theta})t_1(\underline{\theta}, \underline{\theta}) + \Pr(\sigma_2 = \phi/\sigma_1 = \underline{\theta})t_1(\underline{\theta}, \phi).$$

If he proposes to hide his signal for the maximal bribe that the firm can offer $(\Delta\theta\bar{q})$, his expected utility[12] is:

---

[11] The reader may object that there is never corruption in equilibrium. To have corruption at equilibrium it is enough to introduce some form of incompleteness in the contract that the regulator can use or to distinguish between regulators of different propensity to be corrupted, as in Laffont and N'Guessan (1999).

[12] We assume that a regulator must decide his collusive behavior before knowing what the other regulator has observed. Otherwise, they could coordinate their collusive offers and collusion-proof constraints would be written: $t_1(\underline{\theta}, \underline{\theta}) \geq \frac{1}{2}k\Delta\theta\bar{q}$; $t_1(\underline{\theta}, \phi) \geq k\Delta\theta\bar{q}$; $t_2(\phi, \underline{\theta}) \geq k\Delta\theta\bar{q}$. Then, the expected cost of ensuring collusion-proofness would be the same as with a single regulator. Here again we assume that the regulators have all the bargaining power in the side contracts. This is without loss of generality – the firm could have the bargaining power – as long as the timing is as specified above.

$$\Pr(\sigma_2 = \underline{\theta}/\sigma_1 = \underline{\theta})t_1(\phi, \underline{\theta}) + \Pr(\sigma_2 = \phi/\sigma_1 = \underline{\theta})$$
$$\times (t_1(\phi, \phi) + k\Delta\theta\bar{q}).$$

Indeed, if the other regulator has observed $r_2 = \underline{\theta}$ and has informed the government, the offer of collusion will be rejected. However, if the other regulator has observed $r_2 = \phi$, it will be accepted.

Given the limited liability constraints $(t(\cdot, \cdot) \geq 0)$, the government will obviously set $t_1(\phi, \underline{\theta}) = t_1(\phi, \phi) = 0$ and the collusion-proof constraint reduces to

$$p_{11}t_1(\underline{\theta}, \underline{\theta}) + p_{12}t_1(\underline{\theta}, \phi) \geq p_{12}k\Delta\theta\bar{q}, \qquad (8.10)$$

and similarly for regulator 2

$$p_{11}t_2(\underline{\theta}, \underline{\theta}) + p_{21}t_2(\phi, \underline{\theta}) \geq p_{21}k\Delta\theta\bar{q}. \qquad (8.11)$$

These incentive payments for regulators produce the additional expected social costs

$$\lambda\nu k(p_{12} + p_{21})\Delta\theta\bar{q}.$$

This leads to the optimal collusion-proof regulation characterized[13] by

$$S'(\bar{q}_{II}^{\phi}) = (1 + \lambda)\bar{\theta} + \lambda\frac{\nu}{1 - \nu}\Delta\theta(p_{22} + k(p_{12} + p_{21}))$$
$$\bar{t}_{II}^{\phi} = \bar{\theta}\bar{q}_{II}^{\phi}$$
$$S(\underline{q}_{II}^{\phi}) = (1 + \lambda)\underline{\theta}, \underline{t}_{II}^{\phi} = \underline{\theta}\underline{q}_{II}^{\phi} + \Delta\theta\bar{q}_{II}^{\phi}.$$

The activity of each regulator creates a negative externality on the other regulator. Reporting the informative signal

---

[13] We have considered an equilibrium in which it is profitable for a regulator to report truthfully when the other regulator also reports truthfully. One may wonder if there is also an equilibrium in which both regulators hide their signals. To avoid such a situation, it is enough to have, say for regulator 1,

$$p_{11}t_1(\underline{\theta}, \phi) + p_{12}t_1(\underline{\theta}, \phi) = t_1(\underline{\theta}, \phi) \geq p_{12}k\Delta\theta\bar{q}.$$

In the payments characterized above ((8.10), (8.11)) we can always choose $t_1(\underline{\theta}, \underline{\theta})$ and $t_1(\underline{\theta}, \phi)$ such that this inequality holds at no further cost (take $t_1(\underline{\theta}, \underline{\theta}) = 0$ and $t_1(\underline{\theta}, \phi) = k\Delta\theta\bar{q}$).

prevents the other regulator from striking a side deal. It is not internalized when separation of powers occurs and it allows the government to economize $\nu k p_{11} \Delta \theta \bar{q}$ in expected incentive social costs for regulators. This saving on regulatory costs enables the government to afford a rent–efficiency trade-off more favorable to efficiency, hence a higher level of production for the inefficient type $(\bar{q}_{II}^{\phi} > \bar{q}_{I}^{\phi})$ and a higher information rent for the efficient type $(\Delta \theta \bar{q}_{II}^{\phi} > \Delta \theta \bar{q}_{I}^{\phi})$, when it is not identified.

Proposition 8.3: *Separation of powers saves on incentive payments for regulators and entails higher-powered optimal regulation.*

It is worth stressing that the gain from separation is not only due to the eventual correlation of signals σ_1 and σ_2.

Suppose that the signals are independent, and $\Pr(\sigma_1 = \underline{\theta}) = \xi = \Pr(\sigma_2 = \underline{\theta})$. Then

$$p_{11} = \xi^2 \qquad p_{12} = p_{21} = (1 - \xi)\xi \qquad p_{22} = (1 - \xi)^2.$$

All propositions hold for this case. What does the correlation of signals change? Take a particular stochastic structure

$$p_{11} = \hat{\xi} - \varepsilon \qquad p_{12} = p_{21} = \varepsilon \qquad p_{22} = (1 - \hat{\xi}) - \varepsilon.$$

When ε goes to 0, the correlation becomes perfect.

The gain from pure informational competition is related to p_{12} (compare (8.5) and (8.6)). It decreases as correlation of signals increases.

The gain from separation of powers is related to p_{11}. In this example, it increases with the correlation of signals. But it need not. Take, for example,

$$p_{11} = \hat{\xi} + \varepsilon \qquad p_{12} = p_{21} = \varepsilon \qquad p_{22} = (1 - \hat{\xi}) - 3\varepsilon.$$

If we define the "quality" of the technology of the two signals as the probability of discovering $\underline{\theta}$, i.e. $p_{11} + p_{12} + p_{21}$ then, for a given quality, the separation of powers effect increases with the correlation of signals. When the correlation becomes perfect, separation of powers achieves the optimal regulation with benevolent regulators, i.e. eliminates completely the opportunism of regulators.

8.6 Separation of powers in developing countries

Let us denote W^{II}, W^{I} the expected social welfares with two or one regulator, ignoring momentarily the cost of duplicating regulators. The question we ask is, then, how does the gain from separation $\Delta W = W^{II} - W^{I}$ vary with the level of development?

Consider first the transaction cost of collusion k that, we argued, is higher in less developed countries. We obtain immediately:

Proposition 8.4: *The gain of separation increases with k for low values of k since*

$$\left.\frac{d\Delta W}{dk}\right|_{k=0} = \lambda v \Delta \theta p_{11} \bar{q}_I^\phi > 0.$$

In the appendix (p. 243) we show more generally that the gain increases as the transaction cost of collusion decreases.

We obtain a similar result for increases in $\bar{\theta}$ and λ.

Proposition 8.5: *The gain of separation increases with $\bar{\theta}$ for low values of $\bar{\theta}$ and with λ for low values of λ since*

$$\left.\frac{d\Delta W}{d\bar{\theta}}\right|_{\bar{\theta}=\underline{\theta}} = \lambda v p_{11} k \bar{q}_I^\phi > 0$$

$$\left.\frac{d\Delta W}{d\lambda}\right|_{\lambda=0} = v p_{11} k \Delta \theta \bar{q}_I^\phi > 0.$$

(See the appendix.)

On the contrary, the gain of separation decreases when the quality of the supervision technology decreases. To show this simply, consider an increase of p_{11} which leaves $p_{12} + p_{21}$ constant. Then, we have:

Proposition 8.6: *The gain of separation increases with p_{11} since*

$$\left. \frac{d\Delta W}{dp_{11}} \right|_{p_{12}+p_{21}=Cte} = \lambda v \Delta\theta [\bar{q}_{II}^{\phi} - (1-k)\bar{q}_{I}^{\phi}] > 0.$$

We can conclude that the value of separation of powers to fight capture appears even higher in developing countries where regulators have supervision technologies of the same qualities.[14] The result becomes ambiguous when we take into account the fact that developing countries have poorer supervision technologies. Furthermore, the cost of implementing such a structural policy also varies with the level of development.

8.7   Implementing separation of powers

Separation is successful only if regulators do not collude.[15] The probability of such collusion is not independent of the level of development. To model this problem, simply suppose that the probability of collusion $\pi(k)$ depends on the transaction cost parameter k to express the fact that the less developed the country is, the higher k and the higher the probability of collusive behavior of regulators.[16]

---

[14] This conclusion was also obtained in Laffont and Martimort (1999) in a model with no correlation effect.

[15] This is particularly bothering because the symmetry of the situation makes reciprocal favors easy (see Laffont and Meleu, 1997).

[16] One can also argue that the probability of collusion between regulators should increase with the stake of collusion, which is $p_{11}k\Delta\theta\bar{q}_{II}^{\phi}$. This would reinforce the result below except when we take into account the regulatory response which entails a level $\bar{q}_{II}^{\phi}$ which decreases with k.

When setting up two regulators the constitutional designer knows that with probability $\pi(k)$ the regulators will collude and behave as a single regulator.

Let $W^{II}(\bar{q}^\phi)$ and $W^I(\bar{q}^\phi)$ be expected social welfare with two or one regulators as a function of the production level required from the inefficient type, $\bar{q}^\phi$. The optimal design entails a level of $\hat{\bar{q}}_{II}^\phi$ which maximizes

$$(1 - \pi(k))W^{II}(\bar{q}_{II}^\phi) + \pi(k)W^I(\bar{q}_{II}^\phi).$$

With one regulator we have $W^I(\bar{q}_I^\phi)$ with $\bar{q}_I^\phi$ determined by (8.9).

So far, we have neglected the direct cost of regulators. If K is such a direct cost, including the social cost of one regulator, $(1 + \lambda)K$, or two regulators, $2(1 + \lambda)K$, helps us determine when the welfare gain brought about by one or two regulators is worth it.

It has also been argued[17] that the transaction costs of collusion decrease when the regulator is more specialized. Let us denote $\delta k, \delta > 1$, the transaction cost parameter of side contracts with two regulators. Finally, let us index also K and λ on k ($\lambda'(k) > 0$, $K'(k) > 0$) to have a single parameter.

When we differentiate with respect to k the gain in welfare due to the presence of two regulators, we have in addition to terms similar to these of section 8.6 (and therefore positive), several negative terms

- $\pi'(k)[W^{II}(\hat{\bar{q}}_{II}^\phi) - W^I(\hat{\bar{q}}_{II}^\phi)] - \lambda'(k)K$
- $(1 + \lambda)K'(k)$
- $(\delta - 1)[p_{12} + p_{21} + \pi(k)p_{11}]\lambda\nu\Delta\theta\hat{\bar{q}}_{II}^\phi.$

Indeed, in a less developed country the likelihood that separation will be bypassed by colluding regulators is higher (first term), the financial burden of another regulator is higher

---

[17] See Neven, Nuttall, and Seabright (1993).

(second and third terms), and the higher transaction costs of collusion for specialized regulators are magnified (fourth term). Hence we have

Proposition 8.7:   *The implementation of separation of powers is more costly in a developing country.*

This last result is important to moderate the enthusiasm of recent development economics which sees institution building (rightly) as key to development. Even though improvements in institutions are even more valuable in developing countries than developed ones, it is unfortunately more difficult to implement them in such countries and they are bound to be less efficient.

8.8   Separation of powers as an endogenous institution

Separation of powers can sometimes be recommended as an institutional change which increases expected social welfare. However, this normative approach is somewhat naïve and one may want to model the political economy constraints imposed on such institutional changes. We will assume that institutional changes are chosen by the majority in power and we consider for this purpose the random majority model (Laffont, 1996).

There are two types of voters and the proportions of these two types fluctuate. Type 1 voters are stakeholders in the regulated firm and share the information rent. They will be less inclined to decrease the information rent than a utilitarian social welfare maximizer would be. Type 2 voters are not stakeholders in the regulated firm and will want to decrease the information rent more than socially desirable.

With probability $1/2$, type 1 is in proportion $\alpha > 1/2$ and it is in proportion $1 - \alpha$, also with probability $1/2$.

Then, under majority 1 and a single regulator, the following objective function is maximized

$$\alpha[\nu(p_{11} + p_{12} + p_{21})(S(\underline{q}) - (1 + \lambda)\underline{\theta}\underline{q} - \lambda k\Delta\theta\bar{q})$$
$$+ \nu p_{22}(S(\underline{q}) - (1 + \lambda)\underline{\theta}\underline{q})$$
$$+ (1 - \nu)(S(\bar{q}) - (1 + \lambda)\bar{\theta}\bar{q})] + [1 - (1 + \lambda)\alpha]\nu p_{22}\Delta\theta\bar{q}.$$

Members of the majority share the expected information rent $\nu p_{22}\Delta\theta\bar{q}$ between themselves and therefore overvalue it socially. We obtain $(\underline{q} = \underline{q}^*)$ and

$$S'(\bar{q}_I^1) = (1 + \lambda)\bar{\theta} + \frac{\lambda\nu}{1 - \nu}\Delta\theta$$
$$\times \left[(p_{11} + p_{12} + p_{21})k - p_{22}\frac{(1 - (1 + \lambda)\alpha)}{\lambda\alpha} \right],$$

where we assume $(1 + \lambda)\alpha < 1$ for simplicity, so that majority 1 still wants to minimize the firm's rent.

Similarly with two regulators we have:

$$S'(\bar{q}_{II}^1) = (1 + \lambda)\bar{\theta} + \frac{\lambda\nu}{1 - \nu}\Delta\theta$$
$$\times \left[(p_{12} + p_{21})k - p_{22}\left(\frac{1 - (1 + \lambda)\alpha}{\lambda\alpha}\right) \right].$$

On the contrary, with majority 2 in power, the objective function with one regulator is

$$\alpha[\nu(p_{11} + p_{12} + p_{21})(S(\underline{q}) - (1 + \lambda)\underline{\theta}\underline{q} - \lambda k\Delta\theta\bar{q})$$
$$+ \nu p_{22}(S(\underline{q}) - (1 + \lambda)\underline{\theta}\underline{q} - (1 + \lambda)\Delta\theta\bar{q})$$
$$+ (1 - \nu)(S(\bar{q}) - (1 + \lambda)\bar{\theta}\bar{q})],$$

hence

$$S'(\bar{q}_I^2) = (1 + \lambda)\bar{\theta} + \frac{\lambda\nu}{1 - \nu}\Delta\theta$$
$$\times \left[(p_{11} + p_{12} + p_{21})k + \frac{(1 + \lambda)}{\lambda}p_{22} \right],$$

and similarly with two regulators

$$S'(\bar{q}_{II}^2) = (1+\lambda)\bar{\theta} + \frac{\lambda v}{1-v}\Delta\theta\left[(p_{12}+p_{21})k + \frac{(1+\lambda)}{\lambda}p_{22}\right].$$

If we now include the direct costs of regulators it is clear that majority 2, which is more interested in cutting down information rents, will choose separation of regulators more often than majority 1, which overvalues socially information rents.

Consequently, the way to promote separation of powers when it is socially useful is not to advocate it from a normative point of view, but to favor the emergence of majority 2. However, it is clearly a form of political interference.

8.9 Conclusion

We have shown that the institution "separation of powers", which can be useful to mitigate the costs created by the opportunism of regulators, is even more valuable in developing countries. This is because these countries suffer from high costs of public funds (due to inefficient tax systems), from low transaction costs of collusion (due to poor auditing and monitoring), and from less efficient technologies. However, the implementation of this institution is more difficult and more costly for the same reasons, leaving us with an ambiguous result if the various weaknesses of these countries are not addressed simultaneously.

We believe that this type of result is quite general,[18] but more research is needed to go beyond the indeterminacy stressed in this chapter. Also, by making the analysis static, we have lost an essential dimension of institutions, namely the credibility that they are associated with. We hope to pursue our analysis in dynamic contexts to assess the difficulties

---

[18] Laffont (1999) argues similarly that competition policy is also more useful in developing countries, but more difficult to implement.

of implementing credible long-term institutions in developing countries.

Appendix

$$W^I = (p_{11} + p_{12} + p_{21})v(S(\underline{q}^*) - (1 + \lambda)\underline{\theta}\underline{q}^*)$$
$$+ p_{22}v(S(\underline{q}^*) - (1 + \lambda)\underline{\theta}\underline{q}^* - \lambda\Delta\theta\bar{q}_I^\phi)$$
$$+ (1 - v)(S(\bar{q}_I^\phi) - (1 + \lambda)\bar{\theta}\bar{q}_I^\phi)$$
$$- \lambda v(p_{11} + p_{12} + p_{21})k\Delta\theta\bar{q}_I^\phi$$

$$W^{II} = (p_{11} + p_{12} + p_{21})v(S(\underline{q}^*) - (1 + \lambda)\underline{\theta}\underline{q}^*)$$
$$+ p_{22}v(S(\underline{q}^*) - (1 + \lambda)\underline{\theta}\underline{q}^* - \lambda\Delta\theta\bar{q}_{II}^\phi)$$
$$+ (1 - v)(S(\bar{q}_{II}^\phi) - (1 + \lambda)\bar{\theta}\bar{q}_{II}^\phi)$$
$$- \lambda v(p_{12} + p_{21})k\Delta\theta\bar{q}_{II}^\phi.$$

From the envelope theorem

$$\frac{dW^I}{dk} = -\lambda v(p_{11} + p_{12} + p_{21})\Delta\theta\bar{q}_I^\phi$$

$$\frac{dW^{II}}{dk} = -\lambda v(p_{12} + p_{21})\Delta\theta\bar{q}_{II}^\phi$$

$$\frac{dW^{II}}{dk} - \frac{dW^I}{dk} = \lambda v\Delta\theta p_{11}\bar{q}_I^\phi + \lambda v\Delta\theta(p_{12} + p_{21})(\bar{q}_I^\phi - \bar{q}_{II}^\phi).$$

There is a first-order effect $\lambda v\Delta\theta p_{11}\bar{q}_{II}^\phi$ which represents the gains from saving incentive costs for regulators with probability p_{11}. However, this saving leads to a higher production level with two regulators than with one regulator, and therefore to a countervailing effect

$$\lambda v\Delta\theta(p_{12} + p_{21})(\bar{q}_I^\phi - \bar{q}_{II}^\phi) < 0.$$

However, this effect is of the second order in $\Delta\theta$ while the other is of the first order.

Furthermore this second effect is of the order of the difference in transaction costs between the two types of regulation while the first one is of the order of the level of production. For example if $S(q) = q - \frac{q^2}{2}$, inserting the values of $\bar{q}_I^\phi$ and $\bar{q}_{II}^\phi$ we obtain:

$$\frac{dW^{II}}{dk} - \frac{dW^I}{dk} \propto \bar{q}_I^\phi - \frac{\lambda v}{1 - v} k\Delta\theta(p_{12} + p_{21}).$$

Therefore, it is fair to say that propositions 8.4–8.7 are valid in general and not only locally.

Similarly

$$\frac{dW^{II}}{d\bar{\theta}} - \frac{dW^I}{d\bar{\theta}} = \lambda v p_{11} k \bar{q}_I^\phi + (\bar{q}_I^\phi - \bar{q}_{II}^\phi)$$

$$\times ((1 + \lambda)(1 - v) + \lambda v(p_{22} + k(p_{12} + p_{21})))$$

$$\frac{dW^{II}}{d\lambda} - \frac{dW^I}{d\lambda} = \lambda p_{11} k\Delta\theta \bar{q}_I^\phi + (\bar{q}_I^\phi - \bar{q}_{II}^\phi)$$

$$\times ((1 - v)\bar{\theta} + v(p_{22} + k(p_{12} + p_{21}))) \Delta\theta).$$

9

Concluding remarks

This book is only a sketch of what a book on regulation in LDCs should be. Ideally, such a book should provide a general model of regulation which fits the institutional characteristics of LDCs, give empirical evidence of the relevance of such a model, and derive policy implications. Many obstacles need to be removed before such an ambitious goal can be achieved.

9.1 A more general model

Developing economies are often described as "economies with missing markets." In the contractual world of regulation, this translates into incomplete contracts. Contracts are incomplete because of players' bounded rationality as in any economy, but also because of institutional weaknesses in enforcement, commitment, auditing, etc. Accordingly a theory of regulation viewed as a contract between the regulator and the regulated firm is bound to be more complex than a theory with complete contracts. Furthermore, as we have argued, institutional development proceeds by stages which call for different theories.

A given developing country is characterized by specific values of some crucial parameters such as the cost of public funds (which reflects the quality of the tax system), or the propensity to corruption (which reflects the lack of education, among other things), but also by the quality of institutions such as the quality of democracy, the quality of the judiciary, or the quality of auditing.

Policy recommendations for such a country should be based on a model which incorporates all these features. The work needed to obtain the mapping from the characteristics of the country to the policy recommendations is daunting, and probably beyond the capacity of the few researchers in this area.

Our contribution to this vast progam can be described as follows. Chapter 2 uses a classical model of regulation designed for developed economies and explores how the optimal contract is affected by the values of some parameters which are specific to LDCs. In chapter 3, we depart from a normative approach which assumes that the government maximizes social welfare to account for corruption at the governmental level. This enables us to provide a theory which relates the level of privatization to the level of corruption. Chapter 4 models the imperfection of enforcement and derives an endogenous level of enforcement which depends on the characteristics of the country, including the level of corruption. Chapter 5 is more policy-oriented and uses the recent literature on access pricing to derive some policy recommendations for access pricing in LDCs. However, this is done in a rather informal way – i.e. by trying to adapt the available theory to the characteristics of LDCs. Chapter 6 uses the complete contract approach to deal with the provision of USOs in LDCs, where the investment decision in rural areas is more important than in developed economies but does not require a new methodological step. The design of regulatory institutions is the topic of the last two chapters. Chapter 7 uses historical evidence and the theory of organizations to suggest some principles of organizational design adapted to LDCs. Again, the approach here is rather informal. On the contrary, chapter 8 discusses formally how the characteristics of LDCs affect the choice of one or two regulators to regulate a given industry when capture of regulators by the regulated firm is an issue.

9.2   Empirical validation

Testing theories of regulation is already extremely difficult in developed economies because of a lack of appropriate data. This state of affairs has even led some (see Gasmi, Kennet, Laffont, and Sharkey, 2002) to use engineering data partially to overcome this lack of data.

The data situation in LDCs is even worse, because regulatory reforms in LDCs are very recent and because no systemic data collection has been undertaken in most countries.

Serious empirical studies in LDCs are not really feasible today. Nevertheless, I have included a number of tests which use various data sets from the World Bank and in particular the data set put together by Luis Guasch (2001). They are just illustrative of the type of empirical results that are specific to the economic conditions of LDCs.

9.3   Policy implications

The difficulties of the econometric analyses in the realm of regulation, in particular for LDCs, force us to derive policy implications from our knowledge of historical experience, theory, and case studies. It is a difficult exercise that I have attempted extensively only in the case of access pricing and design of regulatory institutions. However, these recommendations are very far from the grandiose mapping I alluded to above.

We have covered, admittedly very imperfectly, the main issues of regulation, with perhaps the exception of financial issues. Obviously, a lot of work remains to be done and I simply hope that this little book prompted by the Caffè Lecture will encourage further research. Economists of the developed countries owe that to the people of the developing world.

References

Abdala, M. (2001), "Institutions, Contracts and Regulation of Infrastructure in Argentina," *Journal of Applied Economics*, 4, 217–254

African Development Indicators (1997), Washington, DC: World Bank

Aghion P. and J. Tirole (1997), "Formal and Real Authority in Organizations," *Journal of Political Economy*, 105, 1–29

Armstrong, M. (1998), "Network Interconnection," *Economic Journal*, 108, 545–564

Artana, D., F. Fernando Navajas, and S. Urbiztando (2002), "Regulation and Contractual Adaptation in Public Utilities: The Case of Argentina," in Basanes and Willig (2002)

Aubert C. and J.-J. Laffont (2001), "Multiregulation in Developing Countries," IDEI, mimeo

Auriol, E. and J.-J. Laffont (1992), "Regulation by Duopoly," *Journal of Economics and Management Strategy*, 1, 503–533

Bacon, R. and J. Besant-Jones (2001), "Privatization and Reform in the Global Electricity Supply Industry," *Annual Reviews Energy and the Environment*, 2, 119–143

Bardhan, P. and D. Mookherjee (1999), "Relative Capture of Local and Central Governments: An Essay in the Political Economy of Regulation," University of California, Berkeley

Baron, D. and D. Besanko (1986), "Regulation, Asymmetric Information and Auditing," *Rand Journal of Economics*, 15, 267–302

(1992), "Information, Control, and Organizational Structure," *Journal of Economics and Management Strategy*, 1, 237–275

Baron, D. and R. Myerson (1982), "Regulating a Monopoly with Unknown Cost," *Econometrica*, 50, 911–930

Basanes, F. and R. Willig (2002), *Second Generation Reforms in Infrastructure Services*, Washington, DC: Inter-American Development Bank

Becker, G. (1968), "Crime and Punishment: An Economic Approach," *Journal of Political Economy*, 76, 169–217

Becker, G. and G. Stigler (1974), "Law Enforcement, Malfeasance, and Compensation of Enforcers," *Journal of Legal Studies*, 3, 1–19

Bennedsen, M. (1996), "State Ownership versus Private Ownership under Incomplete Taxation," Harvard, mimeo

Berg, S. and L. Gutierrez (2000), "Telecommunications Liberalization and Regulatory Governance: Lessons from Latin America," *Telecommunications Policy*, 24, 865–884

Bernheim, D. and M. Whinston (1986), "Menu Auctions, Resource Allocation and Economic Influence," *Quarterly Journal of Economics*, 101, 1–31

Besley, T. and R. Burgess (2001), "The Political Economy of Government Responsiveness: Theory and Evidence from India," London School of Economics, mimeo

Besley, T. and S. Coate (1998), "Centralized versus Decentralized Provision of Local Public Goods: A Political Economy Analysis," Working Paper, 7084, NBER

Bhatiani, G. (2002), "Independent Regulation of Infrastructure Services in India: A Review," *International Journal of Regulation and Governance*, 2.

Biais, B. and E. Perotti (1997), "Privatization Underpricing, Social Inequalities and Popular Capitalism," IDEI, mimeo

Bitran, E. and P. Serra (1998), "Regulation of Privatized Utilities: The Chilean Experience," *World Development*, 2, 945–962

Bolton, P. and G. Roland (1997), "The Breakup of Nations: A Political Economy Analysis," *Quarterly Journal of Economics*, 62, 1057–1090

Border, K. and J. Sobel (1987), "Samurai Accountant: A Theory of Auditing and Plunder," *Review of Economic Studies*, 54, 525–540

Boycko, M., A. Shleifer, and R. Vishny (1996), "A Theory of Privatization," *Economic Journal*, 106, 309–319

Caillaud, B., B. Jullien, and P. Picard (1996), "National vs European Incentive Policies: Bargaining, Information and Coordination," *European Economic Review*, 40, 91–111

Campbell-White, O. and A. Bhatia (1998), *Privitisation in Africa*. Washington DC: World Bank.

Campos, J., A. Estache, and J. Trujillo (2003), "Processes and Accounting Matter for Regulators: Learning from Argentina's Railways Privatization," *Journal of Network Industries*, 4, 3–28

Carlin, W. and P. Seabright (2000), "The Importance of Competition in Developing Countries for Productivity and Innovation," mimeo

Chisari, O., A. Estache, and C. Romero (1999), "Winners and Losers from Privatization and Regulation of Utilities: Lessons from a General Equilibrium Model of Argentina," *The World Bank Economic Review*, 13, 357–378

Chisari, O., A. Estache, and C. Waddams-Price (2003), "Access by the Poor in Latin America's Utility Reform: Subsidies and service obligations," in C. Ugaz and C. Waddams-Price (eds.), *Utility Privatization and Regulation: A Fair Deal for Consumers*, Northampton, MA: Edward Elgar.

Congleton, R. (1984), "Committees and Rent-Seeking Effort," *Journal of Public Economics*, 25, 197–209

Cremer, H., F. Gasmi, A. Grimaud, and J.-J. Laffont (2001), "Universal Service: An Economic Perspective," *Annals of Public and Cooperative Economics*, 71, 5–42

Cremer, H., M. Marchand, and P. Pestieau (1990), "Evading, Auditing and Taxing: The Equity–Compliance Trade-Off," *Journal of Public Economics*, 43, 67–92

Crémer, J. and R. McLean (1988), "Full Extraction of the Surplus in Bayesian and Dominant Strategy Auctions," *Econometrica*, 56, 1247–1258

Crémer, J. and T. Palfrey (1996), "In or Out? Centralization by Majority Vote," *European Economic Review*, 40, 43–60

Dana, J. and K. Spier (1994), "Designing a Private Industry: Government Auctions with Endogenous Market Structure," *Journal of Economic Theory*, 53, 127–147

Dewatripont, M. (1989), "Renegotiation and Information Revelation over Time," *Quarterly Journal of Economics*, 103, 589–620

Dewatripont, M., I. Jewitt, and J. Tirole (1999), "The Economics of Career Concerns, Part II: Applications to Missions and Organization," *Review of Economic Studies*, 66(1), 199–217

Dewatripont, M. and G. Roland (1992), "Economic Reform and Dynamic Political Constraints," *Review of Economic Studies*, 59, 703–730

Dewatripont, M. and J. Tirole (1999), "Advocates," *Journal of Political Economy*, 107, 1–39

Dobbin, F. (1994), *Forging Industrial Policy: The United States, Britain and France in the Railway Age*, Cambridge: Cambridge University Press

Estache, A. (2001), "Privatization and Regulation of Transport Infrastructure in the 1990s," *The World Bank Research Observer*, 16, 85–108

——— (2003), "Argentina Privatization: A Cure or a Disease?," in C. von Hirschlausen, *Proceedings of a Workshop on Applied Infrastructure Research*, Berlin University of Technology

Estache, A. and M. Rodriguez-Pardina (1997), *The Private Sector in Infrastructure: Strategy, Regulation and Risk*, Washington, DC: World Bank

——— (2000), "Reforming Electricity in the Southern Cone," in L. Manzetti (ed.), *Regulatory Policy in Latin America: Post-Privatization Realities*, Miami: North–South Press Center at the University of Miami, 171–199

Estache, A., T. Valletti, and M. Manacorda (2002), "Telecoms Reform, Access Regulation and Internet Adoption in Latin America," *Economia*, 2, 153–218

Faure-Grimaud, A., J.-J. Laffont, and D. Martimort (2000), "Collusion, Delegation and Supervision with Soft Information," IDEI, mimeo

Fels, A. (1996), "Decision Making at the Centre," speech on April 19, 1996, Workshop on the Implementation of Antitrust Rules in a "Federal" Context, European University Institute, available at http://www.accc.gov.au

Freixas, X., R. Guesnerie, and J. Tirole (1985), "Planning under Incomplete Information and the Ratchet Effect," *Review of Economic Studies*, 52, 173–192

Galal, A. (1996), "Chile: Regulatory Specificity, Credibility of Commitment, and Distributional Demands," in B. Levy and P. Spiller (eds.), *Regulation, Institutions, and Commitment:*

Comparative Studies of Telecommunications, Cambridge: Cambridge University Press, 121–144

Gale, D. and M. Hellwig (1985), "Incentive-Compatible Debt Contracts: The One Period Problem," *Review of Economic Studies*, 52, 647–663

Gasmi, F., D.M. Kennet, J.-J. Laffont, and W.W. Sharkey (2002), *Cost Proxy Models and Telecommunications Policy*, Cambridge, MA: MIT Press

Gasmi, F., J.-J. Laffont, and W. Sharkey (1999), "Competition, Universal Service and Telecommunications Policy in Developing Countries," *Information Economics and Policy*, 12, 221–248

Gilbert, G. and P. Picard (1996), "Incentives and the Optimal Size of Local Jurisdictions," *European Economic Review*, 40, 19–41

Gilbert, R. and D. Newbery (1988), "Regulation Games," Working Paper, 8879, University of California

Green, R. and M. Rodriguez-Pardina (1999), *Resetting Price Controls: A Manual for Regulators*, Washington, DC: World Bank

Greenwald, B. (1984), "Rate Base Selection and the Structure of Regulation," *Rand Journal of Regulation*, 15, 85–95

Guasch, L. (2001), "Concessions and Regulatory Design: Determinants of Performance – Fifteen Years of Evidence," World Bank, mimeo

   (2003), "Granting and Renegotiating Infrastructure Concessions: Doing it Right," WBI Development Studies, Washington, DC: World Bank.

Guasch, L., J.-J. Laffont, and S. Straub (2002), "Renegotiation of Concession Contracts in Latin America," IDEI, mimeo

Guasch, L. and P. Spiller (2002), *Managing the Regulatory Process: Design, Concepts, Issues, and the Latin America and Caribbean Story*, Washington, DC: World Bank

Guesnerie, R. and J.-J. Laffont (1984), "A Complete Solution to a Class of Principal–Agent Problems with an Application to the Control of a Self-Managed Firm," *Journal of Public Economics*, 25, 329–369

Haggarty, L. and M. Shirley (1999), "Telecommunication Reform in Ghana," World Bank, mimeo

Heller, W. and M. McCubbins (1996), "Politics, Institutions, and Outcomes: Electricity Regulation in Argentina and Chile," *Policy Reform*, 1, 357–387

Henisz, W.J. and B.A. Zelner (2001), "The Institutional Environment for Telecommunications Investment," *Journal of Economics and Management Strategy*, 10, 123–147

Hills, J. (1986), *Deregulating Telecoms, Competition and Control in the United States, Japan and Britain*, Westport, CT: Quorum Books

Jones, L., P. Tandon, and I. Vogelsang (1990), *Selling Public Enterprises: A Cost Benefit Methodology*, Cambridge, MA: MIT Press.

Karhl, W.L. (1982), *Water and Power – The Conflict over Los Angeles Water Supply in the Owens Valley*, Berkeley: University of California Press

Kaufmann, D., A. Kraay, and P. Zoido-Lobaton (1999a), "Governance Matters," World Bank, mimeo

(1999b), "Aggregating Governance Indicators," World Bank, mimeo

Kerf, M. and D. Geradin (1999), "Market Power in Telecommunications," *Berkeley Technology Law Journal*, 14, 919–1020

Kerf, M. and W. Smith (1996), "Privatizing Africa's Infrastructure: Promise and Challenge," World Bank Technical Paper, 337

Khalil, F. (1992), "Auditing without Commitment," Discussion Paper, 92–15, University of Washington

Klitgaard, R. (1988), *Controlling Corruption*, Berkeley: University of California Press

Kovacic, W.E. and C. Shapiro (2000), "Antitrust Policy: A Century of Economic and Legal Thinking," *Journal of Economic Perspectives*, 14(1), 43–60

Krasa, S. and A. Villamil (2000), "Optimal Contracts When Enforcement is a Decision Variable," *Econometrica*, 68, 119–134

Laffont, J.-J. (1996), "Industrial Policy and Politics," *International Journal of Industrial Organization*, 14, 1–10

(1999), "Competition, Information and Development," in B. Plescovic and J. Stiglitz (eds.), *Annual World Bank Conference on Development Economics 1998*, Washington DC: World Bank, 237–257

(2000), *Incentives and Political Economy*, Oxford: Oxford University Press

(2001a), *Theoretical Incentive Theory*, Peking: Peking University Press

(2001b), *Applied Incentive Theory*, Peking: Peking University Press

Laffont, J.-J., A. Estache, and X. Zhang (2000), *Regulation and Competition in Network Industries*, Beijing: Chinese Academy of Social Sciences

Laffont, J.-J., S. Marcus, P. Rey, and J. Tirole (2003), "Internet Interconnection and the Off-Net-Cost Pricing Principle," *Rand Journal of Economics*, 34, 370–390

Laffont, J.-J. and D. Martimort (1997), "Collusion Under Asymmetric Information," *Econometrica*, 65(4), 875–911

(1999), "Separation of Regulators Against Collusive Behavior," *Rand Journal of Economics*, 30(2), 232–262

(2000), "Mechanism Design with Collusion and Correlation," *Econometrica*, 68(2), 309–342

(2002), *The Theory of Incentives*, Princeton: Princeton University Press

Laffont, J.-J. and M. Meleu (1997), "Reciprocal Supervision, Collusion and Organization Design," *Scandinavian Journal of Economics*, 99, 519–540

Laffont, J.-J. and A. N'Gbo (2000), "Cross-Subsidies and Network Expansion in Developing Countries," *European Economic Review*, 44, 797–805

Laffont, J.-J. and T. N'Guessan (1999), "Competition and Corruption in an Agency Relationship," *Journal of Development Economics*, 60, 271–295

(2000), "Telecommunications Reform in Côte d'Ivoire," IDEI, mimeo

Laffont, J.-J. and J. Pouyet (2002), "The Subsidiarity Bias in Regulation," *Journal of Public Economics*, 88(1–2), 255–283

Laffont, J.-J., P. Rey and J. Tirole (1998a), "Network Competition I: Overview and Non Discriminatory Pricing," *Rand Journal of Economics*, 29, 1–37

(1998b), "Network Competition II: Price Discrimination," *Rand Journal of Economics*, 29, 38–56

Laffont, J.-J. and J. Tirole (1986), "Using Cost Observation to Regulate Firms," *Journal of Political Economy*, 94, 614–641

(1988), "The Dynamics of Incentive Contracts," *Econometrica*, 56, 1153–1175

(1990), "Adverse Selection and Renegotiation in Procurement," *Review of Economic Studies*, 75, 597–626

(1991a), "The Politics of Government Decision Making: A Theory of Regulatory Capture," *Quarterly Journal of Economics*, 106, 1089–1127

(1991b), "Privatization and Incentives," *Journal of Law, Economics, and Organization*, 7, 84–105

(1992), "Cost Padding, Auditing and Collusion," *Annales d'Economie et Statistique*, 25–26, 205–226

(1993), *A Theory of Incentives in Procurement and Regulation*, Cambridge, MA: MIT Press

(1994), "Access Pricing and Competition," *European Economic Review*, 38, 1673–1710

(1996), "Creating Competition through Interconnection: Theory and Practice," *Journal of Regulatory Economics*, 10, 227–256

(2000), *Competition in Telecommunications*, Cambridge, MA: MIT Press

Laffont, J.-J. and W. Zantman (2002), "Information Acquisition, Political Games and the Delegation of Authority," *European Journal of Political Economy*, 18(3), 407–428

Levy, B. and P.T. Spiller (1996), *Regulations, Institutions, and Commitment: Comparative Studies of Telecommunications*, Cambridge: Cambridge University Press

Loeb, M. and W. Magat (1979), "A Decentralized Method of Utility Regulation," *Journal of Law and Economics*, 22, 399–404

Madison, J., A. Hamilton, and J. Jay (1788), *The Federalist Papers*, Penguin Classics edn (1987), Harmondsworth: Penguin Books

Martimort, D. (1999), "Renegotiation Design with Multiple Regulators," *Journal of Economic Theory*, 88(2), 261–294

Mirrlees, J. (1971), "An Exploration in the Theory of Optimal Income Taxation," *Review of Economic Studies*, 38, 175–208

Mishkin, F. (1997), "Understanding Financial Crises: A Developing Country Perspective," in M. Bruno and B. Pleskovic (eds.), *Annual World Bank Conference on Development Economics*, Washington DC: World Bank

Moe, T. (1986), "Interests, Institutions, and Positive Theory: The Policies of the NLRB," *Studies of American Political Department*, •

Montesquieu (1748) *De l'Esprit des Lois*, in *Oeuvres Complètes*, Paris: Editions du Seuil (1964)

Mookherjee, D. and I. Png (1989), "Optimal Auditing, Insurance and Redistribution," *Quarterly Journal of Economics*, 104, 399–415

Mueller, B. (2001), "Institutions for Commitment in the Brazilian Regulatory System," *Quarterly Review of Economics and Finance*, 41(5), 621–643

Mueller, D. (1997), *Constitutional Democracy*, Oxford: Oxford University Press

Neven D., R. Nuttall, and P. Seabright (1993), "Regulatory Capture and The Design of European Merger Policy," in D. Neven, R. Nuttall, and P. Seabright (eds.), *Merger in Daylight*, London: CEPR

New Zealand Ministry of Economic Development (2000a), "Ministerial Inquiry into Telecommunications," New Zealand, available at http://www.teleinquiry.govt.nz/reports/draft/

(2000b), "Ministerial Inquiry into the Electricity Industry," New Zealand, available at http://www.electricityinquiry.govt.nz/reports/issues/

OECD (1999), *OECD Review of Regulatory Reform in the United States*, Paris: OECD

Olsen, T. and G. Torsvick (1993), "The Ratchet Effect in Common Agency: Implication for Regulation and Privatization," *Journal of Law, Economics and Organization*, 9, 136–158

(1995), "Intertemporal Common Agency and Organizational Design: How Much Centralization," *European Economic Review*, 39, 1405–1428

Ordover, J., R. Pittman, and P. Clyde (1994), "Competition Policy for Natural Monopolies in a Developing Market Economy," *Economics of Transition*, 2, 317–343

Perotti, E. (1995), "Credible Privatization," *American Economic Review*, 85, 847–859

Polinsky, A.M. (1983), *An Introduction to Law and Economics*, Boston: Little Brown

Posner, R. (1972), *Economic Analysis of Law*, Boston: Little, Brown

Rey, P. (1997), "Competition Policy and Development," IDEI, mimeo

Rose-Ackerman, S. (1978), *Corruption: A Study in Political Economy*, New York: Academic Press

Sah, R. (1991), "Fallibility in Human Organizations and Political Systems," *Journal of Economic Perspectives*, 5, 67–88

Sah, R. and J. Stiglitz (1986), "The Architecture of Economic Systems: Hierarchies and Polyarchies," *American Economic Review*, 76, 716–727

(1991), "Quality of Managers in Centralized versus Decentralized Economic Systems," *Quarterly Journal of Economics*, 106, 289–296

Saleth, R.M. and A. Dinar (1999), "Water Challenge and Institutional Response: A Cross-Country Perspective," Research Policy Working Paper, 2161, Washington, DC: World Bank

Sappington, D. and J. Stiglitz (1987), "Privatization, Information and Incentives," *Journal of Policy Analysis and Management*, 6, 567–582

Schmidt, K. (1996a), "The Cost and Benefits of Privatization: An Incomplete Contracts Approach," *Journal of Law, Economics and Organization*, 12, 1–24

(1996b), "The Political Economy of Mass Privatization and the Risk of Expropriation," Munich University, mimeo

Seabright, P. (1996), "Accountability and Decentralization in Government: An Incomplete Contract Model," *European Economic Review*, 40, 1–90

Shapiro, C. and R. Willig (1990), "Economic Rationales for the Scope of Privatization," in E.N. Suleiman and J. Waterbury (eds.), *The Political Economy of Public Sector Reform and Privatization*, Boulder, CO: Westview Press, 55–87

Shleifer, A. (1985), "A Theory of Yardstick Competition," *Rand Journal of Economics*, 16, 319–327

Shleifer, A. and R. Vishny (1994a), "Corruption," *Quarterly Journal of Economics*, 109, 599–617

(1994b), "Politicians and Firms," *Quarterly Journal of Economics*, 109, 995–1025

Smith, W. (2000), "Regulating Utilities: Thinking about Location Questions," World Bank Summer Workshop on Market Institutions, Washington, DC

Spiller, P. and C. Sampson (1996), "Telecommunications Regulation in Jamaica," in B. Levy and P. Spiller (eds.), *Regulation, Institutions, and Commitment: Comparative Studies of Telecommunications*, Cambridge: Cambridge University Press, 36–78

Spiller, P. and I. Vogelsang (1996), "The United Kingdom: A Pace-Setter in Regulatory Incentives," in B. Levy and P. Spiller (eds.), *Regulation, Institutions, and Commitment: Comparative Studies of Telecommunications*, Cambridge: Cambridge University Press, 79–120

Stigler, G. (1970), "Optimum Enforcement of Laws," *Journal of Political Economy*, 78, 526–536

Tiebout, C. (1956), "A Pure Theory of Public Expenditure," *Journal of Political Economy*, 64, 416–424

Tirole, J. (1986), "Hierarchies and Bureaucracies: On the Role of Collusion in Organizations," *Journal of Law, Economics and Organization*, 2, 181–214

(1992), "Collusion and the Theory of Organizations," in J.-J. Laffont (ed.), *Advances in Economic Theory*, Sixth World Congress, 2, Cambridge: Cambridge University Press

(1994), "The Internal Organization of the Government," *Oxford Economic Papers*, 46, 1–29

Townsend, R. (1979), "Optimal Contracts and Competitive Markets with Costly State Verification," *Journal of Economic Theory*, 21, 1–29

Trebilcock, M. (1996), "What Makes Poor Countries Poor? The Role of Institutional Capital in Economic Development," University of Toronto, Law and Economics Program

Trujillo, L. and G. Nombela (1999), "Privatization and Regulation of the Seaport Industry," Research Policy Working Paper, 2181, Washington, DC: World Bank

Ugaz, C. and C. Waddams Price (eds.) (2003), *Utility Privatization and Regulation: A Fair Deal for Consumers?*, Northampton, VT: Edward Elgar

Wallsten, S. (2001), "An Econometric Analysis of Telecom Competition, Privatization and Regulation in Africa and Latin America," *Journal of Industrial Economics*, 49, 1–19

Wellenius, B. (1997), "Extending Telecommunications Services to Rural Areas – The Chilean Experience," Viewpoint Note, 105, Washington, DC: World Bank

Williamson, O. (1985), *The Economic Institution of Capitalism*, New York: Free Press

Wilson, J. (1980), "The Politics of Regulation," in J. Wilson (ed.), *The Politics of Regulation*, New York: Basic Books

Index

Printed in the United States
by Baker & Taylor Publisher Services